PUSHING

TO THE

FRONT

Published by CelebrityPress™, Orlando, FL
A division of The Celebrity Branding Agency®

Celebrity Branding® is a registered trademark
Printed in the United States of America.

ISBN: 9780983340478
LCCN: 2011930528

For more information, please write:

CelebrityPress™,
520 N. Orlando Ave, #2
Winter Park, FL 32789

or call 1.877.261.4930

Visit us online at www.**CelebrityPressPublishing**.com

PUSHING TO THE FRONT

Front Line Strategies from the World's Leading Experts

Go Lobos!

-Dr Sugar-

TABLE OF CONTENTS

CHAPTER 1
HOW TO TAKE RISKS
BY BRIAN TRACY 11

CHAPTER 2
OWN THE ROOM EVERY TIME
BY ALISON (ALI) HAMNER CRAIG 19

CHAPTER 3
MAXIMIZE YOUR BUSINESS BY MANAGING YOUR ENERGY
BY DR. CAROLYN ANDERSON 27

CHAPTER 4
CHOICES
BY WILLIAM (BILL) LAM 37

CHAPTER 5
HOW TO BRAINSTORM YOUR WAY TO NEW MARKETS
BY NANCY PHILLIPS 45

CHAPTER 6
THE PASSION PRINCIPLE
–THE FOUNDATION FOR YOUR SUCCESS
BY MICHAEL E. BUDOWSKI 53

CHAPTER 7
PASSION AND PURPOSE
– GO WHERE THE ENERGY IS!
BY LOULIE KEY SCHARF 59

CHAPTER 8
UNLEASH YOUR POWER NOW:
ELEVEN KEYS TO SUCCESS
BY SUGAR SINGLETON, M.D. 69

CHAPTER 9
RIDE PURPOSE, ATTITUDE & WORK ETHIC TO THE FRONT
BY MICHAEL D'ADAMO 79

CHAPTER 10
FREEDOM THROUGH LIMITS
– HOW SETTING BOUNDARIES CAN EMPOWER YOUR TEAM AND YOUR LIFE
BY MIKE CONDUFF 87

CHAPTER 11
ELEVEN STEPS TO MAKE YOUR DREAMS COME TRUE
BY RENATA KRONOWETTEROVA 95

CHAPTER 12
YOUR LIFE LISTS
BY TRACEY PLYMPTON 103

CHAPTER 13
FROM BELIEVER TO ACHIEVER
– BRING FORTH THE BEST OF WHO YOU ARE
BY JOHN STUCKENSCHNEIDER 109

CHAPTER 14
GLOBAL CONNECTIONS MEAN ALL THE WORLD
BY YING HAN 121

CHAPTER 15
MENTORS IN MY LIFE
BY CHARLES SIKORA 129

CHAPTER 16
THE POWER OF CONSCIOUS CHOICE
BY ROBERT VITELLI 137

CHAPTER 17
THE THREE "R'S" FOR SUCCESS
BY DR. PAUL TOOTE 145

CHAPTER 18
THE 5 CRITICAL INDICATORS THAT LEADERS MUST EXECUTE TO KEEP RELEVANT IN TODAY'S CHANGING ECONOMY
BY DR. JON SARVER 153

CHAPTER 19
UNCLE FRANK'S 21 SECRETS OF CREATING A MONEY-MAKING CUSTOMER EXPERIENCE REVEALED!
BY TRACY E. MYERS, CMD 163

CHAPTER 20
THE GOLD STANDARD OF LIFE
– A SIMPLE FIVE-STEP GUIDE TO PUSHING YOURSELF TO THE FRONT OF YOUR FIELD
BY FOREST HAMILTON 173

CHAPTER 21
ENJOY THE GOOD LIFE:
THE GUIDE TO HAVING IT ALL
BY ALAN & BONNIE CASHMAN 183

CHAPTER 22
CHANGE YOUR SALES RESULTS FROM GOOD TO GREAT!!!
BY CHUCK MITCHELL 193

CHAPTER 23
WISDOM FOR PUSHING YOU TO THE FRONT
BY DR. EMMA JEAN THOMPSON 203

CHAPTER 24
CLEARING A TRAIL FOR SALES SUCCESS
BY DAVID DOMOS 215

CHAPTER 25
THE ONLY GAME IN TOWN:
4 POWERFUL SECRETS TO BUILDING YOUR UNIQUE AND EXCLUSIVE MARKETING PLATFORM
BY JW DICKS, ESQ., NICK NANTON, ESQ., AND LINDSAY DICKS ... 223

CHAPTER 26
7 TIPS ON GOAL ACHIEVEMENT
BY TARIK ALSHARAFI 235

CHAPTER 27
GOALS:
THE 11 VITAL STEPS TO ACHIEVING EXTRAORDINARY RESULTS
BY MELISSA D. WHITAKER 243

CHAPTER 28
HOW IMPORTANT IS CUSTOMER SERVICE?
BY DULCEE LOEHN 251

CHAPTER 29
CONQUERING COMPLACENCY
BY DIANE CIOTTA 259

CHAPTER 30
14 SECONDS
BY DOMINIC KNIGHT 267

CHAPTER 31
THE INNATE POTENCY OF THE CRY FOR HELP
BY MFON EKPO 279

CHAPTER 32
THE SECRET TO LUCK!
BY PHAP TRINH 287

CHAPTER 33
THE LEADERSHIP MATRIX
9 HABITS OF BUSINESSES THAT EXECUTE
BY RICK WALLACE 295

CHAPTER 1

HOW TO TAKE RISKS

BY BRIAN TRACY

You've probably heard it said many times that entrepreneurs and business people are risk-takers and that they should be expected to take risks, which imply losses, in the pursuit of their financial objectives. However, quite the contrary is true. Successful business people, entrepreneurs and sales people, as well as others, are not necessarily risk-takers. In fact, they're more often what is called, risk-averse. They're very astute at avoiding risks in the pursuit of their goals. It's the people who are the most capable of taking risks where they do not lose who eventually succeed, and succeed big.

The fact is that all of life is a risk, of some kind. Whenever you engage in any action where the outcome is uncertain, for any reason, you are taking a risk. You take a small risk when you drive to work or walk across the street. You may take a large risk when you start a business or invest a sum of money. You take a risk whenever you venture into the unknown, where your possibilities and probabilities cannot be determined to an exact degree. From the time that you get up in the morning until you go to bed at night, and even when you're sleeping, you're dealing with risk to some degree.

The question is not whether or not you take risks, but how skillful you are, and therefore, how confident you are in taking the right risks for the right reasons in pursuit of the right goals and objectives.

It's a fact that every great leap forward in human life begins with a giant step of faith into the unknown. Men and women who accomplish wonderful things are invariably men and women of great faith and confidence in themselves and their abilities. The better you become at analyzing and assessing risk, and then avoiding as much of the risk as possible, the more competent and more capable you will become and the more successful you will be.

There are basically five types of risk for you to consider.

1. The first type is the simplest. These are *risks that are not yours to take*. These are decisions that you do not have to make or gambles that you do not have to engage in. Since every action has a consequence, and often creates the need for further actions, either to follow up or to remedy what happened, whenever you can delegate a risk or an act entailing uncertainty to another person, you can reduce your possible losses of time and money and can increase your likelihood of long-term success.

2. The second type of risk is defined by those that are *unnecessary*. You engage in unnecessary risks when you act precipitously, without sufficient information, or without taking time to think it through carefully in advance. Peter Drucker said... Action without thinking is the cause of every failure. Many of the mistakes that you have made have occurred because you acted without thinking, that is, you acted without taking the time to minimize the risks involved.

3. The third type of risk is the risk you *can afford to take*. Calling on a new prospect, following up on a lead, or pursuing a new opportunity, are all risks that you can afford to take. The cost of failure in these cases is very low while the rewards of success can be very great. Buying an inexpensive product or service, or going to a new restaurant, or going out with a new person, are all risks, entailing uncertainty that you can afford to take because the downside is limited. The worst that can happen is

that you perhaps experience a little bruise to your ego.

4. The fourth type of risk is the risk that you *cannot afford to take*. The consequences of making a mistake are too enormous. You cannot afford to bet your whole company or your whole bankroll on speculation of any kind. You cannot afford to commit all your resources to a single project and have your entire success or failure hang on the outcome of that project.

   Many sales people make the mistake of working on one very large prospect and gradually curtailing their efforts to develop a series of smaller prospects. From everything that I've heard, and from my own experience, whenever a sales person does that, the large prospect always fails to materialize and the sales person is left with empty hands and an empty pocket book. In the world of investing, they talk about the importance of "spreading your risks." No individual and no company should be dependent upon one or two people for their financial well-being. One of the best ways to minimize risks is to develop alternatives to what you are currently doing. The more alternatives you have, the lower your risk, and the higher your likelihood of success.

5. The fifth type of risk is the risk that you *cannot afford <u>not</u> to take*. The downside may be costly, but the upside is so exciting that it's very much worth taking a chance to go after it. If you are working on a big prospect whose headquarters is a long way from your main office, it's certainly a risk to travel all the way out there and back several times, but it's a risk that you cannot afford <u>not</u> to take. If the prospect materializes, it can make a major difference to both you and your company.

Sometimes you will be given a job opportunity that you cannot afford <u>not</u> to take. Although there is always a potential loss involved, the upside may be tremendous.

One of the best of all exercises, in every situation involving uncertainty, is to assess and evaluate the worst possible outcome. Ask yourself, "What could possibly go wrong in this situation?" "What is the worst possible thing that could go wrong?"

Remember Murphy's Law, "Whatever can go wrong, will go wrong." There are also several additions to Murphy's Law, such as "Whatever can go wrong, will go wrong, at the worst possible time." And, "Of all the things that can go wrong, the most expensive thing will go wrong at the worst possible time." Another sub-law is, "Everything takes longer than your best calculation." In advising business people, we suggest that they take their very best estimate of break-even for any business venture, and then triple it to arrive at a more realistic number. Whenever business people follow this advice, they are amazed to find that, in spite of their best calculations, it takes about three times longer than they thought before they actually start to make money.

Another sub-law is, "Everything costs more than you can possibly anticipate in advance." In minimizing risk in any venture, always add a 'fudge' factor to account for the degree of uncertainty. Whenever I do a business plan, I always add a 20 percent factor to the total of all costs that I can identify – to come up with the actually probable cost. Anything less than this, whether in business or taking a vacation, is probably an exercise in self-delusion.

Once you have identified the worst possible thing that could possible go wrong, make a list of everything that you could possibly do to offset these negative factors. Engage in what is called, "Crisis anticipation." Look down the road, into the future, and imagine every possible crisis that could arise as the result of changing external circumstances.

One of the characteristics of successful men and women is that they are intensely realistic. They do not trust to luck. They carefully think through and calculate every possible risk and then think about what they would do, should it occur. They always have a backup plan in case things do not go as they wish them to. They have a "Plan B," and options to that plan that take all kinds of variables into consideration.

The successful individuals engage in strategic thinking. They minimize risk by continually questioning their assumptions, and always ask themselves what they would do in the case of unexpected delay, costs overruns or unexpected responses from their competitors. They are seldom caught unprepared because they have thought through the kind of uncertainties that create unacceptable risks, risks that they cannot afford to take, or to settle for.

In dealing with risk, a mild degree of fear or anticipation is often very helpful because it keeps you alert and aware of what might go wrong. *The problem with fear is that most people have it to excess and are therefore paralyzed by their fears, rather than motivated by their opportunities.*

The two most common fears that we experience are the fear of failure and the fear of rejection. These two fears, in combination, form the upper and lower limits of our comfort zones. Your natural tendency is to get into a comfort zone, an area of certainty where you feel secure. Once you get into your comfort zone, whether it's in regard to income or occupation or relationships, you have a tendency to rationalize and justify your situation in life because the alternative is to accept risks, to face fear, and to move out boldly into the unknown.

One of the characteristics of leaders is that they are aware of the seductive influence of the comfort zone, so they are always consciously pulling themselves out of the comfort zone into the direction of fulfilling their potentials. The problem with the comfort zone and with fear is that they are both habits of mind. The more we practice, or give in to the emotion of fear, the more fearful we become and the more likely it is that we will avoid even reasonable risks that could lead us on to greater happiness and prosperity. One of your key jobs in life is to fight the magnetic pull of the comfort zone and to push yourself toward the outer boundary of your possibilities by consciously confronting risk and uncertainty, even though it's emotionally uncomfortable.

There is an old saying, "Faint heart ne'er won fair maid." And there is another, "Nothing ventured, nothing gained." Giving into fear makes you fearful while acting boldly makes you courageous. Your actions create your beliefs and your beliefs create your realities. The only solution is to "Do the thing you fear" each time you feel afraid or nervous for any reason. An old man once advised his grandson with these wonderful words, "Act boldly, and unseen forces will come to your aid." Truer words were never spoken.

Most sales people are selling far less and earning far less than is possible for them because of their exaggerated fear of rejection. Even though they have never met the prospective client or customer, they have inordinate fear of that person, and whether or not that person will like them or approve of them. When you actually dissect the fear of rejection of strangers, it seems kind of silly, but for a sales person faced with the need to develop new prospects, it can, and does, paralyze their activities and hold them back.

One of the very best ways to develop your ability to take intelligent risks is to consciously and deliberately do the things you fear, one step at a time. You don't have to leap out of an airplane without a parachute. This is not risk taking. This is simply foolish. What you do have to do is to resist your natural tendency to slip into a comfort zone of complacency and low performance, and push yourself forward. Take any fear that you may be experiencing and treat it as a challenge and as an opportunity to grow and become a better person. Face the fear, control the fear, master the fear, and continue to move forward – regardless of the fear. This is the mark of the superior person. Many of our fears of taking risks are unfounded. They have no real basis in reality. When you test them, you will find that they don't even exist.

Often we are afraid to take the risk of approaching a new person because we fear that this person will not like us, be interested in us, or be impressed enough with us to want to have anything to do with us. However, the simple solution is to get out of yourself and focus all of your attention on the other individual. When you concentrate your attention on the other person and find reasons to like him or her, to be interested in him or her, or to be impressed by him or her, a remarkable thing happens. The other person, in turn, finds that you are likeable, interesting and impressive. And the secret is to ask questions about the other person and then to listen attentively to the answers. Men and women who are popular with others practice this all the time. They eventually find that they have nothing to fear in introducing themselves to new people, either on a personal or business level.

If you are in sales, and you are thoroughly conversant with the benefits that your product or service can bring to another person, you can approach others with calmness and confidence, seeing yourself as a helper rather than a sales person. The very best sales people, in all fields, see themselves as friends and advisors to their customers and prospective clients. They feel that they are in a position to do a favor for a person who can benefit from what they have to offer. Instead of seeing risks in approaching new people, they see opportunities and possibilities. Their attitudes are positive and expectant rather than negative and reluctant. They overcome the fear of rejection by thinking and talking about ways that their product or service can help the other person and can enrich the other person's life or work.

A very good way to overcome the fear of risk-taking is to set clear, written, measurable goals for yourself, and then to review those goals regularly.

According to the work done at Harvard, continuous motivation, which leads to a positive mental attitude, is only possible when you feel that you are growing in a direction that is important to you. And its goals that enable you to grow. So make your goals reasonably challenging. Set goals that have a 50-50 probability of success. Set goals where you can have a major impact on the outcome by applying your personality and your intelligence to the activities necessary to achieve the goals.

When you set reasonable, measurable and yet, challenging goals, and you move toward them, step-by-step, you develop a feeling of confidence and courage that becomes the opposite of the fear of taking risks. With measurable goals, you get regular feedback on your progress which is inherently motivational. It gives you the feeling that you are progressively realizing a worthy ideal. As you do this, you feel that you are growing and fulfilling more of your inherent capabilities. You tend to feel wonderful about yourself.

ABOUT BRIAN

Brian Tracy is Chairman and CEO of Brian Tracy International, a company specializing in the training and development of individuals and organizations. Brian's goal is to help people achieve their personal and business goals faster and easier than they ever imagined.

Brian Tracy has consulted for more than 1,000 companies and addressed more than 5,000,000 people in 5,000 talks and seminars throughout the US, Canada and 55 other countries worldwide. As a Keynote speaker and seminar leader, he addresses more than 250,000 people each year.

He has studied, researched, written and spoken for 30 years in the fields of economics, history, business, philosophy and psychology. He is the top selling author of over 50 books that have been translated into 36 languages.

He has written and produced more than 300 audio and video learning programs, including the worldwide, best-selling Psychology of Achievement, which has been translated into more than 20 languages.

He speaks to corporate and public audiences on the subjects of Personal and Professional Development, including the executives and staff of many of America's largest corporations. His exciting talks and seminars on Leadership, Selling, Self-Esteem, Goals, Strategy, Creativity and Success Psychology bring about immediate changes and long-term results.

Prior to founding his company, Brian Tracy International, Brian was the Chief Operating Officer of a $265 million dollar development company. He has had successful careers in sales and marketing, investments, real estate development and syndication, importation, distribution and management consulting. He has conducted high level consulting assignments with several billion-dollar plus corporations in strategic planning and organizational development.

He has traveled and worked in over 80 countries on six continents, and speaks four languages. Brian is happily married and has four children. He is active in community and national affairs, and is the President of three companies headquartered in Solana Beach, California.

For more information on Brian Tracy programs, go to: www.briantracy.com

CHAPTER 2

OWN THE ROOM EVERY TIME

BY ALISON (ALI) HAMNER CRAIG

When was the last time you walked into a room and you owned it? All eyes were on you. The other guests didn't know you, but they wanted to. Most likely you have never or have rarely experienced such an event. Such was the case with my client Diana.

Diana, like you, is a hard working entrepreneur who loves what she does. She is also a single mom trying to create a work/life balance that works for all. But her clients were not appreciating her talents, and she was not receiving the respect or pay she deserved. Her nightmare clients had her feeling trapped. She was listening to the big name experts, but the results were not there.

Fast-forward two months after working with me for one day, and Diana's business went from frustration to a dream. She proudly dumped her old unappreciative clients and found twice as many new clients who happily paid her and appreciated her gifts. Go forward another six months and Diana is no longer a slave to her business. She travels, spends time with her kids, and lost 30 lbs. She plays, works, and loves life in everything that she does.

So what is the difference between the two Diana's? The Diana of today knows how to authentically share her business and own every single room she enters. So she dominates her marketplace and clients pursue her. She owns her life and business, and not the other way around.

Just like my consulting client Diana, you have a dynamic life-changing message/product that will positively impact lives, but you can't get anybody's attention. You work and work and work on your business, in your business, and study the masters like crazy – mimicking everything they say and do – all with less than stellar results. You are your own best-kept secret. You are an amazing expert in your field, but no one knows it.

The sad truth is that most of the entrepreneurs I meet from around the world feel like an imposter, not a professional. The good news is that the feeling that you are tired of "playing" business ends for you today.

You can be one of those people who seemingly skyrocket to success and influence overnight… one who attracts ravenous fans who love you and can't wait to get more of what you have to offer. All you have to do is discover your "I.T." Factor℠ and let the synergy begin.

Your "I.T." Factor℠ is that indescribable yet highly influential presence that can command a group or an individual without ever saying a word, and all the while coming from a completely authentic, non-sales position. The "I.T." Factor℠ is all about claiming your service, your self, and your success. When you truly own your "I.T." Factor℠ you can simply walk into a room and people want to know you. You own the room and your marketplace.

The "I.T." Factor Synergy℠ is all about communication and connection. I am not talking about verbal communication *per se*, I am talking about how we communicate 50 – 93% of the time – nonverbal communication. No matter if you are saying a word or not, if someone sees you in the store, at a meeting, with a client, in your car, or in a picture, you are communicating nonverbally. So are you even aware of the conversation you are having?

There are 5 simple steps to creating the "I.T." Factor Synergy℠ for yourself and in turn owning every room you walk into.

STEP 1: HEART

Many people, including some of my coaching clients, miss the power of our thoughts and motives, but there is a good reason why being clear in this area is step one. The simple fact is that if all you care about is the money, and you have no desire to serve, help, or bless your clients and customers; then all of that greed, selfishness, and lust will come out through your nonverbal communication.

Scientific studies have shown that only psychopaths can genuinely lie through their nonverbal communication. All the rest of us just end up sending mixed messages to our clients, customers, and ourselves. This miscommunication clouds our message and purpose, making it harder for our ideal clients to find us in the sea of competitors.

So get clear on your "Whys" and you will immediately have clearer communication. Ask yourself: "Why do I love my job?" …"Why do I enjoy my customers?" …"Why am I the best at what I do?" …"Why am I passionate about my profession?" You must be clear about who you are, what you do, and why you do it before anyone else will be.

Think about it this way, you are driving down the road in your car listening to your favorite radio station. Then all of a sudden the radio station jumps. Instead of hearing this crystal clear signal where you understand ever word that is being spoken, you are now getting every other word and a whole bunch of static. What do you do?

Well, it is your favorite station, so you try to dial the station in to regain that crystal clear signal, but you still are only getting every other word drowning in static. Now what do you do? You can change stations and listen to a competitor, put in a CD or plug in your iPod, or you turn the radio off altogether.

This is exactly what your customers do when you are unclear about your "whys." When you don't understand clearly for yourself what drives you at work, your customers are equally unclear on why to do business with you versus going to a potential competitor.

You must be clear on why you are the best at what you do and why you care, so that everyone else can begin to see why you are uniquely the best at what you do.

STEP 2: BODY

Being aware of your body language is a big way to effectively own the room. Once you are clear about the "whys" in your heart, your body language just got ten times easier. Body language really has two main areas: (1) the actual actions your body makes, and (2) how your body feels. Let's face it, if you feel horrible, you aren't going to be expressing your authentic authority and in turn you won't own the room.

What are the areas of your personal wellness that are holding you back? Are you too stressed out? Not getting enough sleep? Eating junk food because it is quick and readily available? Caffeine-overload everyday? Just like with your Heart, your Body must be clean, so that you can make the strongest impact possible on your marketplace.

The second part of your body language is the actual action your body makes. Now, we can't lie through our body language, but we must be aware of mimicking. Mimicking occurs naturally especially when we are trying to relate to somebody. It is a very effective tool when dealing with negotiations or tense situations, but when it comes to owning the room and your marketplace, it is the wrong move to make.

So when you want to really own the room and show everyone why you are the best at what you do, make sure to stay clear in your heart about your "whys." You must be aware of your actions. Are you folding your arms across your chest? Why? Do you feel insecure and are trying to tell people to back off? Or are you mimicking the people around you? Either way, stay present and connected to what makes you completely unique and authentic.

When you come from your genuine place of service, you will always reflect the most powerful representation of yourself every time. In turn, you will naturally attract your ideal clients to you instantly, and you will own the room.

STEP 3: FACE

What do you do when you want to know if someone is lying to you or not? You look at their face. Facial expressions are closely connected to our feelings and our hearts. What I have learned over the last eleven years working with countless people is that though our facial expressions can be genuine, there are some non-genuine looks that we all have. It is these looks that are blocking our true ability to own the room.

The most common generic facial expressions all deal with our smile. Either we plaster a fake smile on, or we are frowning most of the time. Many people don't realize that they aren't smiling or they are unaware that their smile never changes. Authentic facial expressions change, move, and express.

The easiest way to know what your face is saying is to record yourself or watch yourself make sale calls in the mirror. By being aware of your look, you know first-hand what your clients' experience. And by recording a sales presentation, you can see when your mind clicks off and goes into autopilot because your facial expressions lose life, and many times this is when you lose your client's interest as well.

By simply being connected to what makes you unique, and being present in your conversations, your passion shows.

STEP 4: TONE

When looking at the 'big picture view' of your company, what is the tone for your organization? Is it friendly and approachable, polished and professional, elite and aloof? No matter what your overall tone is for your business, you must make sure that everything communicates the same message: staff, website, social media posts, blogs, brochures, etc. Slight variations in how your customers perceive you and your company are the beginning cracks of doubt and confusion for your customer, and their relationship with your company.

Besides the overall tone of your company's message, the tone of your voice is crucial to be conscious of, especially in any situation where you are speaking. Most women speak softer in public situations, yet speak in a higher pitch when they are nervous. Guys can go soft as well, but they also tend to be louder when nervous.

It doesn't really matter how loud or soft you speak, what matters is the conviction behind your voice. Does your passion show through? Are you excited about the information you are sharing? Conviction comes when you are clear, committed, and believe in what you are selling.

Communicating a passionate tone with a consistent message makes ideal clients want to stay connected to your business, and always come back for more.

STEP 5: STYLE

The last step to owning the room and creating that "I.T." Factor Synergy℠ is all about owning your style. Style is more than what you wear or how your hair is cut. It isn't about trends or fads either. Your style is completely authentic and unique to you. It is your Soul Style℠.

Your Soul Style℠ is as different as your DNA. No two people are alike. But more importantly, it covers more than just fashion. Your Soul Style℠ includes your personal style, your space, and your collateral. Your Soul Style℠ deals with everything that has an esthetic edge to it, and yes, your company has it's own Soul Style℠ too.

Your personal style may seem like the easiest place to reflect your authentic self and it should be, but too many of us unintentionally limit ourselves to what we see on TV or to what we think we are supposed to be. The truth is there are no rules in fashion. There are things that you can do to make yourself look "better" depending upon your body's shape, skin and hair color. But when you are truly dressed in a way that expresses who you are completely, it doesn't matter what color you should wear or if that pair of pants is the right cut for your body. When you begin to reflect your authentic heart through your style, it just always works out.

Just like with your style, your space needs to be a reflection of you and your purpose. Your commercial space is one more way to reinforce your branding, but also be reflective of your company's overall tone. Within your space you can feed all of the senses: touch, taste, smell, sight, and sound – making your company's environment highly memorable and desirable not only to your customers, but to your staff as well.

Your collateral is the last area where most, if not all of the five senses can be stimulated, making the bond between your company and your clients even stronger. By using the five main senses in an authentic manner through the use of your Soul Style[SM], you are creating powerful and lasting memories for your clients – which establishes a stronger bond and a more loyal customer.

Owning the room and your marketplace isn't hard, but you must be intentional in your actions. Get clear on what you and your company are all about. By applying the five simple steps to "I.T." Factor Synergy[SM], you and your company will be an unstoppable force commanding your marketplace and increasing your bottom line.

ABOUT ALISON (ALI)

Known as ***The Wonder Woman of Success and Style*** [SM]***,*** *Alison (Ali) Craig shows entrepreneurs how to own the room, command the marketplace, and get their message out with a roar! Ali's low-cost, high-impact strategies help business owners effortlessly stand out from the crowd and attract ideal customers with ease.*

For over 11 years, Ali has worked with countless professionals, from the women of Wall Street to the fresh entrepreneurs just starting out. Through her one-on-one consulting, coaching, events and media appearances, her message of authentic empowerment is revolutionizing businesses, and it can do the same for you.

Ali is a frequently-featured expert on NBC, CBS, ABC, and FOX affiliates, as well as in print publications such as the *Wall Street Journal*, *Denver Post*, and the *New York Daily Newspaper.*

To learn more about Ali, and to receive a complimentary ***Success K"I.T."*** *(a $350 value),* connect with her online at: 3impressions.com and alicraig.com.

CHAPTER 3

MAXIMIZE YOUR BUSINESS BY MANAGING YOUR ENERGY

BY DR. CAROLYN ANDERSON

"I don't have enough time" has become the rallying cry of a generation, as we try to do it all and be all things to all people. But time is the great equalizer; whether we are Oprah Winfrey, Bill Gates, Richard Branson, Howard Schultz or Hillary Clinton we are all given 24 hours in a day, 7 days a week, 365 days a year. Why do some people manage to pull off extraordinary accomplishments while others just make it through the day?

The difference between these two groups of people is not only how they manage their time, but more importantly, how they manage their energy. I have come to realize that energy and not time is the 'hot commodity.' How we manage our energy will dictate how big we play the game of life and the impact that we have.

In this chapter, I'll share with you my system of energy management. This system will revolutionize your life. If you follow the simple steps of the system, your energy will explode off the charts and catapult you to excellence in your business and your life.

MY STORY

It is nearing the end of a busy day in the OR. A stale heat hangs over the room and mixes with the unappealing aroma of disinfectant that typically lingers in a hospital, the boom box at the back of the room is cranking out that old Diana Ross tune "Ain't no mountain high enough", but the reception is so fuzzy I have to strain to make it out. I am on my last case of the day. I move my chair into position and start my first incision, into the shining blue eye of the 81 year old kind gentlemen who has entrusted me to remove his cataract. Suddenly, I feel a kick to my belly from the inside, and a bead of sweat rolls down my forehead. I am exhausted and uncomfortable, but the patient in front of me deserves my best and somehow I have to come up with it. I am 34 weeks pregnant and planned on working the rest of this week and then taking some time to get ready for the baby. Little did I know that the little boy growing inside of me would feel compelled to get an early start on tripping around the planet, and at the time I was doing that last surgery of the day, I was probably in early labor. A few hours later, my beautiful little boy was born and life as I knew it changed forever.

I would consider myself an optimistic and goal-oriented person. As long as I can remember, I always wanted to be a doctor. I finished my medical degree and residency, and started my practice performing cataract surgeries. While still practicing medicine, I opened up a private surgical clinic, a medical spa, a medical consultancy business, became involved in real estate development, and also founded an online magazine for active older adults. While I was busy, I was also happy and felt I was moving forward in life and doing things that mattered to me. I had always been blessed with high energy and optimism, and I seemed to be able to keep all the balls in the air.

I then focused on my next goal in life – to have a child. While I was so excited to pee on a stick that finally turned blue, I had no idea how much it would change my life. It has been the most amazing experience, and it really is like making a decision to have your heart go walking around outside your body for the rest of your life. I love being a Mom, but for the first 18 months after my little man was born, I felt like a 'walking zombie.' Even when my son started sleeping though the night, I still felt constantly run-down and exhausted.

I kept wishing for more hours in a day so I could get everything done. But after accepting that I would never find a magic time-granting genie, I looked for a better solution. I realized that in my desire to be a perfect mom, I had stopped doing all the things that had made me successful in the first place. I wasn't exercising, eating right, planning out my life or taking the time to rejuvenate.

I began incorporating my past habits into my daily routine and immediately noticed a jump in my energy levels. Through extensive research, my own experiences and the experiences of my coaching clients, I've come up with an Energy Management System. I now feel more energetic and productive than I ever have – even while chasing around a toddler. I am convinced that we cannot get to greatness and reach our potential in life without high levels of energy. The most successful people the world over have high levels of energy. This system will skyrocket your energy levels through the stratosphere, and put you on the path to world-class success in both your business and your life.

THE ENERGY MANAGEMENT SYSTEM

The Energy Management System is broken down into six parts that can be represented by the word, 'Energy.'

E – Eating Well & Exercising
N – Now – Living in the Now
E – Everyday Life Management
R – Rejuvenation
G – Gratitude
Y – Your Passions

1. – E – Eating Well & Exercising

There is no question in my mind that when you feel better physically, you feel better mentally, emotionally and spiritually. It extrapolates to all areas of your life and helps you to build momentum. The physical is the foundation on which all other aspects of your life are placed. To feel better physically, you must be eating well and moving your body.

EATING WELL

Just like a machine, our bodies need high-quality fuel in order to function at our highest level. Too often we rely on quick energy fixes like coffee, energy drinks or sweets, which only improve our energy levels for a short time before we crash.

Instead of quick-fixes, focus on eating high-quality foods like whole grains, complex carbohydrates, lean protein and lots of fruit and vegetables. Ingesting foods such as these that trigger a less inflammatory state will not only improve our health and energy, but will also decrease the risk of cancer, heart disease and premature aging. The easiest way to follow an anti-inflammatory diet is to shop around the perimeter of the grocery store. All the real stuff, the good stuff, is on the outside. Avoid processed and fried foods as much as possible.

Action step: ***Eat an anti-inflammatory diet.***

MAKE TIME FOR EXERCISE

We often know what we should be doing but life gets in the way of our good intentions. Part of the reason it can be hard to be motivated to exercise is that we think of it as something we need to do to stay healthy in the long-term and can be put off. But along with the many long-term health benefits, exercise gives you an instant energy boost. Exercise has also been shown to improve your mood and reduce stress.

Make sure to move everyday for at least 20 minutes to get your heart rate up, and weight train 3-4 days a week. Do something you love to keep you fit, decrease stress and boost your energy levels.

Action Step: ***Move for 20 minutes everyday***

Any short-term gains we experience from skipping exercise, sleep or a proper meal will result in decreased productivity a few hours, days or even years later. If you're an entrepreneur, you are the most vital part of your company. If you had a machine as vital as yourself you would be sure to take care of it and get regular maintenance. Treat your mind and body as the valuable investments they are.

2. – N – Now – Living in the Now

In an effort to juggle our roles as entrepreneurs, spouses, parents and friends we often try to multitask. We are texting during dinnertime or thinking about a company problem while spending time with a friend. While we may think we are getting things done faster, the research shows that multitasking leads to lower overall productivity.

A recent study for Hewlett Packard revealed that the average IQ drops by 10 points while multi-tasking, which is equivalent to missing one night of sleep. Another study by Professor David Meyer showed that when switching between two tasks, participants took 50% longer to complete both tasks than when working on each task continuously without any interruption. Multitaskers were also more likely to make mistakes and have increased stress.

How do we stop doing too many things at once and feeling stressed, when it seems there is so much to do all the time?

Try doing just one thing at a time. Really be in that moment, immerse yourself in it and see if it is more enjoyable. Live your life. Really love your life, one moment at a time. Don't waste your energy trying to do everything at once.

I struggle with this constantly. But I do find if we are conscious of living for the now, we are more likely to do it. I am trying to make efforts in little ways to achieve this. For instance, when one of my team members comes into my office to ask me something, I put down what I am doing and physically turn my chair towards the person addressing me. By giving people your full attention in the moment, they feel more valued, you actually hear what they are saying and the issue or question can be addressed more appropriately.

<u>Action Step:</u> ***Do one thing at a time and give it your full attention and focus – before moving on to the next task.***

3. – E – Everyday Life Management

I think because we are all so busy it is imperative that we plan not only our time, but more importantly, our priorities. Life as we know can get so crazy, that unless you actually schedule something to occur, it is unlikely to ever get done. I used to have dreams that were always being put on the back burner – because of more urgent matters that were sometimes dictated by what others wanted.

In order to achieve my goals, I started a weekly planning session. Every Sunday night, I take one hour and plan my upcoming week. I break it down into all my businesses and all the other areas of my life – such as finances, fitness, personal development, spiritual, philanthropic and relationships. For each area I put an ultimate goal on the top of a blank sheet of paper. Then I write down 1-2 small action steps I need to do that week to bring me closer to that goal. By seeing the positive results this planning can bring, you will be energized and able to accomplish more than you ever thought possible.

<u>Action Step:</u> ***Spend an hour on Sunday night planning out the upcoming week.***

4. – R – Rejuvenation

In the midst of our busy lives it is essential to take time for self-rejuvenation. Like the oxygen in the airplane story, you must put the mask on yourself before you can help anyone else.

One of the best ways to reduce stress and rejuvenate is to simply meditate. Studies have shown than even just a few minutes of meditation can significantly reduce stress levels. Meditation can also improve sleep quality, moods and reduce fatigue.

In 2009, West Virginia University researchers taught a group of stressed-out people mindfulness techniques, such as deep breathing and meditation. At the end of three months, the participants had a 54 percent drop in psychological distress and a 46 percent drop in medical symptoms such as high blood pressure. The control group had little reduction of stress and an increase in medical symptoms.

<u>Action Step:</u> ***If you find your mind racing, STOP and take 5 deep breaths in and out slowly.***

5. – G – Gratitude

I think it's important to step back and be thankful. While we should always be striving to do more and be more, we must simultaneously be content with what we have. As Oprah once said, "*Be thankful for what you have; you'll end up having more. If you concentrate on what you don't have, you will never have enough.*"

Another benefit to gratitude is that when you focus on the abundance of possibilities around you, you begin to see more opportunities to expand and improve your business and your life. Researchers from the University of California found that students who kept gratitude journals were sick less often, exercised more and had more optimism than those in the control group.

Action Step: ***Write a gratitude journal. List 5 things you have to truly be grateful for everyday of your life.***

6. – Y – Your Passions

Your passions represent the best of yourself and your full potential. Find them, embrace them and move towards them. Step back and think about what you really do well and what you love to do. What activity or work comes easy to you? When does time fly by and when does it drag? Psychologists label this feeling "*flow*" and it is one of the key signs that you are living your life in tune with your passions and strengths. The key to passion is purpose. Make sure you are living a life you love, and not a life that others would love you to live.

Following your passions will energize you. There is no question in my mind that you will be happier and more successful doing something that you love to do.

Keep searching for your strong moments and imbalance in your life to spend more of your precious time engaging in your passions. In this you will find your truth, your energy and your very best life.

Action Step: ***Take a blank piece of paper and put a line down the middle. On the left side make a list of the things you love to do and on the right make a list of the things you don't like doing. In the following month make an effort to do more of what you love and less of what you don't like to do.***

CONCLUSION

To maximize your energy levels think ENERGY....**E**at well and exercise, live in the **N**ow with mindfulness, plan your **E**veryday around your goals and values, take time to **R**ejuvenate, be truly **G**rateful for all the good things in your life, and follow **Y**our passions. These are simple practices, but success is so often about doing the simple things consistently. Following these practices will elevate your energy and help you reach the highest levels of excellence in your personal and professional life.

ABOUT CAROLYN

Dr. Carolyn Anderson is an expert in managing energy levels. With her medical training, extensive research, personal experience and entrepreneurial background, she self-developed the Energy Management System.

Using the Energy Management System herself has allowed her to run her surgical practice, private surgery clinic, medical consulting business, a real estate development project, speak professionally and publish an online magazine for active older adults.

Carolyn regularly blogs on her own website (CarolynAndersonMD.com) and contributes articles to other websites including the Huffington Post. She publishes an online magazine for active older adults at Impowerage.com and co-authored, *It's Never Too Late to Be Fit* -- an exercise guide for the aging population.

She is currently working on a full-length book on Energy Management. She regularly gives speeches on Energy Management to entrepreneurs, women's groups and physicians. Using the Energy Management system allows these busy groups to improve their work/life balance and succeed professionally. As a medical consultant, Carolyn helps physicians run more effective practices. This allows them to maximize their earnings while minimizing their time at work.

Carolyn lives near Vancouver, BC with her husband and son. To learn more about Carolyn and the Energy Management System, please visit her website at www.CarolynAndersonMD.com. Newsletter subscribers will receive a free report on "10 Essential Steps for High Energy." Carolyn is available for speaking engagements, teleseminars and one-on-one coaching.

www.CarolynAndersonMD.com

CHAPTER 4

CHOICES

BY WILLIAM (BILL) LAM

You are where you are today from choices you have made. You will be where you are tomorrow from choices you make from this point on.

From a very early age until your life ends, everything is a choice. Your attitude, your spouse, your job, where you live, your beliefs, and on and on. Understanding this makes it obvious: choice is one of the biggest gifts you are given in this life. It's also one of the largest responsibilities. Everything is a choice, even not making a choice is a choice. So why is so little written on how and why we make the choices we do? And why aren't we more conscientious about how we make decisions? It is simple, yet complex. Common sense, yet scientific. Lives are changed every day by simple choices, and I am sorry to say not always in a positive direction. Hopefully, as we go through the process of understanding how choices are made, we will create a road map on making better choices and improving the quality of your life.

Time and time again we have seen or heard of someone making a poor choice that changed the direction of his or her life, ended a relationship, cost a fortune, or even ended a life. What enables a person to make a better choice, thus opening the door to live an extraordinary life?

Most successful people understand goals, focus, planning, and time management; yet they often make choices that hinder the process, establishing sayings such as "your actions speak so loud I can't hear a word you're saying," or "behavior never lies." In other words, people often say one thing yet do another, perhaps going back to childhood when we heard "do what I say, not what I do."

This actually brings us to the first step in the process of making better choices. We should establish priorities, I mean life priorities, such as spiritual, immediate family, extended family, and jobs. Then write them out and list them in order: most important to least. Once you have done this, it is important to establish your core values. This includes such things as integrity, loyalty, and work ethic. In other words, those values that determine how people see you and, in fact, how you see yourself and who you want to be. Here it becomes imperative that you understand you are the master of your fate, the pilot of your vessel. In other words, you determine the direction and outcome of your life by choices you make.

Business people, athletes – in fact most all people – understand that without specific, short-term, intermediate, and long-term goals, as well as a certain plan or process, you will never reach your potential. Priorities and core values are just as necessary to make better choices. When your choices begin to live up to your priorities and core values, your life will go in that direction.

Have you ever written down your priorities in life, your core values and thought, "This is who I am, this is how I want to be viewed? This is what I want to be known for?" It's a simple task, yet few have ever done it. It can change your life.

It has also been well established that successful athletes, coaches, and business men have a good self-image, and high self-esteem. Again, this leads to a cycle. When you make choices that are in agreement with your priorities and core values, you like yourself and you continue to make better choices establishing an upward spiral. Conversely, when you make poor choices or choices that go against your core values, you don't like yourself, causing a downward spiral.

This is why it is so important to write out your priorities and core values, take time to examine them and ask yourself, "Is this who I want to be? Is this the legacy I want to establish? Is this the husband, father, boss I want to be?"

The next time you have an important decision, look and see how it lines up with your core values. It will almost make your choice for you. Certainly this will take some time and effort, but soon it will become second nature, developing habits and choices that will change the quality of life, opening the door to an extraordinary life that will bring you happiness and a life you will be proud of.

There is another huge factor at work. That is believing. The law of believing is a universal law. It is like gravity, it doesn't matter whether you believe it or not, it is in action 24-7.

Science can explain how gravity works and even tell you the rate at which something will fall. I will try to explain how the law of believing works. Just as everything is a choice, everything is a form of believing. The law says believing = receiving. You have positive believing and negative believing. Positive believing is to have trust, faith, and confidence. Negative believing is doubt, fear and worry. I believe Henry Ford said it best when he said:

"Believe you can, or believe you can't, either way you'll be right." My point is that your believing will be a very strong influence in your choices. Choose to stay positive. Why? Well, there's another well-known quote: "You don't always get what you want in life, but sooner or later you get what you expect." Even more specific is the biblical verse, "as a man thinketh in his heart, so is he."

Let's look at other aspects that impair or influence your choices. Certainly substance abuse and alcohol can affect the choices you make. To use or not is even a choice at first, yet can become a habit that makes choices for you. It is well established that your choices become habits. Habits that you first control but then they begin to control you.

Perhaps the best way to explain how people make poor choices is to look at the two Greek words – Apastia and Apatheia. Apastia means you haven't been taught, or you haven't been taught fully or completely. In other words, if you've never been taught a law or don't understand it completely, you can make a very poor choice. How many times have you heard, "I didn't know that" after a bad choice? The other word, Apatheia, means you've been taught but you don't care or you are apathetic and don't care about the consequence. Perhaps you've heard, "I don't care, I'm doing it anyway." Another factor that can affect our choices are emotions – fear, love, loneliness, anger, hate, joy – yet establishing our priorities and core values will even effect how we treat each of those emotions. Let's look at some choices and ask why.

- A very wealthy actress shoplifts a necklace, one she could easily afford – yet the choice she made could put her in jail and end her career.
- A prominent coach does not self-report NCAA violations, causing severe penalties and a huge loss of money.
- A very high ranking politician has an affair causing a divorce and the end of his career.

Had each weighed the choices, and checked priorities and core values, they would have different lives today.

Many successful businessmen have stated after a great accomplishment that it was the right thing to do. Often, their actions created heroes and grew a business exponentially.

One more factor that comes into play when making choices is risk. As we have seen, all choices have consequences or rewards. Again, understanding priorities and values, even risks pale, for when you are passionate about a choice and it falls in line with your priorities and values, great things can happen. I gave a couple of examples of negative outcomes or consequences from choices that were not in alignment with values. Here is a success story of a choice made that involved great risk.

I met Roy Williams in the late 1970's when he came to the University of North Carolina to be a part-time assistant coach and was to receive no pay. Why would a person quit a paying job to work for nothing, especially considering he was married with children? I am sure many were saying, wow, what a poor decision or choice. It was a big risk, but Coach Williams wanted to work under and learn from one of the best – and Dean Smith was that coach. His first year, Coach Williams had to sell basketball posters and deliver films to the TV station to support his family. Later he became the head coach at Kansas and then in 2003 returned to North Carolina to be the head coach. He has won two National Championships since his return and has a multi-million dollar contract. A far cry from selling posters. All because of an early choice to learn from the best. Why was it a great choice? He wanted it with all his heart, and it lined up with his priorities in life and his core values. Even if it hadn't worked out, he would have felt good because he was living the life he was supposed to live – he was finding and developing his purpose.

Choices made with high priorities, standards, and values will take your life to the top. I would be amiss if I didn't add one more note about Coach Williams. He is the same man now that he was when he began his profession receiving no pay. He has high morals, high standards, and a great heart for people, which is attested to by what his former and current athletes say about him. In short, he is a giver who has not lost sight nor changed his priorities and core values. He still makes choices by keeping them in alignment .

Not all people have handled success this well. Many change their priorities and lose sight of their core values. I am certain you can rattle off the names of many great athletes, business men and leaders who made poor choices after they reached the top, thinking they were above this law then saw their world come tumbling down. Still others have come from ashes to glory by learning the lessons and raising their priorities and core values, then making new choices with those new priorities and values. It reminds me that experience is not always the best teacher, for it gives the test before the lesson. My hope is that some of you learn this lesson as you read this chapter.

Everyone has difficult times, some from other peoples poor choices, some from our own and some just from life. The one final choice I would urge is to never give up. It is never over until you quit. Most people quit because they feel sorry for themselves. Just or unjust it doesn't matter, quitting ends it. So how do you stop feeling sorry for yourself? Get thankful for all you have. My mom shared a saying with me when I was very young and I have never forgotten it. "I cried because I had no shoes, and then I met a boy who had no feet." Being thankful for what you have where you are at this moment will change your outlook, it will actually change your behavior and you will start giving to others and low and behold, you have stumbled on another law. When you give you always receive. So the final choice I would ask you to consider is to never give up!!

Be thankful!! Choose to be a giver, understanding that it will always come back. Perhaps not immediately, maybe not in the form you expect, but always in a way that will improve your life.

I am thankful for the life I have had. I have had great success, been on the top of mountain peaks and I have had lows; I've been in the trenches, and when I look back, it was all from making good or bad choices – choices which honored my core values, or those times I turned away from them.

I still have much I wish to accomplish in this life, but I pray I have learned the lesson to make choices that stay in alignment with my priorities and core values.

In closing this chapter I would be foolish to think that you won't make some bad decisions, and to that I would say "winners don't always make the right decisions but they make their decisions right."

The more you understand priorities and core values, the more you keep your choices in alignment with those values, and the greater your chance to enjoy the extraordinary life – a life that is more than abundant – and that is a promise from a much higher source than me.

ACTION EXERCISE: Write out your priorities and rank them from top to bottom. Then list your core values. Read and re-read them as you think of important decisions that are coming your way. Then make a wise choice and start living and enjoying an extraordinary and meaningful life. (Blessings)

ABOUT WILLIAM

William Lam owns and operates "Wrestling with Life," a business and coaching consultancy through which he helps individuals and organizations succeed. Bill received his bachelor's degree from the University of Oklahoma, earning his master's degree in counseling and guidance and a master's in psychology. A member of OU's national championship team, he went on to set a team record for most victories.

As head coach for 30 years at the University of North Carolina, Bill Lam became the 'winningest' wrestling coach in the history of the Atlantic Coast Conference. He was honored as national coach of the year and was named National Man of the Year among college wrestling coaches.

Lam's coaching years served as the foundation for his consulting career, in which he provides programs to help managers, executives and CEOs for businesses large and small. His Principles of Success workshops, seminars and programs include sales performance, skill building, team building and evaluation. Headquartered in Brighton, Michigan, Lam serves as a Board Member of the National Wrestling Hall of Fame, of which he is a member.

CHAPTER 5

HOW TO BRAINSTORM YOUR WAY TO NEW MARKETS

BY NANCY PHILLIPS

Imagine yourself walking into a boardroom. There are twelve chairs around a large wooden table and a white board at the front of the room. As you pull out a chair to sit down, you think about your last meeting and the dozens of emails awaiting your response. You just finished two back-to-back meetings and gulped down a sandwich at your desk. Your colleagues enter the room with notepads in one hand; some have coffees in the other. You, like many of your colleagues, have another meeting after this one.

Now, imagine lacing up your running shoes and putting on your sunglasses. You open your front door to the glorious sunshine and literally inhale nature's beauty as you step outside. As you begin to move you can feel the positive energy begin to flow through you.

Both of these scenarios are the beginning of brainstorming sessions. Which will be more productive? Inspiring? Which would you rather be involved in? While we can't all hold our brainstorming sessions jogging along the beach or hiking up a mountain, we can recognize and implement some of the key concepts that occur during periods of "free thinking."

KEY FACTORS TO CONSIDER:

1. Don't limit your thinking by defining market boundaries
2. Think big and think clearly. Be as specific as possible about your purpose and direction
3. After the "why", use "how" and "what" questions. "How can we ....?" "What could we develop that ..."
4. Forget about the competition for the time being
5. Ensure your team truly understands the customer's entire experience and circumstances
6. Ensure your top "front line" people are present to relay customer needs and current frustrations
7. Don't "Fire hose" your own or anybody else's ideas
8. Incorporate "free thinking" time into your creative process
9. Think like a scientist, "Fail fast"
10. Prepare your brain!

ASKING THE RIGHT QUESTIONS

Corporations often talk about taking "market share" from the competition. But to really change the face of an industry, to develop a breakthrough product that changes lives, it doesn't start there. It must start with the belief that there is no limit to the "market size." The only limits that exist on the market boundaries are those created by the people within them. To be truly innovative, the companies must ask themselves key questions including: Why do we do what we do? How can we improve our customer's quality of daily life? What is the real need we are trying to fulfill? What matters most to our customer? How can we make their life easier or more convenient? It's that freedom of thought combined with clarity of purpose that can take your idea, product or company to the next level.

Simply put, the "why" must come first. Purpose inspires creation and ultimately the type of visionary, unique products that change the business landscape. Looking within market boundaries often leads to "me-too" products and services. Many "new" products on the market are simply enhancements of those that already exist – either from one's own company or the competition. As many corporate teams have found out, products that are line extensions or enhancements to previous products are not inspiring to either the customer or the sales team. Perceived lack of time and "market pressure" often lead companies down this default route. In a rush to gain market share, many organizations miss the opportunity to create a valuable, leading-edge answer to the customer's true needs.

One of the most powerful lessons an entrepreneur can learn is to break out of the "competition" mindset and think purely in creative thoughts. There needs to be definitive clarity in the goal, the end deliverable to the customer, but the "what" should be given freedom to develop, grow and emerge from ideas of what is possible.

UNDERSTANDING YOUR CUSTOMER

Researching the entire customer experience within your field is critical. Focusing only on the stage of their experience that involves your potential product is limiting and can force you to miss the opportunity to deliver greater outcomes. Looking at what the customer does before, during and after they use your product or service will help clarify where you can step in and add value. This will ensure you have the critical information necessary to solve more of the customers' needs.

In the development of a piece of protective sports gear for college and pro football players, a design team missed one key piece of information. The product was designed considering only a player's typical practice and game schedule. However, when the gruelling "Two-a-Days" practice schedule began, certain parts of the product didn't leave time for the sweat to dry between practices and it began to slip. The problem was easily worked out with a slight change of materials, but the example demonstrates the necessity of comprehensively identifying the circumstances in which your customer may interact with your potential product or service.

Who attends the brainstorming meeting is also critical. The top "front line" people should be there, not just the management, IT or engineering team. You will miss out on key customer information if you don't have your top sales and customer service people in attendance. They can give you the most compelling information about your customer's current daily frustrations and unfulfilled needs. Their involvement will also significantly aid in the successful implementation of the new strategy.

NO "FIRE HOSING"

Brainstorming as a large group in a meeting room isn't always the most creative atmosphere, but there are many lessons we can all take away. "Fire hosing ideas" is *a definite no-no* in any creative process. It is critical for everyone to listen to all ideas and not give any negative feedback. This should continue until an exhaustive list is created. One of the biggest mistakes many companies make is to try to come away with "the" idea, at the end of one, long, brainstorming meeting.

Why is this a mistake? Because there hasn't been time for everyone's subconscious mind to digest and incorporate all the ideas, to combine them in infinite combinations, to pull them apart and put them back together again – to solve the puzzle. Researchers in brain science have found that the part of the brain responsible for decision-making and control of emotions, called the dorsolateral prefrontal cortex can, and frequently does, go into overload. In scientific studies, when subjects were given continuous information over time, there came a point when the activity in the dorsolateral PFC essentially shut down and people began to make silly mistakes. Not surprisingly, their emotions then escalated skyward. Studies have also shown that memory increases after a sleep. Through sleep, the subconscious is given the opportunity to organize the new information along with the old, so the lessons and knowledge can "relate" to each other. This is how our brain learns, by relating recognized information to each other.

QUIET TIME IS KEY

This is why, in my opinion, it is so important to take the time to let your brain "digest" the information presented at a brainstorming session. Often the best ideas are combinations of several different ideas presented, and these combinations may be difficult to pick out immediately because our decision-making and "factual" part of the brain work very differently. A relaxed brain is crucial for the best ideas to come forward. This is the reason so many people have their best ideas when driving, having a shower, jogging or in the middle of the night. Bottom line – the mind needs quiet time to make its best decisions and to effectively use the years of knowledge and experience that already exists in the subconscious. Entrepreneurs and corporate executives can, and should, create that time.

Once the team works towards narrowing down and combining decisions to come to the "final few," encourage a feeling of excitement about all the ideas, so there is as little bias as possible going into the trials. Although you want to have a good decision-making process, it is unrealistic to expect you will always hit the target on the first try. This is where the concept of "failing fast" and thinking like a scientist comes in. As long as each "failure" is looked at as a learning opportunity which provides more information and gets you closer to the final destination, the team will stay inspired and driven towards producing a high quality product for the customer.

AT THE MEETING

Funnily enough, when most of us come to brainstorming meetings we completely forget to think about the state of our brains!! To maximize its effectiveness stand up! This increases the oxygen flow to your brain and ultimately your memory. This is precisely why many Fortune 500 CEO's have stand-up desks. Standing up has also been proven to make meetings run more productively because people are more alert. Focus is critical for the creative process – so all phones should be off. Any interruptions not only affect the person receiving the communication, but also the people around them. Scientific studies have shown that humans don't actually "multi-task." What really happens is the brain switches tasks very quickly. During this switch, vital information can get forgotten, ignored or completely missed.

One other important consideration for brain performance is based on the fact our brains are composed of 78% water. Most people in our society have chronically dehydrated brains from drinking coffee, tea, or soda. Your brain will be in a much better state and you will be more effective, if you drink water *throughout* the day. It takes two hours for the water to get to your brain so don't wait until you feel thirsty!

In summary, there are many factors to consider when brainstorming to expand a market or create a new one. True "breakthrough" products often have less to do with what already exists and more to do with things people need without even realizing it. Too often the focus is on the "total market" and taking a piece of that market from the competition. If instead we approach it from the position of growing the market or better yet, creating a new one, we have the opportunity to offer our customers something truly grand.

As an entrepreneur, you have the opportunity to develop valuable, meaningful products that can improve people's lives. Give yourself the freedom of thought to create these "blue ocean" products. It will drive your passion and creativity – while allowing you to provide your customers with innovative, valuable solutions.

ABOUT NANCY

Author and entrepreneur, Nancy Phillips is the creator of the Zela Wela Kids financial literacy and life skills products for children and teens. With a BS in Human Kinetics as well as an executive MBA, she has a formal background in both the biological sciences and business. While working in the corporate world for almost twenty years, she held positions in product development, portfolio management and international marketing for three of the world's leading medical companies.

Since becoming a mother, her new passion is to research and create fun resources to inspire and help children and young adults to reach their full potential. She also coaches parents who want to learn more about teaching their children good financial habits and life "success" skills. She is the author of *The Zela Wela Kids Learn about Becoming Entrepreneurs, The Zela Wela Kids Build a Bank, The Zela Wela Kids Learn about Needs and Wants* and *The Zela Wela Kids Learn about Money*.

Nancy has been interviewed on radio stations throughout North America. She has appeared on T.V., written numerous magazine articles, and been interviewed by both magazine and newspaper reporters on this very timely topic.

CHAPTER 6

THE PASSION PRINCIPLE

–THE FOUNDATION FOR YOUR SUCCESS

BY MICHAEL E. BUDOWSKI

Show me a passionate businessperson and I will show you a successful business. Passion is the key to creating extraordinary businesses. What is passion? The dictionary definition is: a strong and barely controllable emotion • an intense desire or enthusiasm for something.

Many "experts" convey that to follow your passion requires labor. I disagree; following one's passion precludes you from being a laborer, as passion is not a conscious thought or action, it is an intangible emotion that is an unconscious reaction. It is what wakes you up early in the morning in excited anticipation of another day. Passion fuels your thoughts and actions. This is why it is critical to find your passion in business and then begin your entrepreneurial quest. Passion is a conviction that is not governable; you can't just pick something and arbitrarily decide "I am going to be passionate about this," any more than you could say 'I love you' to someone, and truly mean it from looking at their resume. It does not work that way, whether in business or in your personal life.

So how does all this apply to my business? Glad you asked. Finding your passion means never having to work again in the traditional sense. It makes work pleasurable, not work. Your passion can be anything, from being the best bug killer (more on that in a moment), to aspiring to be the world's most innovative technology company, à la Apple®. The key is the conviction that comes from being passionate about what you do. It is important to be cognizant that passion may come from many places. It could be something you are born with, something that you were exposed to, or something that frustrated you to the point that you were determined to do something better.

Passion from frustration? Absolutely. James Dyson became so frustrated with weak vacuum cleaners that lost suction that he began trying to create an incredibly strong vacuum that would never lose suction. The power of this passionate frustration drove him for 5 years – until he finally achieved the Dyson® vacuum that would turn into a 6 billion dollar business! His estimated net worth is in excess of 2 billion dollars. Pretty frustrating indeed!

In 1984, I co-founded my first company, a commercial exterminating company. Sure, being a bug killer might not excite a lot of people, (I now find the vacuum cleaner to be quite exciting), however, out of frustration we were determined to create a new kind of exterminating company. We became even more determined after meeting with industry icons including representatives from the industry's National Association; all of whom said what we wanted to do could not be done. This added more fuel to our passion. We developed a guaranteed pest elimination program for restaurants, hotels and other food establishments. We quickly became a multi-million dollar company operating in 8 states and servicing 3000 commercial properties in 20 business days of every month. In an industry where restaurants or hotels would change exterminating companies every 11 months, our average customer retention was 7.2 years! Our passion and reputation caught the attention of a multi-billion dollar public British company that purchased our business.

Passion is derived from the Latin word for suffering. This is a different type of suffering than an injury or illness. The suffering of sacrificing your time to realize your passion's potential with all the setbacks that go with it. Think about Michael Jordan's endless basketball practicing, the first one at practice and the last one to leave. James Dyson after 5000 plus attempts to get his vacuum design right. The setbacks propel us to continue, and make no mistake whatever the endeavor – there will always be setbacks and challenges to overcome.

President Calvin Coolidge was quoted as saying: "Nothing in the world can take the place of persistence. Talent will not; nothing is more common than unsuccessful men with talent. Genius will not; unrewarded genius is almost a proverb. Education will not; the world is full of educated derelicts. Persistence and determination alone are omnipotent. The slogan 'Press On' has solved, and always will solve, the problems of the human race."

So how do we make passion work in our business?

- Spread Your Passion – It is contagious, a perfect example is Pixar® and Apple®. Steve Jobs did not do it alone. His passion became their passion, all working together for a common goal to create something extraordinary. Shrek®, Toy Story®, the iPhone®, enough said. Success fosters yet more conviction and passion.

- Environment – Create an environment for your team to excel. Remember they are not you and do not have the same commitment and resolve as you do (yet). For this reason you must take the time to create extraordinary systems for ordinary people to thrive. One of the best examples of how to accomplish this is Michael Gerber's book series *The E-Myth*®. People are inherently more committed when they are thriving in their jobs.

- Commit to EverLearning™ – You have to stay ahead of the game. For this reason alone you must be constantly refueling your subconscious with new ideas. Set aside time each day and commit to learning something new that may aid in the execution of your vision. Passion without some control and discipline can lead to disastrous results. Manage your time wisely. One of the best books on time management is *Eat that Frog, 1 & 2* by Brian Tracy. Remember, business and life are not static. You are either moving ahead or falling behind in all areas of life; there is no "*status quo*."

- EverTeaching™ – Since you are constantly learning and improving, it is critical for you to continuously pass along lessons learned to your team. One thing I witness from passionate entrepreneurs is they forget at times how much they have assimilated into their brains, and think everyone should know what they know. Well guess what? They don't, and it's your job to be constantly teaching and encouraging them to teach others.

- Manage Expectations – This applies to your staff, and your customers. This is an area of control and discipline. While your passion and vision is to be, do, and create, you have to manage expectations. It is not realistic to tell your staff you will be a billion dollar company in a year. This undermines the confidence they have in you and will keep them from "catching" your passion.

  From a customer's perspective, a great example of control and discipline is Apple's® first iPhone. They chose not to put 3G on the phone. Not because the technology for 3G was not readily available, in fact most Smartphones at the time were either 3G or coming out with 3G. The issue was the battery drain from the 3G. Apple® decided the feature was not worth potentially disappointing their new customers, especially with this being their first cell phone in the company's history. We all know what has transpired since. The iPhone's user satisfaction is unparalleled, they have created loyal customer advocates, plus sold a few phones –more than a 100 million iPhones worldwide!

You will know when your passion presents itself. It does not matter the field or endeavor – from bug killer, plumber, doctor, lawyer, vacuum designer, athlete, musician, artist, to 'you name it.' When it does appear, you will move forward as if you are on autopilot with an endless supply of fuel. Passion is intoxicating, it becomes an obsession. By exercising discipline and control, you will attract other passionate individuals that will not only expedite the achievement of your goals, they in turn will attract more passionate individuals, both staff and customers. When that happens, not even the sky becomes a limit.

To read more case studies on business passion, or to learn more about Ever-Learning™ and EverTeaching™, please visit: www.mikebudowski.com.

ABOUT MICHAEL

Michael Budowski is a serial entrepreneur and sales and marketing expert. He has had successful as well as unsuccessful ventures. He believes the latter is where humility and wisdom is derived – most notably in his case as President and CEO of a dot.com that did SuperBowl® advertising during the Internet boom and subsequent crash. Michael was drawn to business at an early age. He co-founded his first company in 1984, which later sold to a multi-billion dollar public British company.

He has spoken at National Conventions, and has been a panel member at several Universities as well as a former Dale Carnegie Sales Instructor. He has appeared on or in over 80 television, radio and print publications, including Your World with Neil Cavuto, ABC World News Tonight with Peter Jennings, NPR, CNN Headline News, CBS MarketWatch, MSNBC, FOX News Channel and articles from Business Week, USA Today, New York Times, Wired Magazine and a host of others.

He is a consummate learner, avid reader and particularly enjoys the case method. His obsession with sales, marketing and persuasion started when he was 19 and attended a five-day boot camp with world-renowned sales trainer Tom Hopkins. He has also attended Executive Education programs at Harvard, Harvard Law School and The Wharton School. Michael recently founded EverLearning™ and EverTeaching™ to spread his philosophy of 'forever learning' and 'forever teaching.'

Michael recalls his early fascination with the Internet when it was only text. He was fixated on search engines before the term SEO was invented. His fundamental approach to web positioning has achieved over a decade of consistent top rankings, and has weathered countless algorithm changes.

He believes that all successful businesses and marketing campaigns begin with passion and focus. For more information on his business, Internet marketing services and speaking engagements, go to: www.mikebudowski.com.

CHAPTER 7

PASSION AND PURPOSE

- GO WHERE THE ENERGY IS!

BY LOULIE KEY SCHARF

Fourteen years ago, I attended the first in a series of workshops that would alter the course of my life. The workshops, hosted by a California-based nonprofit called The Painting Experience, taught me a simple principal that I have come to live by.

As participants, we explored "process art," a mode of painting in which the emphasis remains on the creative journey and pure expression. My greatest takeaway from these workshops has become one of my mantras: "Go where the energy is!"

What does this phrase mean? In the workshop, it meant allowing our deepest feelings to guide our creativity. It meant coming face-to-face with ideas and images that intrigued us, thrilled us, and sometimes terrified us. In life, it means following our passions. It means pursuing those things which resonate most deeply within us. It means chasing the trail of the things that stir us most deeply. It means riding a vein of energy, and staying with it to see where it leads.

"Go where the energy is!" echoes in my mind and shapes my day-to-day life. If something thrills me, I follow its direction. Likewise, if something terrifies or disgusts me, I know I probably have some work to do around that, and I try to explore that further. But that's a different chapter!

Through the workshops, my husband and I became friends with the co-founder of The Painting Experience, Stewart Cubley. Stewart is a fantastic example of someone pursuing his passion and using his gifts to make the world a better place. Stewart has created a life he loves, helping others to discover and follow their own unique paths. He nurtures participants as they face fears and transformation, and he encourages them as they experience ecstasy and bliss. Stewart lives an amazing life, traveling to the world's most beautiful locales to conduct his workshops.

Do you love your work? Besides home with your family, is your workplace your favorite place to be? Is there nothing you would rather be doing? Is your work a blessing because it makes you feel good? Does your work reward you handsomely, both emotionally and financially?

Sadly, most people trudge through their workdays and only pursue their passions in their spare time. In the past few years, I have noticed a constant, discontented buzz. Acquaintances and strangers alike complain of boredom and restlessness, saying they want to DO something important, something that matters. They long for a way to contribute to the world.

Unhappiness in the workplace is more relevant today than ever before. CBS News reported in 2010 that 55 percent of Americans are dissatisfied with their work. The survey showed the most dissatisfaction in 20 years.

Most people believe they have a higher calling, which might contribute to their restlessness with their current work. A 2007 Gallup survey asked adults in 84 countries, "Do you feel your life has an important purpose or meaning?" More than 80 percent replied, "yes." Among those who affiliate themselves with a religion, roughly 90% answered "yes." This is because faith and purpose are strongly connected. People who believe in a higher power usually believe they are divinely chosen for a certain mission.

Certainly, the challenging economy fuels mass unhappiness. There are lots of stressed-out people in our society, and negativity can be contagious. The pace of our world has accelerated too, heaping added stress upon our shoulders. The Earth is spinning more quickly, and society is on the hamster wheel, spinning furiously. "Down time" is a rare luxury. We race around at a frantic pace, and we still cannot catch up. In a society frenzied by this pace, those of us who spend our time doing exactly what we want to are truly blessed.

Every person comes into this world with unique talents and gifts. I believe we each have a divine purpose in life, aligned with our talents. Our true work utilizes our talents to contribute to the greater good of the world. It is our job to discover our highest mission in life, and then find a way to make that our daily work.

How can you tell if people are living their divine purposes?

If they are not engaged in their chosen work, they are dragging themselves through life. Their misery is readily apparent.

On the other hand, when people live their true purposes, they ride veins of energy. They are excited, passionate and energetic, because they are pursuing the causes that matter most deeply to them, in alignment with their values. They are "following the energy," and they are on fire with their work.

If you seek them out, you will find shining stars all around you who are living their purposes, and therefore bettering the world. Surround yourself with these people! We become who we hang around, so spend time with positive-minded people who use their gifts to contribute to the world.

As I move through my day-to-day life, I cross paths regularly with fortunate folks who are pursuing their passions while contributing to society. In other words, they are living their true purposes.

For starters, I am endlessly grateful that I lead a life built around my passions. I am a mother and a wife, and these two roles make me happiest of all. Our family includes lots of four-legged critters, too, who bring us endless joy. We are very active in animal rescue, fulfilling a deep-seated desire to help animals. I am an artist and a writer, and I work on creative projects that engage and thrill me. I love to learn, and my graduate school studies ensure that I continue to grow in my creative pursuits. I am thankful to live an enriched life, surrounding myself with the people, critters and activities I love.

My husband, Matt, spends his day pursuing his passions while making a contribution to our community. Matt renovates historic properties, the ultimate form of recycling. He exercises his creative muscles to find new uses for dilapidated properties, and the challenge thrills him. He also manages to carve out time in his busy schedule to volunteer in our kids' classrooms, chaperone field trips, and join them during school lunches. I am so blessed to have a husband so devoted to his family!

While our kids are in school, I stop at the gym to exercise, and the fitness instructors' chiseled physiques are clear indications of the passion they feel for what they do. The gym is their second home, and it is where they love to be, improving their own bodies while they help others achieve physical fitness.

When I pick up our kids at school, I am constantly in awe of their teachers' passion and devotion. They truly cherish their roles as educators and role models, and the kids and parents love and appreciate them for it.

We drive from school to the tennis courts, and again we meet passion face to face. My kids' tennis coaches would rather be on the courts than anywhere else, which is a great measuring stick for passion and purpose.

The question of whether you are living your purpose comes down to this: Is your work selfish, or is it selfless? Are you giving of yourself, using your talents and gifts to better the world? A true purpose is selfless in nature. However, the financial rewards can be massive!

There is a lot of truth in the saying, "Do what you love, and the money will follow." A 2011 issue of Forbes Magazine named Bill Gates as America's richest person and the world's second richest person. Gates' technological genius contributes tremendously to society, and he makes the world a better place through his global philanthropic efforts. Did he also make a tremendous fortune? Absolutely, beyond his wildest dreams!

Two extraordinarily creative "givers" on the Forbes list are Steven Spielberg, dynamo film producer, and George Lucas, creator of Star Wars. They clearly follow their passions, and in so doing, they entertain the world. And the riches follow.

When I think of enormously successful people, I think of Tony Robbins, self-help guru who improves the lives of millions through his work.

Oprah and Ellen DeGeneres are two more shining examples. They educate and entertain the world, bringing smiles to millions of faces.

Walt Disney's contribution to the world lives on even larger now that he is gone, as does Dr. Seuss' creative genius, which has enriched the lives of countless children, near and far. I also admire writers such as Brian Tracy and Louise Hay, who use their craft to raise awareness. Another favorite of mine is Jack Canfield, coauthor of the Chicken Soup series. Is he rolling in the riches? Yes! Does he deserve to be? Yes! His positive impact on humanity is massive.

Those are celebrity examples. While most people living their true purposes may not make a global impact, there is tremendous good to be found in small communities across the world. In our friendly coastal town of Wilmington, North Carolina, the population is hardly more than 100,000 people, yet we have more than 700 nonprofit organizations. Our community is working for the greater good!

Higher callings may entertain, educate, enlighten, beautify, create, heal, assist, encourage or teach. True purposes come in all shapes and sizes. My father is a master woodworker. His perfectly turned wooden bowls are exquisite objects of beauty, and they bring pleasure to those who admire them. At this stage of his life, woodworking is both his passion and his contribution.

My friend, local artist Pam Toll, is blessed with true God-given talent. She paints breathtaking paintings and teaches art at our local university. She co-owns ACME Studios, a building housing dozens of working studios. She is cofounder of No Boundaries International Art Colony, a nonprofit organization that brings a group of international artists together yearly to make art for two weeks on nearby, beautiful Bald Head Island. Pam uses her gifts and follows her passions, and in doing so, she has created a life filled with creativity and interesting people.

Tracy Wilkes, another friend of mine, created a nononprofit organization called Dreams, which provides art education to children in need. Through Dreams, she has changed the lives of hundreds of local kids. I had the privilege of teaching art at Dreams, and I experienced firsthand the rewarding feeling that fills Tracy up on a daily basis.

"I feel like I have woven together all that I love best into this program:

children, the arts, my experience as a social worker and therapist," says Tracy. "When I began the program fourteen years ago, I remember feeling like I had come full circle, bringing all of my talents to bear on a mission that I was passionate about. There is no better feeling than waking up everyday and knowing that the work that you do is also the work that you love."

Another local program I admire for its commitment to improve the lives of kids through creativity is Kids Making It. Started by Jimmy Pierce in the mid-90s, Kids Making It teaches woodworking and offers mentoring to children in need.

When I asked Jimmy what inspired him to start Kids Making It, he said, "Parenthood hit me like a ton of bricks. Your whole world changes. Your perspective changes. Your priorities change."

Driving his family home from a vacation late one night, with his baby son sleeping in the back, Jimmy had a revelation about starting a program to help the city's most needy youth. After some time spent putting his plans in place, he left his successful law practice to start Kids Making It, his higher calling.

Jimmy says, "I love woodworking because it puts me in a zone. I lose track of time. I absolutely am living in alignment with my true purpose. My dream is to be in the shop, doing woodwork with the kids, every day, all day long."

Jimmy's journey from lawyer to nonprofit founder illustrates an important point. It's OK to change your path! Think of Robert Frost's two roads in a wood, with one road leading toward your true purpose, and one toward less meaningful work. If your work is not aligned with your higher purpose and ideals, it might be time to consider a path change.

Sometimes it takes a radical path change. I have had a couple in my life. Right after college, I had the privilege of living and working in Sydney, Australia. I felt I landed the ideal job when I got an internship with Coca-Cola South Pacific, a few steps away from the Sydney Opera House, overlooking Sydney Harbor. Though I adored my time there, I ultimately learned that a clean desk policy and the corporate world did not light my fire. This discovery moved me closer to my true purpose. Within a year, I rediscovered my childhood passion for art, which has defined my life and work ever since.

After my Australian experience, I daydreamed for years about owning a far-reaching art studio. Eventually, I opened "Make Art," a buzzing, 5,000 square foot art school that became a local hub for artists, instructors, kids and creative folks. While it was a wild, wonderful and necessary chapter in my life, I realized early on that the tremendous workload was taking me away from my family. I decided to switch paths, and I have not looked back since. That was the right move, and it brought me even closer to my true purpose.

You might already have a clear vision of your higher calling. Maybe you just need to fine-tune your mission. Or, you might be starting with a blank slate. If so, persistent soul searching and self-reflection can lead you to your true purpose.

Discovering your purpose, and therefore your ideal life's work, is like solving a riddle. Reach deep inside yourself to find answers to some core questions. Your answers are your clues. To begin the process, I suggest settling down into a comfortable spot with a notebook and pen, and free-writing your "gut answers" to the following questions:

What excites you?
What drains you?
What do you do in your spare time?
What do you daydream about?
What are you good at?
How could you use your natural talents to contribute to the world?
What are you passionate about?
What do you collect?
What would you do for no compensation?
What activities make you feel good about yourself?
If you were a teacher, what would you teach?
What do you want to learn more about?
What do you stand up for?
Who and what do you surround yourself with?
Who inspires you?
What brings you joy?

As you ponder your passions, remember to think about WHO you want to help, as well as what you want to do.

Another strategy for discovering your life's purpose involves hiring your nocturnal subconscious mind. Ask your subconscious mind upon going to sleep: "What is my true purpose? What am I on this Earth to do?" Put a pen and paper beside the bed, and jot down any thoughts you have during the night. Upon waking, spend the first 20 minutes free-writing, using the above questions as your prompts. When you discover gold, you will know it. Your cork will pop, and your energy will flow.

I love to journal. I have stacks of journals filled with thoughts, concerns and ideas from the last 20 years of my life. When you devote time and energy to the writing process, your intuition comes to your aid and helps to solve your toughest dilemmas. As you soul search for your divine purpose, common themes will appear. My common themes are family, animals and nature, as well as art and writing. These have been my great passions for as long as I can remember.

Writing is just one way to discover your purpose, but it can work wonders. I can attest to the magic of journaling. Write and reflect. Then, repeat. Discover more about yourself through your writing! Do you surround yourself with artists? Maybe your inner artist is begging to be set free. Do you love to wander the aisles of your local home improvement store? Do you tinker in the garage every chance you get? These are clues.

After you unveil your higher calling through soul searching and self-reflection, you will want to begin visualizing your success and the positive impact that your work will have on society. Goal setting is key, and there are plenty of excellent books on the topic. I recommend Goals! by Brian Tracy. A list of action steps will also help you stay on track. Endless resources are available to help you use visualization, goal setting and action steps to manifest your dreams.

We are all faced with countless choices each day. Make choices that align with your passions! *Go where the energy is!* When you live your life's purpose, you not only help the world, you help yourself. Just like endorphins keep us wanting more exercise, the energy surge we feel when we pursue our chosen work keeps us energetic, wanting more. The more we help the world, the better we feel! We lead by example, and those around us are inspired to make their

own unique contributions to the world. It's a tremendously positive cycle. Imagine a world in which all of us passionately pursue our purposes. Harmony and peace abound, because everyone enjoys a blissful state of mind. When we all unite to help each other accomplish our higher callings, what a wonderful world it will be!

ABOUT LOULIE

Loulie Key Scharf was born and raised in Columbus, Georgia and currently resides in Wilmington, North Carolina, with her husband, two children and nine rescued animals. Besides her top role as mother and wife, Scharf is a writer, artist, art teacher, environmentalist, animal rescuer and animal advocate.

Loulie has studied positive living and personal development for 20 years. A self-professed "workshop junkie," Loulie has participated in dozens of intensive workshops, including The Hippocrates Health Institute, The Painting Experience, SARK, The Feng Shui Institute of America, *You Can Heal Your Life* conference, No Boundaries International Art Colony and Common Boundaries.

While obtaining a journalism degree from the University of Georgia, Loulie began her writing career as a journalist for the college newspaper, *The Red and Black*. She later studied fine art at The University of North Carolina at Wilmington, and she is currently pursuing a Master of Fine Arts through The Academy of Art in San Francisco, California.

Loulie's corporate experience includes working in marketing for Coca-Cola South Pacific in Sydney, Australia and public relations for The Atlanta Apparel Mart. She and her husband now own and operate a multi-million dollar real estate investment business.

Loulie's life purpose combines two decades' worth of studies with her passions for family, creativity, the Earth and animals. Her higher calling is to raise kids' self-esteem and environmental awareness through creativity. She is using her artistic and writing skills to develop a forthcoming line of books and tools to help parents "Raise Happy Kids Who Care."

For complimentary reports on positive living and parenting, visit: www.Loulie.com.

CHAPTER 8

UNLEASH YOUR POWER NOW:

ELEVEN KEYS TO SUCCESS

BY SUGAR SINGLETON, M.D.

I have always learned best and remembered more when a story was at the heart of the lesson. I offer you eleven keys to success from my heart to yours.

1. FIND YOUR PURPOSE AND THEN COMMIT TO IT.

I had many health challenges and nearly died as a child and again as a teenager. Through these challenges, a doctor was always there to save my life. Even as a child, I felt this second chance at life was given so that I could help others as I had been helped. So I set on my journey to become a medical doctor.

There was never any doubt in my mind that I would do it. I was an avid reader and a voracious learner, and I decided early on that I wanted to learn something new every single day. This is a commitment that I still follow today, and to which I attribute much of my success.

2. EVERY DAY TAKE LITTLE STEPS TOWARDS THE DREAM.

I committed to take little steps toward my dream every day, and this goal has been important in my journey to becoming a doctor. Along the way, there were times when I went the wrong way and even times when I fell down. The important thing to remember is that each time I got out of the groove, I stood back up and continued taking little steps toward my dream.

With this strategy well in place, I breezed through school. My journey to becoming a doctor, while sometimes difficult, was never a journey that I questioned until I actually got into medical school. I had been accepted to one of the best medical schools in the country. I was so happy. I remember bonding with the other students over the smell of formaldehyde as we dissected cadavers and laughing as we looked under microscopes learning how to tell if the tissue on the slide was brain or kidney. All of my dreams were in the palm of my hand.

One night I was sitting home with my nose stuck in a big medical book, just about to doze off. Suddenly the phone rang. It was my dad. He said, "Sugar, the doctors say your mom has cancer and it is very advanced. . . . She has two months to live."

It took my breath away to hear those words. I felt like I had been kicked in the stomach, and my eyes began to sting with tears. The phone slid from my hand and hit the floor I heard myself scream, "Why! It is not fair. NO! Not my mom!" I cried through the night as my heart broke into a million pieces.

The next morning I had a big decision: go home to care for my mom or stay in school and follow my dreams. Of course, I left school and returned home to become daughter and caregiver. I deeply loved my mom. I remember sitting at her bedside as she said to me, "Sugar, I am not ready to die." I took her hand in mine, looked her in the eye, and said, "Mom, I need you to do one thing for me. I need you to believe with all of your heart and soul that you will get better, and don't worry about anything else."

3. IF YOU BELIEVE... ANYTHING IS POSSIBLE.

These were hard times. I was devastated at the thought of my mom dying and I was devastated to be away from school. During the next few years I stayed with my mom… caring for her, wiping her brow, protecting her as she had done for me so many times. Because of her incredible strength & belief even during those unbelievably difficult times, she was able to turn that 2-month medical deadline into 10 wonderful years!

4. THE BURDEN OF WASTED POTENTIAL IS THE BIGGEST BURDEN OF ALL.

During this time, we were blessed with our first-born child. I had done my best being a daughter, and now I was doing my best being a Mom, which I loved! Yet one night, I realized that there was something missing inside. It felt like I had let go of a part of me. Somehow deep inside I knew that if I didn't become a Doctor to do for others what was done for me, I would carry the burden of wasted potential on my shoulders for the rest of my life.

5. WHEN THE DREAM IS BIG ENOUGH, THE FACTS DON'T MATTER.

This realization came to me at 2:00 a.m. I woke my husband with these words, "Honey, I have to become a doctor." He rolled over and took me in his arms while looking deeply into my eyes. In that moment I understood exactly how much he loved me and how much he was willing to give up for my happiness. He said, "My love, if that is what you want to do and what will make you happy, then that is what you will do and we'll make it work."

In that moment none of this made sense. These were the facts: The nearest medical school was 180 miles away. We had a little baby boy! It seemed impossible; but sometimes when the dream is big enough the facts don't matter.

6. CHALLENGES WILL MOLD YOU AND MAKE YOUR STRONGER.

For the next seven years I commuted back and forth to school weekly. During that time we were blessed with a little girl. I'm not sure how that happened when I rarely saw my husband! For seven years I saw my family only on weekends. I got my heart broken every Sunday as I would look into my husband's eyes and then get into the car. For seven long years I kissed my babies good night on the telephone. Knowing that my goal was not just to have the initials M.D. after my name, but how I'd be able to help others was the only reason I was able to continue…

I learned many things during this journey. The most important is to have the courage and the strength to follow your passion, to move forward regardless of the circumstances and challenges that can sometimes arise.

7. CONNECT WITH AND COMMIT TO YOUR PASSION.

Fast-forward a few years: I am a wife, mom and doctor. Yet I came to a point of not knowing who "I" was on the inside. I began to do some self-analysis, and through this experience I realized that my purpose and my passion lay in something much deeper than just the routine practice of medicine. I realized I was passionate about working with women on a very deep level. I began to see that women everywhere have unconscious blocks that stop them from truly being happy, healthy, fulfilled, confident, and from really thriving.

8. RELEASE YOUR UNPRODUCTIVE CELLULAR MEMORIES.

I had to learn how to release my unproductive cellular memories – those subconscious blocks that we all have that hold us back from truly becoming prosperous and living an abundant life. The process, once discovered, was incredible, fast, easy and powerful! I remember experiencing it for the first time and knowing that the woman I used to be was going to leave transformed. I recall looking into my own eyes in a mirror and seeing someone that had been waiting to blossom out of me! I had discovered how to shift on a Cellular level! I gave birth to a WOMAN who was waiting inside of me that I didn't even know existed, and let me tell you, it wasn't even painful! I just had never known how to do that before!

That's when I fell in love with the concept of CELLULAR memory and what it took to release my own personal blocks. *The interesting thing is that I was UN-aware of most of these blocks on a conscious level, I just had a sense of knowing that my greatest work was yet to be done!*

So I began a very committed and meaningful journey into the world of *cellular memory release*. I learned what it meant to release my own unproductive cellular memory. That's when a whole new level of me emerged! It was the beginning of an abundant and thriving life for my family and me.

9. FIND YOUR TRUE SENSE OF FULFILLMENT.

It was during this time that I had my most profound realization yet. I recognized that I was called to be a healer not just a medical doctor!

That is my purpose… That is what "FOR ME" brings the ultimate connection to Self that every woman I know looks for, even if she doesn't know it consciously. A true sense of FULFILLMENT!

You see sometimes when we, as doctors, just practice traditional medicine, it can almost become a bit superficial. It's like a band-aid. Fix what is wrong today, but you never really get to work on the root of the problem. When I allowed myself to listen and follow my ultimate purpose, I began to see that I needed to pay attention to the cause of the malfunction! If you put a tight rubber band on your finger, the flow of blood will be blocked. As a result, the tip of your finger will start to turn blue because it's struggling to receive sufficient blood flow. Now, if we were to only pay attention to the symptom, we'd want to fix it. By doing what? Perhaps rubbing a cream on the tip of the finger, would we inject the finger, take a pill? Nothing will allow the flow to return to its optimal capacity unless the rubber band itself is removed! That's the cause, that's the block! As a healer, I now go for the cause! And working with releasing cellular blocks, I teach women how to release their deepest blocks toward fulfillment, purpose, and the flow of prosperity.

10. DISCOVER THE TRUE FOUNDATION OF LASTING CHANGE.

I have seen it over and over again, women who carry subconscious issues in their cells for years (not even knowing so on a conscious level). These unproductive cellular memories serve as blocks that hold them back from being at their best, from being happy, having high self-esteem, and from creating their desired personal and professional results!

Releasing blocks on this level, at the core, going beyond an emotional and mental level, getting right down to the cellular level. <u>That is the FOUNDATION of lasting change.</u> This is where there are no blocks and it just flows!

This process that removes the blocks and stimulates the flow is called RELEASE.

- Releasing unwanted, unproductive subconscious belief systems from the body and the subconscious mind;
- Releasing negative residual patterns that keep on feeding these subconscious blocks;
- Releasing subconscious issues related to money;
- Releasing unwanted negative patterns AND actually stimulating the flow of prosperity;
- Releasing the patterns that get in the way of true fulfillment;

The inner conflicts are blocked energies, which are mostly subconscious. We are holding onto them in the form of cellular memory!

Some general examples of **Inner Conflict:**

On a **PERSONAL** level:

- Obsessive behaviors such as Perfection
- Self Sabotage
- Fear of Abandonment
- Being sensitive and having your buttons pushed by other people
- Fear of owning your voice (have you ever had a burning or choking feeling in your throat when you were about to speak your truth?)

On a **PROFESSIONAL** level:

- Fear of rejection
- Fear of money/success
- Fear of successful people
- Fear or even anger toward other successful/confident women
- Fear of selling or marketing
- Or have you ever felt resistance toward other people who sell something? The feeling of resistance is like feeling emotionally hot in the body combined with a hint of anger! That's an example of inner conflict. It's unproductive cellular memory.

On a **GLOBAL** level – 'global because these blocks are within the collective psyche of the female gender' and therefore at some level, are a part of our individual cellular memory,

- Fear of not being good enough
- Lack of self worth
- Having guilt/worry
- Fear of other beautiful women
- Lack of trust, ...and so many more.

11. LEARN TO THRIVE PERSONALLY AND PROFESSIONALLY.

Most of us have had experiences in our lives that have created memories in our cells that are causing inner conflict/blocks in the form of unproductive cellular memory. Learning to Release is the only way to have the foundation we require to thrive personally and professionally.

Every cell in our body has memory. Unfortunately, much of the cellular memory that we hold onto is unproductive and manifests itself as confusion, depression, unworthiness, worry, lack, struggle, procrastination, lack of fulfillment, relationship challenges, etc. Most women don't know on a conscious level that they are holding on to these unproductive cellular memories. And most women don't know how to release on this level.

Cellular memory release is the foundation of a shift toward:

- A thriving level of self-esteem
- True fulfillment
- And the flow of prosperity

Lets use a computer as an analogy. Our body is the hard drive of the computer. Our lifetime experiences become cellular memory. Cellular memory is the data stored on the hard drive. Over the years we have numerous files that we put on our hard drives called cellular memory. What happens when your computer has a lot of data on its hard drive? It operates slower, has technical difficulties, and maybe it crashes!

When we delete some files or clear the cookies/cache (in computer terms), and do it in the right way, that type of RELEASING unproductive memory RESTORES the computer's ability to operate at a whole new level!

I love being a physician, but looking back, that part of the journey is not what gave me inner peace or even abundance. It meant I could listen to someone's physical symptoms, put a name on their disease and match a medicine to it, write a prescription or even deliver a baby and bring life into this world, but my real education started when I learned to feel joy and happiness on a CELLULAR level. When I learned to embody the feeling that comes when I say 'I LOVE MY LIFE' with all of it's ups and downs, trials, and triumphs, because I have learned to be grounded, to be joyous, to be confident, to be prosperous, and all of it on a deep, deep, level! My cellular memories now work with me instead of unconsciously against me!

Learning how to Release was the best investment I have ever made in MYSELF! It's my purpose to bring this type of cellular shift to you. If you want to make this year the best year you've ever had on a personal level and on a professional level too, it may be time to consider releasing your cellular blocks, and stimulating the energy of fulfillment and prosperity in your cells!

ABOUT DR. SUGAR

Sugar Singleton, MD, is a practicing medical doctor, a loving wife and mother, and a powerful resource for women and their well-being. Dr. Sugar has dedicated her life to helping women break through barriers and transform their lives. Her specialty is "working with women to take their lives to the next level, to achieve the breakthrough that they desire and absolutely deserve to receive."

An exhilarating international speaker and presenter, Dr. Sugar takes women on a journey of discovery to their highest potential. As a cellular memory expert, she conducts regular *Release* experiences in the U.S. in order to assist women to release unproductive cellular memories that are blocking them from achieving true fulfillment, a thriving self-esteem and a flow of prosperity. Her presentations are transformational and can be applied to all aspects of everyday life.

What's unique about Dr. Sugar is that she has a love for true healing as opposed to the traditional ways of just treating disease. Being someone who always follows her heart, she has dedicated her life to being a healer. Today, in addition to saving people's lives in the urgent care, she spends most of her time in assisting women to release the blocks that are getting in the way of their true self-esteem, fulfillment, and prosperity. This passion has led her to become the exclusive expert on cellular healing in the largest online community for inspired women: www.BraveHeartWomen.com.

Every month, women come together from different parts of the world to spend quality time with Dr. Sugar. She helps them to gain clarity about the causes of their resistance, and to learn the tools that give them permanent transformation on a deep cellular level. They soon find out that she's an authentic woman who loves to make a difference and also have fun.

Dr. Sugar is a lifetime member of the prestigious medical honor society Alpha Omega Alpha; she served as Chief Resident at UNM Hospital; she is board certified in Family Medicine and has served as Vice-President for the American Academy of Family Physicians, NM. She is married to her soul mate, Rick, and they have three healthy, beautiful children who reside with them in the Land of Enchantment.

Dr. Ellie Drake, the founder of the BraveHeart Women global community, describes her as "one of the most grounded and purposeful women I have had the privilege of connecting with. She is genuine, intelligent, focused, and above all – inspiring."

To learn more about Dr. Sugar and receive information on the next *Release Experience* visit Dr. Sugar's website at www.sugarsingleton.com, send an Email to: unleashyourpowernow@yahoo.com or call Toll Free: 1-855-Dr-Sugar.

CHAPTER 9

RIDE PURPOSE, ATTITUDE & WORK ETHIC TO THE FRONT

BY MICHAEL D'ADAMO

Nothing in my childhood predicts that I will succeed or even be alive by the time I am twenty-two, when I make my first million dollars. It's some kind of miracle that my older brother Frank, my twin brother Kevin, and I, survived childhood. We grew up in East New York – Brooklyn – back in the day when looking a stranger in the eye could be deadly. The races were sharply divided, and kids fought their parent's ancient and mindless battles. Gang initiation rituals included 'razor-tagging' people's faces. 'Crack' was everywhere. Still, my brothers and I stayed outdoors as much as we could. Home was a painful place – where our father beat our mother, and we were too little to do anything about it. Things got worse the deeper he sank into addiction. We slept with our sneakers on so that he wouldn't sell them when he was 'on a run.'

Was it a lousy way to grow up? Yes. But it taught me what I don't want. Just as the old saying goes, *adversity can be turned to advantage.*

The law finally caught up with our father in a big way on a steamy July night in 1996. I was in the courtroom when the gavel came down. I was numb. I coped the way I'd always coped – I didn't care. I had no idea who I was or where I was going. Not quite six months later, I answered a newspaper ad for a job in a warehouse. I didn't have the confidence to try for anything better. I'd basically been on my own since I was fourteen and had decided school wasn't for me.

Just nine blocks from my home, I learned that the job was really for direct marketing. It opened the door to my future. From that day on, I became a student. Even though I was a drop-out, I learned something new every day. As a rookie, I sold merchandise on consignment. That's the beauty of this business: your work is your investment. Direct marketing provided my first encounter with people whose mental attitude was positive. They showed me an opportunity that could change my life. I had the right stuff, my own version of a **PHD**: I was **Poor, Hungry and Determined.**

Then, the 1997 Nor'easter hit. Snow fell like 'there was no tomorrow.' I was pulling a cart of merchandise through the streets as schools and even subways shut down. My feet were so wet, I sometimes stopped in the middle of the day to buy a change of socks. I always aimed at selling everything in my cart before going back to the office. To this day, my feet are shadowed by the scars of calluses and blisters. On the walls of many direct marketing offices, you'll find something called the 8 Steps, the system of core principles passed down throughout the sales and marketing industry for decades. I remember reading them for the first time. I didn't just learn them – I consumed them. I still apply them daily in every aspect of my life. They were in my toolbox for becoming a successful salesman. I used them in team building, and I used them in starting my first business, T.O.P. Marketing Group, which has grown into a multi-million dollar direct sales network with offices across the nation.

The 8 Steps focus on Purpose, Attitude, and Work Ethic. When I go off track, I use them to get back on. Working hand-in-hand with discipline, the steps guide the choices I make. They require that I give 110 % every day. The 8 Steps opened my eyes to *The Overall Picture*. When you build a team, you earn more income by helping others earn income. Team building is an essential skill. Limitless potential becomes a reality.

Within a year, I went from being a rookie to a manager with fifteen trainees. By 1998, I formed my first company. By the end of 2000, I had earned my first million dollars and was expanding across the country. I had more than 250 sales agents on my team. Then, another couple of years later, I had my first major 'falling out' in business. My mentor left and took our clients with him. He even tried recruiting my own brother. I didn't know what hit me. I was totally unprepared.

I fought back by applying the 8 Steps. I didn't let my emotions bring me down. I rebuilt. I knew direct marketing worked. I just had to fine-tune my vision, my purpose, my why. I knew leadership was key. I recommitted to leading by example. I've rolled with the blows of many other 'ups and downs' on the rocky road to success. I have my battle scars, but most of my wounds were self-inflicted. *Whatever your goals are, success is really an inside job.*

Over the years, my obsession with being early translated into being in the right place at the right time. My team and I went from marketing flashlights on the eve of Y2K to a client list that included Fortune 500 companies, as well as the imaginative products born of new markets from energy, telecommunications, and fiber optics to the jazzy, high-tech marvels that define life on the cutting edge. I developed a knack for finding products and bringing them to consumers who didn't even know they existed as yet.

There's no stopping a man who's found a purpose. When I started out, I was driven by a healthy dose of fear. I knew I wasn't cut out for a nine-to-five job, but I didn't want to walk the destructive paths so many in my neighborhood had taken. I wanted financial success so that I could make a better life for my whole family. In time, money wasn't enough of a motivator. I grew into a larger purpose. Today, I'm driven by love: I love what I do, and I love the people I do it with. I've become a Go-giver not just a Go-getter. I learned that by giving more of myself and being more generous with profit shares, I gained on all fronts. If you think about it, that's not a contradiction. **People are life's true bottom line.**

Take care of your team and your team will take care of you. In our network, we know that. We're loyal to each other and that makes everything possible. Our business has expanded into a multitude of businesses and our team keeps growing.

I do a lot of public speaking, facilitate meetings, and mentor many people. I tell them *it's not where you've been that counts but where you're going.* I teach that achieving success is really based on the choices you make. But choices have to be acted on. You make choices, take chances, make changes and then act with rigid discipline. Discipline is everything. It implies working hard and never quitting. It's no secret that quitters never win. People want short cuts when there aren't any.

The 8 Steps are a foolproof system for hitting your goals. Incorporate them as core principles in business and in life. When you fully commit to them you can't lose. The steps are your daily guideline to success. If, at the end of the day, you haven't hit your goals, walk back through the steps and, inevitably, you will find where you went off track. Whether your goal is having healthy relationships, losing weight or creating a successful business, The 8 Steps are applicable in all areas of life.

Knowing your why – your purpose for what you are doing – is what keeps you going. Hone your vision; make it crystal clear in every detail just like the Olympic athlete keeps the gold medal in mind. The minute you lose sight of your vision, you are in danger of losing your Positive Mental Attitude, and with it your Work Ethic. The athlete knows the only chance of winning is by pushing the extra mile every day. It's important to understand the law of Consistent Time and Energy. Devote your time and energy consistently to your goals. Make sacrifices today for a greater tomorrow.

Think of The 8 Steps as a tree: the roots are your Definiteness of Purpose. The trunk is your Positive Mental Attitude and the branches are your Work Ethic. The fruit is the result of your labor.

The 8 Steps Success Formula

Definiteness of Purpose
+
Positive Mental Attitude
+
Consistent Work Ethic
=
Achievement of Purpose

THE 8 STEPS TO SUCCESS

1. ***Have A Positive Mental Attitude***
   Stay focused on your purpose and your Positive Mental Attitude will follow. It's your best asset, your number one self-discipline. It's the will in you, not the skill in you that will get you there. Begin with the end in mind, sharpen your vision and stay committed to it at all times. Carry it in your marrow and always wear it on your sleeve. Believing is seeing.

2. ***Time Management***
   Time Management is about the strategic thinking that leads to strategic action. Writing your plans down focuses the mind and maps your actions. Time is your most valuable resource; you can't get it back. Invest 80% of your time in the top 20% of your priorities. *Proper priorities and planning produce peak performance, productivity, and profitability.* Where you invest your time you will get your returns. A great manager of time is always a step ahead.

3. ***Be Prepared***
   Adapt. Adjust. Overcome. Be mentally prepared for just two things: anything and everything. Every day brings its own obstacles and roadblocks. Always have a Plan B. A back-up plan. When faced with the unknown, hire an expert. *Know what you don't know so that you can find someone who does.* Don't muddle through because your ego tells you to. Keep a spare tire. Save money for a rainy day. Check the weather forecast so you know what's about to hit you. *As long as you expect the unexpected, nothing is insurmountable.*

4. ***Work A Full Day***
   Do whatever it takes. Work even harder for yourself than you would for someone else. Give the day 110%. Go the extra mile. Develop the habit of doing more than you're expected to do. Erase the laziness and entitlement mentality and replace it with the motivation and work ethic necessary to achieve your goals. Don't look for shortcuts because they always turn out to be detours. Bottom line: you reap what you sow.

5. ***Work Your Territory Correctly***
   There's no substitute for a great work ethic. That's the flat out, hardcore truth. *Great achievements demand great dedication.* Whatever the endeavor, cover your territory completely. Be thorough, research, study and leave no stone unturned. When you cheat, you lose. There are no paved roads to life's greatest achievements. Keep persisting; every "no" leads you closer to a "yes." It's the Law of Averages.

6. ***Maintain A Positive Mental Attitude***
   When **pushing to the front** you are guaranteed to face adversity; seeing The Overall Picture is the key to preserving your attitude. Keep your eyes on the prize. Attitude is so critical; it shows up twice in The 8 Steps. Stay focused on your purpose and develop the mental discipline to protect your attitude when negativity comes your way. The weak allow the situation to change their attitude for the worse, while the strong use their attitude to change their situation for the better.

7. ***Know Why You're Here And Where You're Going***
   We do the things today that most people aren't willing to do, so we can afford to do the things tomorrow that most people can't afford to do! This is the step all the others revolve around. It's about the desire that burns deep in your heart. Success begins with clarity of purpose. Your purpose – your reason why – keeps you **pushing to the front**. In the end, making money is rarely enough to keep you motivated. You have to love what you do and know exactly why you're doing it. Whether you desire to change your family's financial DNA, retire your parents and yourself early, create financial security, create the lifestyle you always dreamed of or leave a legacy, whatever it is – your why has to make you cry. Dream big and never stop dreaming, but remember you have to get out there every day and make those dreams a reality. Bottom line, remember Why You're Here And Where You're Going and do whatever it takes to get there.

8. ***Take Control.***
   Take control of things or they will take control of you. Take control of your life, your attitude, your health, your finances,

in short, take control of everything. *Control is not about physical force but mental discipline.* We don't control our circumstances but we can control our responses. Only you can manifest your own destiny. Self-control and unshakable self-discipline are absolutes of leadership. At the end of the day, you have to lead yourself first. Success is an inside job.

THE UNWRITTEN RULE

HAVE FUN

NEVER BECOME A VICTIM OF YOUR WORK.

LOVE WHAT YOU DO!

ABOUT MICHAEL

Michael D'Adamo is the Founder and C.E.O. Of the T.O.P. Marketing Group a thirteen year-old, direct marketing network with a nationwide footprint. T.O.P. is a leader in serving the cutting edge of Fortune 500 companies as well as small and mid-sized business ventures seeking to expand market share. Turnkey sales solutions bring products and services directly to customers.

Focused on the need for grassroots business leadership, he is on the road much of the year coaching and mentoring talented individuals to become owners of their own businesses. D'Adamo is dedicated to revitalizing the American economy by cultivating a new generation of pioneers in this nation's great entrepreneurial tradition. He believes in self-reliance, self-discipline, hard work, and conscious leadership. Only eighteen years old when he began working in direct marketing at twenty-two he earned his first million dollars. Now, at thirty-three, D'Adamo projects his network will include over one hundred offices by the end of 2012.

Over the years, D'Adamo has exhibited a knack for finding products just as they reached public consciousness, bringing customers 'the best of the best' — from the products created by the deregulation of energy, telecommunications and fiber-optics markets to the jazzy, high-tech marvels that define life on the cutting edge.

T.O.P.'s network functions like an extended family, offering business owners best practice systems, back-office support and ongoing leadership coaching.

In teaming up with individuals to help them fulfill their dreams, D'Adamo has also financed a number of socially-conscious business ventures. For more information about T.O.P. visit: www.topmarketinginc.com or call 855-TEAMTOP.

CHAPTER 10

FREEDOM THROUGH LIMITS

– HOW SETTING BOUNDARIES CAN EMPOWER YOUR TEAM AND YOUR LIFE

BY MIKE CONDUFF

As my youngest granddaughter toddled down the driveway toward our quiet neighborhood street, I positioned myself for a quick rescue if needed, but just as she got to the edge of the sidewalk she stopped 'on a dime,' and turned to make eye contact and giggle at me. "Don't go past the sidewalk," had been our mantra ever since she started walking, and now it was as ingrained as "Don't eat the flowers," or "Don't hurt the kitty." The line of demarcation of the sidewalk had become as much of a barrier for her as if it had a six foot fence in front of it. By staying on our agreed upon side of it, she knew she was safe and in my good graces. If she crossed it she was in imminent danger of losing the privilege of being outside, not to mention being hit by an automobile. She much preferred playing to being scolded, so willingly obeyed.

As adults we have a tendency to think of boundaries or barriers as limiting; something to break through or blow by, when in reality a thoughtful boundary can be incredibly empowering and freeing. For my granddaughter, as long as she stayed on the right side of the sidewalk she could run and play and enjoy the day to her heart's content. She did not have to engage in a series of "Grandad, may I?" questions or guess what it was that she could do today. She simply utilized her energy and enthusiasm to create joy in complete safety and security.

The same principle is true for us and our teams as well. If we know what it is that we are trying to accomplish, and while pursuing those outcomes, goals, and objectives, stay within our boundaries, we can also thrive and prosper and use our creativity, education, training and expertise to great advantage. When we ignore a boundary we do so at our peril.

How many of us know of someone who has lost a career or a marriage or a special relationship because they chose to transgress a boundary? When I ask that question of live audiences, it is not unusual for every single hand in the room to go up. The painful memories are almost palpable. Sometimes for the participants, tears start involuntarily. We all know someone who has suffered through this; perhaps that someone is even us. The fact is that thoughtful boundaries provide safety, security and reward while encouraging everyone to do their best.

So many of these boundaries we know by heart: don't lie, don't cheat, don't steal, and don't take unfair advantage. Some must be agreed upon with others: don't embarrass me in front of your friends, don't tell that story about what we did in college, don't wear orange to a Texas A&M game, don't take credit for the other unit's sales. Some are promulgated upon us: don't drink and drive, don't run a red light, don't 'road rage' that guy that cut you off on the freeway and gave you the 'one finger' wave. Some are self-imposed: don't take a second brownie (well okay, a third), don't talk about someone behind their back, and don't leave early even though others are.

This concept is ageless. King David of Old Testament fame says, "Surely the boundary lines have fallen for me in pleasant places," and pervasive: virtually every sports field has a boundary line. It has also been abused; sometimes the Emperor really doesn't have any clothes on.

About now you are likely pushing back a little. As an enlightened manager, executive, CEO or parent, you probably believe in empowerment and see a boundary as a downer. I often hear, "I would rather tell folks what they can do as opposed to what they can't!"

The challenge of course is that we can never list enough of the things they can do. No matter how long the list of 'can do-s' someone will want to add one, and then we have to take some more time to decide if that one is okay. So, far from being a constraint, a boundary provides ultimate empowerment. We no longer are called upon to micromanage or second guess, and our folks no longer have to manipulate us to get what they want. The boundary provides the security necessary for folks to take risks, try new things and improve performance without fear of a "gotcha." If they come up with something new or experience the unforeseen, they simply address it within the boundary.

BOUNDARIES ARE NOT RULES

In pushing back it is also important not to equate boundaries with rules. Boundaries are very different from rules. A rule attempts to control behavior, but you can never anticipate enough behaviors to have enough rules. In fact, if you have ever raised children or managed a workforce you know this to be true. No matter how detailed the personnel manual someone will always come up with a question or a behavior you did not anticipate. Whole HR departments are engaged every day in developing if/then scenarios that are obsolete almost as soon as they are published. Additionally, no matter how even handed you think the rules are, someone will most certainly complain, often justifiably, that it is "not fair."

In my work as a CEO in multiple organizations with 24 hour responsibilities and multiple lines of business, I never saw a personnel manual I liked. What was fair for a professional police officer or highly-trained firefighter was almost never fair for my talented office workers or a skilled electric lineman or the erstwhile college intern. There never could be enough rules and interpretations of the rules, no matter how many employee committees were utilized or grievances filed or court rulings issued. On the other hand, principles and values could almost always be agreed upon across the multiple lines of business, and with these firmly in hand, appropriate boundaries established. Flexibility within the boundaries empowered employees to use their best judgment and skills to provide world-class service in all areas.

GO FAST BY LETTING GO

My colleagues at OnTarget Governance Consulting, Catherine Raso and Carol Gabanna, and I, have spent the last two decades working with Boards of Directors and their CEOs and Staffs from all over the world. Drawing upon our background in Policy Governance®, we have helped thousands of organizations and individuals think through the power of limits. In our book, the ***On Target Board Member – 8 Indisputable Behaviors***, we talk extensively about how to "go fast by letting go."

Again, kids provide a perfect example. They want to visit their friend. You want to make sure they are safe, and so a long dialogue begins. They ask, "May I go to my friend's house?" You answer with a question of your own, "Who else will be there?" They answer and then you ask, "What will you do?" They answer and then you ask, "Will the parents be home?" They answer and then you ask, "What time will you be back?" They answer and then you ask, "Have you got your homework done?" They answer and then you ask, "What about the chore I assigned you last week?" This goes on and on until you finally render a judgment. (Which, by the way, if it is "no," is immediately met with cries of, you guessed it – "It's not fair!")

While this example is amusing, the same "May I?" dance goes on in almost all organizations every day. "May I attend this training?" "Where is it?" "How long will you be gone?" "How much does it cost?" "Do you have your other work done?" "Who else will be there?" [Sound familiar?] In the end if your answer is no, you are met with… "It's not fair!"

This securing permission dance takes a lot of time, consumes a lot of organizational or family energy and often ends with neither party very satisfied. Enter the power of boundaries. We agree in advance what our key principles and values are. Once these are established it is very easy to determine the boundaries. They simply cascade from the values. If innovation is valued more highly than conformity then we have a different boundary for things like dress, punctuality and work hours. If being mistake-free is valued more highly than speed, then we have different boundaries for redundancy, review and responsiveness.

EASILY CUSTOMIZED

Another excellent feature of boundaries is that they can be easily customized. More or less discretion can be granted based on experience, ability, risk-tolerance and time. My nine and eleven year olds both have cool Razor electric scooters. The nine year old has a different riding limits boundary than his older brother because of his age, temperament and judgment. The employee with ten years of successful experience should certainly have a different boundary than a new hire. An emergency responder will have a different boundary than a part-time clerical worker. By recognizing and adjusting boundaries appropriately, we can exert more or less control in a way that makes sense for all concerned. The organization and the employee can go much faster when we let go of trying to control every situation.

ANY REASONABLE INTERPRETATION

Of course, even with well-reasoned boundaries, we accept that we are not gifted with prescience and cannot possibly imagine every potential scenario; and so, with compliments to Dr. John Carver, the developer of the Policy Governance® model, we extend the concept of "Any Reasonable Interpretation" to really rev up productivity within the boundaries. As long as our colleagues, our staff, or our employees remain within the boundaries, they are free to exercise any reasonable interpretation of the boundary when confronted with unanticipated circumstances. They do not have to check in with us; rather, they are empowered to make a reasoned judgment. If the boundary is a spending limit and by going just beyond it significant per item savings are achieved then we most certainly want that decision made. The test here is a simple one – would a reasonable person when confronted with the facts of the situation make the same or a similar decision. If we disagree with the decision, but find that it was indeed reasonable given the circumstances, then we can always adjust the boundary on a moving-forward basis. However, we do not chastise retroactively. If a boundary is in place and the action is within the boundary or a reasonable interpretation of it, we support it, even if we disagree with it.

Imagine the morale of a group when they know they will be supported, and not even second-guessed as long as they have been reasonable. The productivity and job satisfaction ratings go through the roof.

ADD THOUGHTFUL OUTCOMES TO REALLY GO FAST

Speaking of morale, as you seek to harness the power of setting limits remember that while boundaries are powerful, so are outcomes. What is it exactly that we are trying to accomplish? What is our target? What constitutes success? What is our Super Bowl win? Based on the business unit, organization or corporate objective, these key outcomes are set and aggressively pursued within the confines of the corresponding boundaries. Try this the next time you encounter one of your folks; simply ask them, "What is a homerun for us?" See if they know at all, and if they do, whether or not it aligns with your view.

Most of us have participated in, or at least viewed a tug-of-war contest. Teams on both ends of a rope pull and strain and exert energy trying to get the middle of the rope to move in their direction. Despite these herculean efforts, in most contests the middle of the rope rarely moves very far until one team is worn down or gives up. This tug of war is often going on within your team because there is not uniform agreement on what the team is supposed to be accomplishing. People choose sides and start opposing each other. Much energy is expended for little movement.

Imagine for just a moment the rope with everyone on the same side. It would move incredibly quickly and without much effort at all. The team experiences huge success with all the usual rewards that come with it – accolades, increased self-esteem, and job satisfaction.

Having clear outcomes that are agreed upon puts everyone on your team on the same side of the rope. Having clear boundaries for the behaviors used pursuing the outcomes provides the 'oomph.'

MONITOR RIGOROUSLY

Of course a boundary is not a boundary at all if it is not enforced. Every now and then my granddaughter will test me. While looking at me out of the corner of her eye she will put a toe or even a whole foot across the sidewalk. As soon as I start toward her or just make strong eye contact, she immediately smiles and steps back. The relief on her face is obvious. "Grandad means it. The boundary is still there, I am still safe."

Each of my boys watches to make sure that I enforce each other's boundaries. Since this is expected and in my best interest, it is easy to do. It lets them know I have their best interests at heart and am willing to expend energy to protect them.

Your team wants the same safety. You must make sure adequate safeguards are in place so that violations are quickly detectable and vigorously enforced. The old adage about your poorest performer becoming the standard for the group is absolutely true in monitoring. If you have a boundary and allow your favorite employee or your most challenging employee to transgress it, then you have no boundary at all. Your best folks or your compliant folks may still abide by it, but it has lost its meaning and its safety for the team. Fortunately, the monitoring and enforcing of boundaries is actually pretty easy – much more so than interpreting rules.

CONCLUSION

If you want to see an improvement in innovation, enthusiasm and performance in your teams, discover the freedom that thoughtful limits provide. By letting go you really can go faster – and everyone enjoys the journey more!

For More Information
Mike Conduff
President and CEO
The Elim Group
Tel: 940-382-3945
www.TheElimGroup.com

ABOUT MICHAEL

Michael A. (Mike) Conduff is the President and CEO of The Elim Group – *Your Governance Experts*, a governance, leadership, speaking and consulting firm. Mike has 35+ years of leadership, management and governance experience, having served as the City Manager of four different University communities in the United States.

Mike earned his B.S. in civil engineering at the University of New Hampshire, graduating *Cum Laude.* His M.B.A. is from Pittsburg State University. He is also a charter graduate of the Carver Policy Governance® Academy and is a Past Chair of the Board of Directors of the International Policy Governance® Association. Mike has a number of national not-for-profit, for-profit and local government clients.

Mike is the widely respected author of several books, including *Democracy at the Doorstep – True Stories from the Green Berets of Public Administrators, Bottom Line Green – How America's Cities are Saving the Planet (And Money Too!), The OnTarget Board Member – 8 Indisputable Behaviors,* now in its second edition, and *The Policy Governance® Fieldbook,* a book on the practical applications of Policy Governance. He writes a regular column in the internationally distributed *Public Manager* magazine, and is a much sought after and frequent keynote speaker at national and international events, where he regularly receives "best of the conference" accolades from attendees and conference planners.

Mike is a Fellow of the prestigious National Academy of Public Administration. He has been honored with the 2006 TCMA Mentoring Award in memory of Gary Gwyn, the 2004 International Award for Career Development in Memory of L. P. (Perry) Cookingham from ICMA, and the especially meaningful Joy Sansom Mentor Award from the Urban Management Assistants of North Texas for his commitment to helping others achieve their potential. The Center for Digital Government awarded Mike their coveted "Best of Texas Visionary Award."

A fourth generation Native American, Mike grew up on stories of his Cherokee ancestry, and attributes his love of motivational speaking and telling stories to his grandmothers. He is a Past President of both the Texas City Management Association and Kansas City Management Association. He was one of the original cohort of fully credentialed members of the International City/County Management Association, and is a past member of its Executive Board.

To learn more about Mike or to engage him for your corporate or non-profit event, call The Elim Group at 940-382-3945 or visit: www.TheElimGroup.com.

CHAPTER 11

ELEVEN STEPS TO MAKE YOUR DREAMS COME TRUE

BY RENATA KRONOWETTEROVA

"If you think you can do it, or you think you can't do it, you are right."

~ Henry Ford

More people than ever before are successfully using their mental powers to achieve their goals now. We are living at a very exciting time in human history. Over the past couple of hundred years, civilization has moved through many ages. We moved from Caves to Tribes, from Wilderness to Civilized Cities, from Industrial Age to Information Age. These moves through time and ages are in direct relationship to understanding the laws of our mind. Those who understand these laws and use them have a huge advantage over those who do not understand these laws and do not use them. We could almost call this age the Age of Mind Power. Many people have learned how to use the potential of their mind to attract success and happiness into their lives. And so can you.

In this age we understand that we are the creators of circumstances around us, whether we are conscious of it or not. There are no such things as "co-incidences." What is happening in our lives today is a direct result of our attitudes, beliefs and our past programming. As many scholars have said: "As within, So without." If we wish to change what is happening to us, we have to change what is happening within us. Then we can achieve anything, even things that are regarded as "impossible." And we can do it in all areas of our lives – such as business, career or even health. In this chapter I will show you how. First, let me share a short story.

Several years back, well-known personal development author and presenter, Michael Rowland, delivered a speech on the Gold Coast in Australia. During this event, I heard the words that have changed my life forever. That day I heard for the first time in my life that "we CREATE our circumstances." To be honest, until then I was a very pragmatic person and I believed, like most skeptics, that the circumstances are simply given. That was my paradigm. That was the way I saw the world. However, that evening I dared to question it and I did a little experiment.

I was curious to see if I could really "*create*" my circumstances and I decided to test it on three things. First, I decided that I wanted to find 300 AUD (Australian Dollars) so I could buy a ticket to Michael Rowland's two-day seminar. Second, I wanted to speak to Philippe – a person who had run me over in a car and who later became my spiritual teacher. Third, I wanted to meet one-on-one with Michael Rowland and have the opportunity to discuss with him all the questions I had. That evening, I turned my attention to the universe and I asked for these three things.

Within one week, I opened a box that I packed when I was moving a year earlier and I found there 300 AUD. What a surprise! I bought a ticket to the seminar, and when I went there and took my seat, I turned around to find Philippe right there on the seat next to me. I could not believe it! The next day I was walking through a corridor speaking on the phone and looking down, when I accidently bumped into someone. I looked up and it was Michael Rowland! I apologized and immediately turned off the phone. With a surprised tone of voice he asked me: "Have you finished?" I replied: "Yes, I wanted to talk to you." He responded: "I don't know why, but I'm here to help you, so what do you need?" That day, I had the opportunity to talk with him for about an hour, and put all of my questions to him. Since that day, I stopped believing in "co-incidences."

There are no co-incidences in our lives. We create the world around us whether we are conscious of it or not. This is simply a law. In a way similar to gravity attracting all objects to the Earth, you attract events, circumstances and people to your life. You are truly a remarkable human being and you have capabilities that are far beyond your expectations. We use only a tiny percentage of our brains and minds (5-10%). What would happen if we could increase that? What if the limits really exist only in our minds? Can we cure "incurable" health issues? Can we solve "unsolvable" problems? Of course we can!

Many cancer patients survive despite terminal diagnoses. Call it miracles if you want. The truth is that our outer world is only a reflection of our inner world. Many impoverished people become millionaires. If you follow certain success principles, you will reach your goals whether they are in the area of health, personal life, or business.

It is not important where you are today, what really matters is where you are going from now. Many people started from 'ground zero'. For example, when I started my working life as a self-employed person, I was earning approximately 1000 CZK a day (which is equivalent to 55 USD). One day, someone told me that with regards to earnings, I just needed to add an extra "zero" to my income. I made a shift in my consciousness, and I became curious if it was possible for me to earn 10,000 CZK a day. When I allowed myself to imagine it, I took a different approach. I took extra courses, worked hard on myself and soon it became possible. Of course I have to admit, I did not make those earnings every single day, but I found that it is possible. Years later, this thought came to mind again. Is it possible to earn one zero more per day? Believe it or not, soon afterwards I was invited to speak at a function, where I led a very successful workshop that earned me a clear profit of 100,000 CZK. To my surprise, that person was right – it is just "zeros". The limits are only in our mind. You can do it too.

In the following section, I will introduce you to the eleven principles of making your dreams come true.

STEP 1 – SET A CLEAR GOAL

First, you need to know exactly what you want. Be specific. Clarify and describe your goals in as many details as possible. Write them down. When you know your target, focus on it every day. Create a plan how to achieve it. Take action immediately, and never give up till you get there.

STEP 2 – HAVE FAITH

Create an unshakable belief that you will reach your goal. Like the captain of a ship knows he will cross the ocean and reach the shore, you need to be 100% sure you will arrive at your port, even though you might not be able to see it now.

STEP 3 – CEMENT THE VISION WITH FEELINGS

Create a quiet time for yourself, when you visualize yourself completing your goals on a regular basis. The most important thing is to feel the feelings you will experience when your dreams come true. The best time of the day for this is in the morning after you wake up, and in the evening just before you fall asleep. Do this on regular basis (every single day if possible), and you will experience miracles.

STEP 4 – STAY POSITIVE

Being optimistic will get you much further than being pessimistic. Talk about your goals and what you want to achieve, rather than about the problems you have.

STEP 5 – USE SUPPORT TOOLS

Neuro-linguistic programming (NLP) or affirmations can support you on your way to success. A vision board is another tool that helps you to focus on your goals. You can also write your goals on little cards and put them into your wallet. These tools work for me and for many others. You can even re-write your goals daily and you will have the same results.

STEP 6 – BECOME A CONTINUOUS PROBLEM SOLVER

Will you face problems on the way? Of course you will. Take them as challenges and opportunities for growth. We can all learn from them.

Everyone has problems, your mission is to have better quality ones. Become an expert in solving problems. You know that for every problem, there is a solution.

STEP 7 – UNDERSTAND A PARADIGM SHIFT

If you feel pressured during the problem-solving process, stop and take a break. Try to create a paradigm shift in your mind. By paradigm, I mean the way we see the world around us. When you manage to do that, you often find a solution.

To illustrate, let me ask you a question: which of the following statements do you agree with?

a. I will believe it when I see it.
b. I will see it when I believe it.

The truth is there is no right or wrong answer here. Whatever you believe will be true for you. Change the way you see it and you will experience it.

STEP 8 – WORK ON YOURSELF

What can help us to shift our paradigms? What can help us to see things in different way? The fastest way is to attend personal development seminars and to read such books on a regular basis. We can get a lot of inspiration in this way. When you get new ideas, act on them immediately.

STEP 9 – GIVE WHAT YOU WANT TO GET

Your road to success will be much faster when you focus on what you can give to others rather than on what you can get from them. Find what others need and give it to them in the best possible way. Help others to make money and money will come to you too. Encourage others and you will also receive encouragement. Support others and you will receive support. You will get what you give. Ultimately, success is not about what you have, but about the person you become on the way to achieving it.

STEP 10 – BE GRATEFUL

Practicing gratefulness for everything you already have is a very important step. Focusing on it evokes further feelings of gratitude, and through the law of attraction, those feelings attract more good into your life. The law of attraction works, so use it!

STEP 11 – LISTEN TO YOUR INTUITION

Every single person has intuition that guides us. Some of us rely on intuition more than others. When you use intuition, it can get you to your goals faster than you imagined. I would like to end this chapter with a short story illustrating that anything is possible, if you utilize the steps listed above.

Three years ago, the famous Japanese scientist Masaru Emoto had a seminar in Prague. Because I did not have a camera with me, I asked one of the participants to take a picture of Mr. Emoto and me and e-mail it to me. It never arrived. Recently I decided that I would like to have that picture. My logic told me: "There are ten million people in the Czech republic, you have no chance to get it." I stayed positive and optimistic and I asked the universe to organize the circumstances in a way that I could receive the picture. I had full faith that it would happen. Within two months, I went to a seminar given by Jack Canfield and my intuition told me to go and thank the translator for doing such a brilliant job. It turned out to be the very person who took the picture of Mr. Emoto and me three years ago, and I have the picture now.

You can have pretty much anything you want in your life if you truly believe it, and if you practice all of the steps outlined above on a regular basis. If you can live the life of your dreams in your mind, you can also live it in reality. It is just a matter of time. I wish you success and happiness!

ABOUT RENATA

Renata Kronowetterová is an expert in the area of personal and professional development. She has been helping companies and individuals around the world to reach their full potential since 2001. Renata was privileged to deliver programs to people worldwide. She was also teaching the subject of training and development at Griffith University, Australia.

Renata's expertise in coaching, firewalking, soft skill training, teambuilding, outdoor training, has seen her organizing conferences and incentive travel. She is the founder of three companies: AZ Teambuilding s.r.o., AZ Training s.r.o., and AZ Firewalking s.r.o. Renata's programs are tailored to her clients' specific needs. She often uses experiential learning to create opportunities for clients to step outside of their comfort zone to discover their full potential.

Would you like to find out more about the success principles, law of attraction, power of the mind, NLP or firewalking? To learn more about Renata Kronowetterová and the ways she can help you to achieve your goals faster and more efficiently, visit: www.renatainternational.com or email: info@renatainternational.com

www.renatainternational.com

CHAPTER 12

YOUR LIFE LISTS

BY TRACEY PLYMPTON

The day starts with what feels like a million things to get done. Ugh! You start towards the first task and remember you need to make a phone call first. Now you need to find the phone number and all the information you will need for the call. Fifteen minutes later, you have everything in one place. Oh no! You forgot to give the dog his pill this morning. You go into the kitchen to get a piece of cheese to hide the dog's pill, only to find you are out of cheese. You can't hide the pill in anything but cheese since the dog can find medicine hidden in every other type of food. Off to the store you go! On the way to the store, you feel the car pull to the right and you think, "When was the last time I rotated the tires or had the oil changed?" There is an oil change place next to the grocery store, so you pop in there for a quick oil change. Two hours later, you pull out with fresh oil and a shiny new filter.

While pulling out of the parking lot, you notice a letter tucked in your car's visor that needed to be mailed last week. You run over to the post office and have to go inside because you have no stamps. You stand in line patiently waiting to buy your favorite kind and bump into a friend of yours that you haven't seen in months. You chat for a little while and enjoy the sunshine as you catch up. Stamps in hand, you go back to your car and remember the phone call you started to make this morning! You race back home to get the information you needed to make the call that you left on the table. Finally making the first call, you think of several other phone calls that you need to make, only to forget them before you hang up. What was the first task you started to do? That's right, give the dog his pill, but you never made it to the store. Still no cheese.

I know this is a little extreme for most people, but I know we can all identify to some extent. We get sidetracked by the little things in life. Time slips away and next thing you know your day is gone. It can be difficult to keep up with all the tasks it takes to keep your business and personal life running smoothly.

By compiling Your Life List, you are able to free your mind for other things. So, what is Your Life List? It is a list that helps you keep track of your life. You no longer need to worry about keeping track of all the tasks in your day. You don't keep track of just daily tasks, but you keep track of business goals. Break down your goal into bite-sized pieces and accomplish sections of it every day! *Success isn't just a lucky break. You have to work towards it consistently every day.* This is where Your Life List comes into play every day.

First, you need to figure out when you do your best work. Are you an early bird or a night owl? Of course I am talking about the times you function best. Most of you know when you are at your best. Do you prefer to get up with the sun or do prefer to wake without the alarm around noon? Let's talk about when you are going to be making Your Daily Life List. You will either make it in the evening before bed or in the morning when you get up. Your choice! This won't be the only time of day you look at your list, but it will be the time when you are able to spend time and organize everything on the list. Of course, you will also be adding things to your list throughout the day as well. I like to make my list at night. I rest better knowing that I don't have to try to remember everything to get done the next day. Some people like to do theirs in the morning because it allows them to get ready for the day.

Not everyone has the luxury to be at work when they are at their best, but recognizing when your energy is at its highest will make you more productive. For example, if you are a night owl, but you are scheduling most of your work in the morning. You constantly feel like you are dragging yourself to your next task. Just imagine if you shifted your schedule to work when you are at your best. You will feel energized and projects will just flow! That energy will radiate through your work and bring more energy to you! I am not suggesting you change your business hours to be open until midnight, but instead, work on demanding tasks later in your workday. Take advantage of your high-energy times!

Now that you know when your energy is at its highest, let's make that time your most productive. Picture yourself at work. You are feeling great. You are ready to rock and roll – however, you aren't sure what you needed to get done first. Your energy starts to fade fast! Next thing you know, you have only accomplished a couple of things and you feel frustrated. Now picture yourself back at work, but this time you have a list. Not just any list, but Your Life Lists, one that is prioritized in order of importance. A list with all the information you need to get your tasks completed. A list that has daily, weekly, and large goals in one place for easy reference, these are Your Life Lists!

You start working down your daily list checking items off as you go. You are on a roll! Next thing you know you have completed your list. Your energy has remained high throughout your tasks and you feel great satisfaction at a job well done. Not only are you accomplishing your daily tasks, but you are working towards large goals that you have broken down to smaller tasks. You can actually see everything you completed for the day. You are able to celebrate the things you have accomplished!

The things that need to be included on Your Daily Life List are everything you need to accomplish for the day. Include phone calls to be made, errands to be run, and things to accomplish. It is very important that you include one or two tasks that are setting you up for success towards your big goals. You are not allowed to put tasks that are HUGE on your daily list! Those belong on your weekly, monthly, or yearly goal lists. You wouldn't put 'write book' on your daily list. You would put a time to write or specific research to be done for the book. Breaking your large goal into smaller attainable goals allows you to celebrate your success along the way. This keeps your energy high through all of your HUGE projects.

Your 'write book' would go on Your Life List for goals and you would make it even more specific. For example, write book regarding time management, etc., etc.

When you are making your daily life list, you need to be very specific. For example, under your section of calls to be made, don't just put someone's name. You need to put everything you need to make the call. The person's name, phone number and reason for the call keeps you from wondering who Steve is, and why are you calling him!

Now that you have everything on a list that needs to be done for the day, you need to prioritize! What is the most important thing that has to be done? Is there anything on the list that would make you just fall over dead if it didn't get done? If so, that should probably be at the top. Tasks that get you closer to any life-changing goals should be in your top five. Of course, the things that need to get done, but won't cause economies to crumble, should round out the rest of your list.

What happens if you don't get everything done on your list? Most importantly, don't beat yourself up. Life happens and you are lucky enough to have life happening with you. Take the task that was not finished and add it to your list for tomorrow. However, this does not give you the right to keep putting that task off, day-after-day. Take a hard look at it. Did that item not get done because you are dreading doing it? Or, did you just run out of time? If you are dreading it, then it may need to be broken down into several smaller tasks that aren't quite so daunting.

If you were supposed to get 5 new contacts but didn't, try getting 2 or 3 the next day. You would be setting yourself up for failure if you took the task of getting 5 new contacts and added it to the next day's allotment of getting 5 more new ones. Now it is even bigger! Ten new contacts! Are you kidding me! You might think to yourself that if you couldn't get 5 names yesterday, what makes you think you could get 10 new contacts the next. This would only further destroy your ability to network and let negativity creep in to your thoughts. You may need to rebuild your confidence by only getting 2 or 3. That's okay! Just keep working towards your goal and build to 5 new contacts a day. You may surprise yourself and become comfortable enough to start getting more!

This list will also act as a gatekeeper for you. It will allow you to truly evaluate if something is important to your overall goals. If it won't allow you to work towards your larger goals, then does it deserve to be on your list? If there is something that comes up during the day that needs to be done, you must look and see where on the list it gets to be added.

There are several questions you need to ask yourself if this occurs. First, is it something that has to be done today? If not, write it on your list for tomorrow. If it needs to be on today's list, where does it need to be added? Second, is it going to the top of your list? Should it be somewhere in the middle or at the very bottom? Only you can decide where these tasks are allowed to be on your list!

Now that we have taken a look at how to make Your Daily Life List, let's take a look at how to make Your Goal Life List. This is your list that has your big weekly, monthly, and yearly goals. You can extend it out to your five-year goals as well! For example, if you are planning a party for your child, the party would be on either your weekly or monthly goal list. Which list the party goes on depends on how much time you have to prepare. Let's think of all the things you need to get done to make this a great party. You will need invitations, party favors, balloons, a cake, a camera, and of course… presents! Looking at the camera, you would need to make sure you have the battery charged and enough memory space to take your pictures. This would go on your daily list by writing 'put camera with party supplies.' Under that, write 'check battery and memory space.' Now you can add the other items the same way. If you are making your invitations, then you would need to list all the supplies needed to make them. Not only will you have things needed to get done for the party, but you also have to make a shopping list so nothing will be forgotten, including the present(s)!

Your Life List is a living, breathing thing. It will constantly evolve – just like you! You will get better at making your list and keeping it current the more you use it. It will help you to stay on task and make better use of your time. By consistently using Your Life Lists, you will see yourself become more productive.

ABOUT TRACEY

Tracey has been known as the go to girl for keeping your life organized and helping people to attain their goals. She has shown hundreds of people how to make their Life List and use it to simplify their lives. She has mentored and trained individuals to attain success and leadership roles in several direct selling companies. Direct sales and time management continue to be her passion.

Tracey has been involved in direct selling for over 20 years. During this time she was also a flight attendant with a major airline for 15 years and a public safety dispatcher for police, fire and medical for 6 years. She is married to her best friend, Steve, and has an 18 year old beautiful daughter, Chelsea. She has 2 dog children, Tinker and Samson, that she loves to take for hikes and exploring. They recently moved to Maine to enjoy the outdoors as much as possible.

For more information on Tracey Plympton programs, go to: www.yourlifelists.com

CHAPTER 13

FROM BELIEVER TO ACHIEVER

– BRING FORTH THE BEST OF WHO YOU ARE

BY JOHN STUCKENSCHNEIDER

The setting and achievement of goals is one of the most talked about, yet most misunderstood, keys to success. In fact, many of you reading this probably have thoughts running through your mind like, "Oh, no! Not another chapter on goal setting." The irony is that those of you having those thoughts are also the ones most frustrated with your own lack of progress in that very area. Hey, I get it! I, like many of you, have lived a large part of my life completely and totally frustrated with my own progress in setting and realizing my goals. It was not until I discovered and implemented the strategies that I will share with you here, that I began to realize my life's calling and potential and some really awesome results.

What follows are seven key strategies and ideas that have literally transformed my life, followed by an action plan which I hope will transform yours.

SEVEN SUCCESS STRATEGIES FOR GOAL ACHIEVEMENT

SUCCESS STRATEGY #1 – *TAKE RESPONSIBILITY FOR THE LIFE YOU ARE CREATING*

It was not until I realized that absolutely everything I was experiencing in my life, both good and bad, came as a result of my own thoughts, feelings and actions. Once I accepted responsibility for this, I was able to create a new path, a new life. I discovered and devoured Napoleon Hill's writings during one of the most emotionally and spiritually challenging times in my life. His works led me to the books and programs of Bob Proctor, featured in the movie "The Secret". This led to an opportunity to be personally mentored and trained by Bob, which completely changed my life.

I discovered that every result I was experiencing in my own life was the effect of my own prior thoughts and the emotions or feelings that I associated with that particular way of thinking. Together, these thoughts and feelings created my life's results. I knew that to change the results I was getting, I had to first accept responsibility for those results – then I had to change my thinking.

This can be a hard pill to swallow for the masses. Many feel that the results they are experiencing in life are created somewhere outside of themselves. That if they're getting a raw deal from life, it must be someone else's fault. Since they continuously focus their thoughts on the negative results they are experiencing, they are doomed to create more of them. Some become like hamsters on continuous wheels of negativity. Is this you?

SUCCESS STRATEGY #2 – *CHOOSE YOUR NEW THOUGHTS, A NEW FOCUS*

In order to change your results, and therefore your life, you must decide on something new to think about, a new focus. Here's where this really gets exciting! If you can change your destiny by changing your focus, how truly empowering this is! You literally have all control and therefore can design your own new life. So how do you choose your new focus, your new goal, your new path in life? You break through the barriers of your own comfort zone. Many people choose goals with no power to cause them to grow or stretch. They choose something they know they can reach, or worse, something they have reached before. These are not the types of life-changing goals we are talking about here. If you never challenge yourself by doing things you've never attempted before, then you are doomed to live a life of repeats. Read that line again!

As Les Brown says, "*We are all born with greatness in us, but we must step into it.*" Yes, we are definitely born into greatness and, unfortunately, conditioned into mediocrity.

So, how do you make decisions about whether or not to do something, to step out? I asked Bob Proctor that same question and he replied, "If the thought of stepping out and doing something scares the hell out of me, I know I'm on the right track." In order for me to grow, to become more, I had to step out of my own comfort zone. I've come to ask myself a couple of questions when faced with big decisions.

1. Would doing this move me farther along my path in the pursuit of my purpose?
2. If money were not a concern, would I step out and do this?

If the answers to these two questions are "Yes", then I go for it!

SUCCESS STRATEGY #3 –
IT'S NOT THE GOAL THAT MATTERS

The reason that we set goals in the first place is so that we grow and stretch as individuals through reaching higher and higher levels of achievement. As with all forms of life, if we are not constantly in a state of growth, we are dying. There is no stagnation. There is no standing still. In fact, in business as in life, if you are standing still, the world and your competition will literally pass you by. The true power in goal setting, then focused persistent action through the achievement of that goal, is not in its achievement at all. The true power is in the transformation of you.

SUCCESS STRATEGY #4 –
CREATE A VISION AND VISIT IT OFTEN

Many people do this, and, unknowingly, create a vision that lacks power to create a new reality in their lives. Your vision should be of you having "arrived" at your goal and your "world" at that time, including differences created by your new achievement.

Where the visions of most lack power is in the fact that they view their vision as if looking through the lens of a camera watching a movie of their life, always seeing themselves in the picture. This type of vision is always of a life that they're "watching" rather than "experiencing."

As you create your achievement vision, see it as if you are there looking through your own eyes, seeing what you will see when you have arrived. In doing this, you should not see yourself in the picture at all; but you should rather see and experience things through your own senses.

I encourage you to write a fully-detailed description of your experiences in this new place. Use all of your senses. Make it as detailed as possible and we will utilize what you have created here when we get to the action plan.

SUCCESS STRATEGY #5 – *DECIDE TO FULLY INVEST YOURSELF IN THE EFFORT*

If you are going to reach the goals you've identified and create the life of your dreams, you must invest yourself fully in the effort. In Malcolm Gladwell's book, *Outliers: The Story of Success*, he points out that if you want to master anything, you have to put 10,000 hours into it. The truth is, most people won't put the 10,000 hours in. They take the only life they have and they waste it living the way they don't want to live, doing the things they don't want to do, and not earning enough to live the way they really want to live. Decide today that this will not be your story.

Everyone wants the great results. But few are willing to invest the time, dedication, perseverance and bulldog determination it takes to literally become the originator, the cause, of the results they seek. It's never crowded along the extra mile or at the top of any mountain. And nobody labeled "normal" ever made it into the history books, either.

SUCCESS STRATEGY #6 – *EXPECT LIFE'S OBSTACLES, LEARN TO EMBRACE THEM*

Don't expect success to come easily. An extraordinary life only happens as a result of extraordinary effort. Unexpected problems or challenges will come along on the way to reaching our goals to blindside us. Those challenges that come to all of us are what I've come to call "character building moments," and I've learned to be thankful for every one of them and the personal growth that's come with each one.

You see, your challenges or problems do not define you, but the way that you react and respond to them does. In your quest to reach your goal, accept that almost no one ever does anything absolutely correctly the first time they try it. None of us walked the first time we tried, or drove a stick-shift car like a pro the first time we gave it a shot. There will be challenges you will face, and with the right mindset, will conquer along the way. Embrace those experiences for what they are...NECESSARY!

SUCCESS STRATEGY #7 – *GET TO WORK! THE POWER OF NOW!*

Though it is imperative that you have a vision of your life as it will be, it is important that you are aware that it will never move into reality without you taking advantage of your opportunities to create that vision here in the present. Many people are always in the "I'm going to do this" mentality, future tense. Others live in the past. What you must realize is the past is sealed and only exists in your mind through your memories. The future is fantasy, not yet reality. The only time in your life over which you have complete control is this moment, right now. The way you think, feel and act in this moment determines every moment to come. Therefore, it is critical that you make each decision in your life based on where you're going instead of where you are now. Be present in every moment and ask yourself if you are moving closer to, or farther from, your vision for your life.

You cannot live any moment of your life over again. You are giving every moment of your life for something, for that moment's experience. Make sure it's a good trade.

YOUR ACTION PLAN – SEVEN ACTION STEPS TO GOAL REALIZATION

ACTION STEP #1 –
SUSPEND YOUR OWN DISBELIEF BY CONTROLLING YOUR FOCUS

Once you decide on your goal, the next question is, "How do you control your focus?" By forcing yourself to see only how your goal CAN be accomplished and never how it can't.

Try this exercise:

1. On a piece of paper draw a large capital "T" down the center of the page. Across the top of the page write your goal. At the top of the left column write, "Why I Can't"and on the right side, write "How I Can."
2. Now, in the entire left column of the page draw a big "X", so there is absolutely no room for ideas about why you can't accomplish your goal.

We can all focus on the reasons why we can't do something. When we focus on those, we close off our ability to focus on how we can do something. If we can only focus on one thing at a time, doesn't it make sense to focus in ways that serve us and bring us closer to achieving what we desire?

3. Now, down the right side of the page, create your list of "How I Can" and focus only on ways you can achieve your goal. Make it a real brainstorming session! No idea is ridiculous! List everything that comes to mind. You can refine this later. When a thought about "Why I Can't" comes to mind, just dismiss the thought by mentally saying "Dismissed" or "Next."
4. Review the "T" chart you've created along with your vision daily.

ACTION STEP #2 –
FOCUS ON ENDS RATHER THAN MEANS

Some people allow themselves to become paralyzed by the fact that they don't know everything they need to know to accomplish their goal. Well, no kidding. If you already knew all of the unknowns associated with achieving your goal, you would have already reached it, wouldn't you? Some people allow the fact that they don't know how to do something to become the fatal blow that kills their dream of accomplishing something extraordinary.

Success is not about your resources, or knowledge at hand. It's about your resourcefulness. If you don't know how to do something that's critical to accomplishing what you've set out to do, then go out and get the knowledge you need. All the knowledge we could ever hope to need is as close today as our nearest web browser. Every successful person is a lifelong learner. A successful life is built by on-the-job training with learning and growing experiences. Decide to seek out and secure any new knowledge necessary to take you to the heights of where you want to go.

ACTION STEP #3 – *STRUCTURE YOUR DAY AROUND YOUR GOAL*

I've found the following technique to be extremely effective in holding my focus and determination in check. Charles Schwab credited this strategy as the single-most important action plan he'd ever seen put into daily practice.

1. Write your goal on a 3x5 index card and carry it with you, reviewing it several times throughout the day.
2. On the opposite side of the index card list six action items to be completed today. All should be chosen based on each completed action's ability to move you closer to your goal. They should be listed in order of importance, with number 1 as the most important, down to number 6 being the least important of that day's tasks.
3. Go about your day completing the action items in order, but never moving on to the next before completing the task at hand in its entirety.
4. At the end of the day, items not completed are moved to the top of the next day's list, which you should create anew each evening.

ACTION STEP #4 – *UTILIZE "BACK FROM THE FUTURE" THINKING*

I've put into practice an incredibly effective way to determine what needs to be done – one that I first learned about from one of Brian Tracy's talks. Give it a try yourself.

1. Take out a sheet of paper. Envision yourself five years into the future, having achieved the goal you now seek. Take a look at every area of your life both professionally and personally, and describe what you see, the success you are now experiencing.
2. Now, back it up to three years and look at your life again. Maybe you've achieved the goal at this point or maybe you're on the verge of its accomplishment. Again, describe what you see.
3. Repeat the process for one year from now.

At each of these points in your future success vision, ask yourself, "What action would I have had to take in my life professionally and personally five years ago, three years ago, one year ago – in order for me to have arrived at this milestone in my journey?" and… "What steps and actions did I take at the very beginning that made all of this success possible?"

I found this a very powerful way to get inside my own head and help me to identify which of my decisions and actions are of paramount importance right now. I hope you'll find this exercise as empowering as I have.

ACTION STEP #5 – *DEVELOP AN ATTITUDE OF GRATITUDE IN ADVANCE*

This action step was born out of a very frustrating and even overwhelming time in my life when I was faced with a barrage of very complex and life-changing decisions. There were decisions involving a career path change with me stepping out into something I'd never tried before along with matters in my personal life that needed attention – and all required decisions NOW! I wasn't sleeping, I was incredibly stressed, and, of course, I was taking it out on everyone around me. The difference came when I decided to get alone with myself and ask a series of empowering questions.

1. "How can I step back and look at this situation in a way that serves and empowers me?" Then...
2. "What if I could move beyond this decision-making moment to a time, mentally, where I am living with the results of these decisions?" Then, the big question that made all the difference...
3. "How much better is my life one year from now because of the action I took today?"

As I saw my life in my mind's eye one, three, and five years from now, I saw how much better my life was going to be. Gratitude overwhelmed me! Gratitude for the power of the choices that I would make today and that I could now see would dramatically improve my life. This "Gratitude in Advance" exercise has become an invaluable tool in helping me to step out into new territory with new faith and belief in myself and my abilities.

ACTION STEP #6 –
BE A GIVER

The law of sowing and reaping is definitely alive and well in the universe. Throughout history, all highly successful people have been great givers. They've consistently given more than anyone else around them. They've given more of themselves, of their time and energy, their efforts, and their resources. The best in business know that, as far as compensation goes, it's a 10 to 1 deal. Winners always give ten times more value than what they ask in return. Life is just like a boomerang. What happens when you throw a boomerang? It comes right back to you. If you throw it with a lot of energy, a lot comes back at you. If you give out a little, little comes back. How many people do you know who are giving out a little, yet expecting a lot to come back?

We've heard about this in school as the law of cause and effect, or karma. We've heard, "What goes around, comes around" and "As you sow, so shall you reap." Successful people realize that giving is a principle that operates in the universe and it also greatly influences our success or lack of it. Remember, what you put out will eventually come back to you, just like the boomerang.

ACTION STEP #7 – *DEVELOP THE HABIT OF SUCCESS*

In Dr. Maxwell Maltz' groundbreaking book, *Psychocybernetics*, we learn what it takes to form a new habit. Habits are things we do naturally and automatically, without thinking. These habits have been conditioned into us and come directly from our subconscious mind. According to Dr. Maltz, if we want to change our lives, we must begin to form new habits. In other words, we must change the things we do automatically, without thinking about them. Behavioral scientists tell us that it is possible to recondition or form new habits within 21 days.

In order to develop the habit of success by utilizing the success strategies and action steps laid out in this chapter, you must condition these new responses, or new ways of thinking and acting, for at least 21 days. In order for this new information to change your life, it must become habit in your life. Success never happens by chance, but it does leave clues. The success strategies and action steps in this chapter have been utilized by some of the most successful people in the world. If we know these techniques work, who are we to try and reinvent the wheel?

What we're talking about here is thinking and acting in a certain way, a way that produces successful results. There exists a successful thought-process, one that highly successful people do "inside their heads" that causes them to take the actions they do. Let's develop a habit of success by building new habits and new ways of thinking and acting, because thinking and action guarantee success and results.

We all have greatness within us as well as an untapped gold mine of potential just waiting to be unearthed. Make the decision today to bring forth the very best of who you are.

"God's gift to you is more talent and ability than you will ever use in this lifetime. Your gift to God is to develop as much of that talent and ability as you can in this lifetime."

~ Steve Bow

ABOUT JOHN

John Stuckenschneider is a successful motivational speaker, author, seminar leader, and certified Life Success© coach. He is the founder of several companies. Real Success Investments, LLC was founded by John as a resource designed to match single-family homes with financially-challenged home buyers.

Creative Wealth Solutions, LLC was co-founded by John to help retirees and people approaching retirement age with 100% safe investment and wealth transfer options.

John is also the founder of Think Into Success, LLC, a company dedicated to providing the very best in personal development resources, seminars, and programs. Having been personally mentored and certified by Bob Proctor, of the movie "*The Secret*", as one of Bob's Life Success© Consultants, John became aware of a greater purpose for his life. He became aware of the real power of the life-changing information as it created new results in his own life. John had just began a new career in sales, coming from a 14 year background in Law Enforcement, and through applying what he had learned from Bob, had been experiencing extraordinary success. Within two years of beginning his new sales career he became the highest producing representative in an organization of 1500 salespeople.

His new purpose and mission became to share what he's learned and experienced with as many people as possible to give them the skills and tools to change their own lives as well.

John's grasp of the techniques and strategies which maximize human potential, gleaned from Bob's more than 50 years in the personal development industry, make him a valuable contributor to any corporate workshop or training event.

Available Life Success© workshops and live events include *You Were Born Rich*, *Mission In Commission*, *The Goal Achiever*, *The Success Puzzle*, *A Winner's Image*, and the *Thinking Into Results* Corporate Training Workshop. In addition to the live versions of these events presented by John, these programs as well as others are available in audio and video formats for individual or group use. Personalized coaching is also available. For more information, as well as John's latest Free Offer, please go to: www.thinkintosuccess.com.

CHAPTER 14

GLOBAL CONNECTIONS MEAN ALL THE WORLD

BY YING HAN

"Each friend represents a world in us, a world possibly not born until they arrive, and it is only by this meeting that a new world is born."

~ Anais Nin

You never know what will change your life – but, unless you open yourself up to your passion and open yourself to new possibilities, that change might never come.

In my case, it was a small purple bracelet that prompted the change in a very unexpected way. I'll reveal exactly what that bracelet was all about – and how it made such a huge difference in my life – a little later.

But first, let's talk about you. Are you looking for profound change in your own life and not finding it? Perhaps it's because you're limiting your search to the all-too-familiar usual places.

Now that technological advances have made communication and connections so much easier, your change could come about from anywhere in the world. Remote cultures teach us how to be creative in different ways and how to find new and exciting opportunities through sharing globally.

As someone who immigrated to the U.S. from China when I was younger, I am probably a little more aware than most of how global connections can inspire new pathways to new careers – especially since that is just what happened to me. In this chapter, I'd like to share how my search for a brand new vocation ended happily, through a combination of luck and effort – the two most important ingredients to any success story.

FINDING SUCCESS IN THE U.S.

When I was 21, I quit the top graduate school in China where I was a student, and came to the U.S. with my husband. Once here, I studied science and technology – this was easiest for me, since I, at that time, could not speak or write English very well, even though I had studied the language back in my home country. Even now, I still work with a linguistics coach to improve my English-speaking ability.

I continued my studies here until I received a Master's in Computer Science from Northeastern University. Even though I studied graphics design, artificial intelligence and other technical subjects, I still wanted to work with people more than with machines – so I decided to enter the I.T. field, figuring it would at least enable me to interact with top business people. I ended up as the I.T. manager at Harvard University, and then went to work for Fidelity Investments as an I.T. consultant – I thought that company would help me learn about the financial world. After that, I went to Cornell University and received my MBA. I was really good with finance, as I was with computer science, and I knew I could have a lucrative career in either field – but, again, my passion was still for working with *people.*

After Cornell, I was recruited by EMC, a technology company that specializes in data storage, and I worked there for the majority of my professional life, a total of 8 years. My focus was on finding new market opportunities with new products and new technologies for the company. All the while, however, I yearned to have my own business and my independence – and most of all, I really wanted to play a role on the international stage between America and China. The question was how to put all those elements together in a satisfying (and, of course, profitable!) way.

I took the first steps towards my ultimate goal by starting my own business on my own time while I was still at EMC. That business was a hi-tech consulting company which developed video analytics algorithms for specialized video equipment, such as red light cameras and other surveillance video systems. At the time, Google's rapid growth had made video data search a potential market need. This was a business with a future.

That video software consulting company was the beginning of my new life as an entrepreneur. In the next few years, I founded a Tae Kwon Do studio, invested in two Chinese restaurants (one failed, one succeeded), started an import/export company in Japan, and also expanded my video software consulting company into China.

But I still was not satisfied. I still wanted to go beyond the usual business dynamics and find something that really inspired me in a new and exciting way.

THE BRACELET THAT BROUGHT A NEW BEGINNING

In July of 2010, I was visiting China. I had been going back and forth between my home country and my adopted one frequently on business over the past three years – but this visit turned out to be something special.

I was visiting my brother and his family – and I discovered that all of them, including his daughter, were wearing a distinctive purple bracelet. I had no idea what this was all about – until my brother shared with me their copy of Will Bowen's book, "A Complaint Free World," that had been translated into Chinese. Apparently the book had become very popular in China, so they bought his book, which featured the same purple bracelet on the cover.

When I read it, I was as taken with the book's vision as my brother's family was.

Bowen believed that most of us spent too much time complaining about the mundane things in our lives, instead of taking positive action to improve those lives. By putting so much energy into what we disliked, we were creating a negativity that held us all back. And something that really stood out to me? It was his preface to the book, in which he wrote that he was very interested in coming to China at some point in the future.

His complaint-free message really hit home when I returned to the U.S., when, within a week, my ten year-old son seemed to be constantly complaining – about *everything*. I gave him Will Bowen's book and, together, we visited his website at: www.AComplaintFreeWorld.org. I was happy to see that my son also took the message to heart – and he suggested we email Will Bowen to thank him. At the same time, I took the opportunity to casually mention that I could help him with his ambitions for a China speaking engagement.

Will personally called me a few days later, to my surprise, and told me he had just returned from China. He said that he didn't have a person booking him for appearances in China yet, but there was somebody very interested in signing him – but he wanted to talk to me first. That did it for me – I began to see that this just might be what I was looking for. Very shortly after the call, I went to see him in Kansas City, where he lived.

I told him that China would be very receptive to what he said – that was already evident from how well his book was selling in its Chinese translation. The explosive economic growth in China has thrown many people off-balance. People are increasingly feeling pressured and stressed out. Everyone needs to be more competitive, creative and willing to challenge traditional and conventional thinking. In such a social environment, some people turn to complaining as a way of venting. Just in time, the book "A Complaint Free World" has helped many people to bring balance back to their lives.

Will could see that I understood both cultures very well, and how his message could best be presented in China. He also knew that I was professionally trained in the business world and had the Chinese connections that would help him to succeed over there. Even though I had no idea what I was doing when it came to booking a speaker or setting up the financial arrangements, he picked me to represent him in China.

That vote of confidence was enough to propel me forward into this new arena I was incredibly excited about. I researched the speaker industry to find out what I needed to know – and a couple of months later, I was already thinking I needed to build a team of speakers to create a real business around this idea.

But, again, I had no idea where to start.

SEEKING OUT SPEAKERS

The route I took this time was straight to the bookstore – where I went through the "Management" section, taking down the names of popular authors who seemed likely candidates on my Blackberry. Over the next few days, I did some online research on the names I had come up with and emailed a couple of them. One wrote back and said no, he didn't want to go to China. But someone else wrote back and said that he *was* interested in going to China.

That person's name is on the cover of this book – Brian Tracy.

To be entirely accurate, Brian did not write back personally that first time – instead, it was the president of Brian Tracy International, Ib Moller, who told me they had an agent for China already, but they could use someone to book Brian in the rest of Asia, if I wanted to do that. I agreed, even though my strongest connections were in China, and they sent me many of Brian's books and CDs to review.

When I called to ask what to do if I had a good lead for Brian in China, Ib informed me that they were going to give me all of Asia, including my home country, because they really wanted to work with me. They realized that my cultural knowledge, combined with my business experience, made me someone who could really do the job for them.

So I had my second client – and I was doing very well with my first. At a New Year's Eve event, I booked Will Bowen at a Chinese event where he spoke to 3,800 people. That really opened the door, and many deals suddenly became available to me and my speakers.

This year, I'm looking at phenomenal and explosive growth for my new speakers' agency. I want to have a stable of three to four American speakers who can bring their own cultural vision and products and share them with China. I'm especially anxious to bring Brian over to China. He already has over 30 books translated there, but, to really create a high-profile presence, coming to speak in person will make a big difference.

WHAT AMERICANS CAN TEACH THE CHINESE

Although there's been a lot written and said about China's incredible business growth over the past few years, America is still a leader in terms of ideas for running and managing businesses successfully. That's because China's business economy is still relatively new and unsophisticated.

For example, a few years ago Brian did speak in China – but, at the time, the content really wasn't as relevant. Learning was very mechanical and theoretical; some simple management lessons made their way there from Japan and America, but this material was very limited. In addition, the timing was not as good as it now is. Chinese were then mechanically copying techniques learned from the Americans and the Japanese, and they were busy capturing the newly found economic opportunities. Now that they have had experience in making new history, they have found that they need to artfully learn and creatively experiment with lessons learned from others, including Americans.

China's economic development has now progressed much further and there are many more entrepreneurs who want to learn both higher management theories and the secrets to business success. The Chinese have also found it's not that easy to learn by reading translations of this subject matter – they really want to learn this content directly from the original authors; that's why my speakers are already in such demand.

With these speakers, I really want to bridge our cultures. Americans are very good at creating processes and management systems – they're also very positive, optimistic, open and democratic. Many Asians, on the other hand, are "repressed and depressed" – and need the American "can-do" message to deal with their new economic reality.

People like Brian Tracy enjoy working with me because I do understand these cultural differences and how best to tailor their messages to this huge new audience. There are also not many native Chinese people like myself who can effectively work directly with Americans between the two cultures; and there are even fewer who understand the complete picture of technology and business as well as what both countries are all about.

I will be working on a book with Brian Tracy in the coming months; the book will be translated by me into Chinese, with additional thoughts added by me to make his content more relevant to the people of China. We will then translate the book back into English for the American market.

I have recently signed my third speaker. I'm very anxious to build my "dream team" of speakers – but I am going to be choosy about whom I work with. Other important thought leaders such as Zig Ziglar and Dennis Whitley have much to offer the Chinese business community, and I really want them to share their wisdom while it is still available.

The important lesson I've learned from all this is one I want to pass on in this chapter. If I had not asked about the bracelets my brother's family was wearing – and if I had not followed up on that information – I would not be realizing my professional goals at this minute. How many opportunities do we all walk past every day – just because we don't recognize and act on them?

Through global connections, I feel I am helping to influence the Chinese business community in an exciting and proactive manner – as well as helping it to the next level. My dream of working with people in a profound way is finally coming true.

The whole world is our marketplace now – and by exploring it to the fullest, we can find amazing new prospects we never even dreamed existed.

ABOUT YING

Ying Han is an established entrepreneur, business consultant and best-selling author. Her life mission is to be the bridge between US and China for technology and cultural exchange. Her speakers bureau exclusively represents some most well-known American speakers (such as Brian Tracy and Will Bowen) for personal develop and corporate training in Asia. Ying has become an effective broker and consultant for businesses in US and China with her drive for people to cross-share intellectual and technology advancements. Her business has been exploding in the past year. She is becoming a rising star in the rapidly growing executive training market in China.

Ying has founded various companies around the world, including one software company in US, one technology solution provider in China, one consumer product trading company in Japan and two service providing companies in US. She has worked with a number of companies as a strategist for their international business development.

Prior to starting her own businesses, Ying had worked at EMC Corp., Fidelity Investments and Harvard University. She holds an MBA degree from Cornell University and a Master's in Computer Science from Northeastern University.

Have you been thinking globally? Technology advancements have made things move fast and far easily. Learn from remote cultures to be creative, find opportunities through sharing globally. If you have things to offer to the vast, fast-growing Chinese market, please contact Ying at (508)529-9012 or visit www.speakerstoasia.com.

CHAPTER 15

MENTORS IN MY LIFE

BY CHARLES SIKORA

Think back and try to remember the first time you were guided or taught. You might say it was a sibling who taught you how to ride a bike or play a game, but most likely you were mentored before you were old enough to remember. As a child you learned to take your first step and say your first word. Who was there holding your hand and giving you the encouragement to take those first steps? Was it a parent, guardian or sibling? They perhaps said, "Look at him! He's starting to walk. Keep it up, put one foot in front of the other." We may not be able to remember those words of encouragement we received so early on in life but, it is because of them that we kept on trying until we could walk. These early experiences are just the beginning of many steps down the pathway of life.

Along the path I have followed, I have built many relationships. Some were short-lived and others are still playing a significant role. The encouragement I received from these relationships inspired me to achieve many goals and reach for the dreams in my life. Throughout school years in the 60's and 70's, special teachers made going to school a positive event. I remember being in the third grade and the thought of having to write in cursive was intimidating. I just couldn't get several letters correct, so my teacher sent me home with many sheets of the "special" triple lined paper to practice. Even though I still can't do a capital Q or Z in cursive, the positive encouragement I received from my parents and teacher gave me the confidence and help I needed to succeed.

In Junior High, my gym teacher was also the sports coach. I attempted to play football, but he steered me into running track. Being lean, track came naturally to me and several of the running events became my favorites. Watching me run the high hurdles must have been a real sight. My coach never said to me, "You dummy, your style is all wrong," or offered any other discouraging remarks. In fact, his enthusiastic remarks often were about how I would be faster in the next event, and maybe even shave several seconds off before next week. Even though many times I knocked down 7 of the 8 hurdles, I learned quickly that in order to finish the race I would need to dust myself off and get back up and continue. One cannot succeed by staying down once you hit a hurdle. You've got to have the courage to get up and persevere to finish the race. This teacher taught me that even though my style was not correct, I was able to get over the hurdles and grew to understand how meaningful this simple lesson in perseverance was.

The summer after junior high, all of the stories that I heard had me terrified before I even stepped a foot into High School, but it wasn't nearly as bad as I thought it would be. Track, once again, was my sport. Only this time I was competing against those seniors who were larger and faster than I was. Our track coach, also the wrestling coach, was All-State and Regional Champ and everyone was terrified of him. I'm sure you have seen a coach like him. He wore his tee shirts a size or two smaller than he should have and he looked like the Amazing Hulk. Being a freshman, I should have been afraid of him but, I looked up to him and soon developed a good relationship. Respectable times in track would get a smile from him and the first year running track with his coaching was a successful year. In PE, he watched me dribble a basketball and I know he worked hard to keep from laughing. Coach even told me that the only way for me to pass PE was to join the wrestling team. Coach mentored his way – no B.S. and directly to the point – and he had a lot of respect from the team. About halfway through the first year, I began to notice that I was getting better. When Coach needed someone to assist him in showing a new move or what someone else had done wrong, I was his practice partner. He put me into positions that I never knew my body could bend. I was bounced off mats, put into half nelsons, and I would get pinned quickly as he demonstrated all the practice moves with me. Looking back, I was being mentored so that I would be better in the years to come. Even though most of the team would comment on how I must have screwed up or upset the coach because he always used me for his personal practice dummy, I never let it bother me. I recently ran into him and he immediately recognized me and said, "Hi Chuck, how's everything going?" It's been nearly 40 years and it felt like just yesterday that we were sweating and tired in that practice room. Now this is not a sequel to "Rocky," but wrestling was a part of my high school years. I may not have received any big trophies or awards but I didn't quit. As our Coach told the team, "A quitter never wins and a winner never quits."

I began my career at the Ford Motor Company Dearborn Engine Plant in the crankshaft department, slinging crankshafts for V-8 engines. I was 140 pounds and each crankshaft weighed approx. 60 pounds — talk about "throwing your weight around!" The job involved lifting and putting the crankshafts in the grinding machines, and this was before ergonomics was required. Running two machines with a run cycle of about 120 seconds I was lifting about 14,000 pounds per hour. I went from that 140 pound kid to a muscular 160 pound man. The factories in the 70's were rough places to work. They were hot and humid with very slippery steel plate floors and many unique individuals. My department was made up of a younger group who were led by several older and more experienced men. These men were our protectors and mentors. If you wanted to know about anything, they were the guys to ask. If they had warned you to not do something and you did it anyway, they never yelled, instead they would only shrug their shoulders and walk away saying "I told you so." There were many days I felt like quitting. But, Joe, one of the senior guys, would say something like, "Son, if I can put up with this for 42 years, you can too!" Even though he was old, grouchy, and yelled and complained, he had a heart of gold that very few got the chance to see. One experience with Joe stands out in my mind the most. One day at the plant, I saw a posting by the union about testing for the skilled trades apprenticeship and I downplayed it. Joe kept mentioning that I should take the test and I came up with all the excuses in the world as to why I did not want to. Well, Joe "shamed" me into signing up for the test that I knew for sure I was going to fail.

Joe informed me that he was going to drive me to the test site just to make sure that I didn't go the other way. Well, he drove me and I said "Don't worry, this won't take long, you don't need to hang around." After the test was over and it was being graded, I felt that I might just have passed it. The instructor came back into the room and started calling names and mine wasn't one of them, and I thought for sure I had failed the test. Then he said "Good luck, try again" and dismissed all the people whose names he had just called. A good feeling overcame me and I realized that I did pass! Not only did I pass, but also I had the second highest score! **Joe taught me to believe in myself.** Several months went by, and I was called up to start the apprenticeship for electrician, a small party was held and off I went. Four years later, I graduated and went back to see Joe to tell him how much it meant that he had believed in me and all that I could achieve, but he retired several months before I got there to see him.

Joe was just one of the many memorable people I met while working at the historic Ford Rouge complex. I met characters who will always be subjects for stories to tell my grandchildren (whenever they arrive). My work experience at the Rouge complex was one of many. I was on the start-up team for two new plants, I worked on the renovation of the WHQ Board Room, and I was even a part of the complete renovation of the World Headquarters building.

Another memorable experience at Ford was working in the Research and Engineering Center the year the east coast power grid failed. I was given a unique job assignment by my Supervisor, Jim, to keep two large generators running. They powered the portable air conditioners in the design studios, which was home to clay model cars. If the temperature was to exceed 75 degrees, the clay would start to fall off the models. We had to work quickly to save the hard work that the modelers had done. At the time, I didn't realize the importance of this assignment, but Jim knew that I had the knowledge to get the job done quickly. Because of making sure the clay models kept cool and didn't fall apart, many of the Ford vehicles you see on the road are there now because of Jim's leadership and my knowledge to keep them cool.

I spent my last few years at Ford working with Jim as my supervisor, and he left a huge impression on me. During my long stint at Ford, I was getting older and more independent. I thought I knew it all. One day, Jim came into my office, closed the door and told me, "You know, you will go a long way in life if you stop and smell the roses once in a while." He then got up and walked out. I thought about what he had said for several days and decided to ask Jim what he had meant. He then told me that he had noticed my patience was not what it used to be, and that I needed to slow down and think things through before jumping into action. Jim's knowledge was far beyond his years. I still get together with him at least once a month, and he always brings up something I did and we all have a good laugh. Jim taught me to think things through and ask if you don't understand. The experiences learned throughout my years with the Ford Motor Company will always be etched in my mind. After being taught and mentored by some of the best, I retired at the age of 53.

After retirement, I was still very active and I wanted to keep busy. With the knowledge and experience I had gained throughout my school and work years, I decided to go on a search to purchase a franchise. I had heard that franchises have a proven record of success and all of the business practices you need to get started. Before I decided to go through with it, I called up an old friend who had been a very successful businessman for many years. I asked him if he thought I should purchase this franchise and he told me that I was talented enough and didn't need to. Well, I didn't take heed of his advice and clearly thought I knew it all. At first, everything was going really well. Business was growing and the outlook was promising, and then the unexpected happened. The economy took a nose dive. I contacted the franchise and asked for their advice on what to do next. Their response was something like, "We haven't gone through a downturn like this before, so keep advertising and investing in your business and customers will find you." Well, it didn't work, and after I closed the business, I ran into my longtime friend who looked at me and calmly asked, "Did you learn anything?" Well, I sure did. I learned that before you start a business, you need a mentor who has 'been there and done it' before you.

As you go through life, it is amazing the people that cross your path and have the ability to see a lot more in you than you are able to see in yourself. The people we meet may come into our lives for short moments and others may stay around. They may be our family, friends, teachers, coworkers or just passersby; however, they often guide and teach us a lot about who we are and who we want to be become. Either you learn and listen to the people who were there before you or you learn from the school of hard knocks. We are not always aware of the guidance we are being given at the time, but through reflection we can remember the lessons, whether big or small, that made lasting impressions on us. It is this guidance that can pick you up when you've fallen, help you pass a test you never thought you could, or even open a successful business.

I now have a mentor who has been, and still is, a successful entrepreneur and business woman. She is the leader of a MasterMind group that I recently joined to surround myself with like-minded individuals, who are all entrepreneurs in similar businesses. I now have business associates in ten states and two countries. I am the CEO of two Internet-based businesses that are well on their way to grossing $1 million per year.

Advice for utilizing mentors:

1. Listen and take their advice, because they can offer an outside perspective that you may not be able to see. Remember to ask questions if you don't understand, because your mentor will always take time to teach.
2. Mistakes are only mistakes if you do not learn from them. Keep in touch with your mentor, because they anticipate an issue before it happens.
3. Always keep your focus ahead. You may know where you want to go now, but as your business grows, you can lose track of your key principles and objectives. Your mentor can help keep you on the path so that you never lose your focus.
4. Remember, a mentor is a wise and trusted counselor or teacher. They are there to help and guide you along your journey, wherever it may lead.

ABOUT CHARLES

Charles (Chuck) Sikora retired from Ford Motor Company as an Electrical and Skilled Trades Supervisor where he worked for 34 years. He has also been an avid motorcyclist since 1974 and in 2007 became a Certified Motorcycle Education Coach. Traveling over 500,000 miles across the US and Canada, Chuck has had the opportunity to see a lot of this country up close. One of the highlights of his many trips was being in Southern Alberta, Canada when Mt. St. Helens erupted in 1980. Traveling southwest without listening to a radio he rode into the fallout from the eruption.

Currently Chuck is the CEO of two web-based businesses. One focuses on personal development and the other offers visual aids to various online channels. Having 5 years of experience in the Network Marketing, Multi-Level Marketing and Direct Sales Industries has made his transition from the corporate world to online business an easy one.

Chuck can be found at www.fireforceonepartnership.com. Fire Force One Partnership is a group of like-minded entrepreneurs assisting other entrepreneurs who are lost or in of need direction.

Giving back is a very important part of life to Chuck. He is active with the Ride For Kids fund raiser as well as the Pediatric Brain Tumor Foundation, which raises funds for children afflicted with brain tumors. The funds go to research and scholarships.

Having just returned from a Destiny Conference in Cusco, Peru, Chuck also learned more about the Inca culture. He helped raise money to purchase two llamas to help (give back to) one village high up in the mountains.

Please visit www.CharlesSikora.com for more information.

CHAPTER 16

THE POWER OF CONSCIOUS CHOICE

BY ROBERT VITELLI

I was at my dad's house in New Jersey one weekend night watching TV when the phone rang. I jumped up to answer it — it was my mom. Her voice sounded very strange. "You're going to be staying with your dad, honey," she said "Mommy's going to heaven tonight. I just wanted to say goodbye."

Though I was only eight, I knew instantly what that meant. Mom had been severely depressed for a long time; she was a stressed out single mom, running herself ragged working seventy-five hours a week and in a pretty unhealthy relationship to boot.

"Dad," I shouted, panicked. "I think Mom's trying to kill herself." He rushed to the phone. "Are you okay? What's going on?" he asked. I heard her crying on the other line. "Stay where you are. You're going to be alright." He hung up with my mom and immediately called 911. An ambulance rushed to our apartment in New York just in time; she had downed several bottles of prescription medication. They pumped her stomach and just barely saved her life.

I spent the next ten-plus years trying to save my beloved, fragile mom from hurting. In our co-dependent relationship, I was the enabler—her support system, her cuddle-machine, the one to bring her up whenever she felt down.

Instead of being driven to self-destruct as a teenager, I became deeply motivated to work on myself. I started reading motivational literature, and at the age of twenty, I attended my first personal growth seminar with Brian Tracy. I saw my dad occasionally, but I didn't have a role model, or a mentor. So I was always seeking to fill that void within me, always looking for someone to show me the road to success.

Fast-forward to my mid-twenties, and I was experiencing an incredible level of financial success. Traveling the country, tossing money to the wind, I was living in an atmosphere of fame and glamour. But I was also completely miserable. I was working seventy hours per week and my health was deteriorating rapidly. One night, while driving cross-country through Nebraska with my girlfriend, the car in front of us lost control and started flipping end-over-end. We pulled over and ran to the car; its two passengers had been killed instantly. Their ruined bodies hung from the doors. We called 911, and waited for the ambulance to arrive.

In shock, we drove a little further, to a motel, and stopped for the night to decompress. We turned on the TV to watch a movie and *Frankie and Johnny* was playing on cable that night. Halfway through the movie, I broke down and started bawling my eyes out. It freaked my girlfriend out—it kind of flipped me out, too. But this was the first time I'd ever seen people die, and it made me re-evaluate, instantly, what was important to me. "What's wrong?" she asked. "I'm miserable," I answered.

I'd bought into the myth of money and fame, and what had it brought me? This gig was a sure two to three million a year, and I'd be looking at double that the next year. But I wasn't enjoying my life. I was exhausted, I had no friends, and I felt no joy. My greed-based mentality had led me to a desolate place. And I realized: *I'm just what Mom did to herself.* Unconsciously, I was sabotaging myself by duplicating her patterns.

In the days that followed, I quit my job. My lifestyle had come with massive overhead expenses, and I was forced to claim bankruptcy. I gave my BMW back to the bank and bought a Ford Fiesta for a couple hundred bucks. Living at the financial bottom of the barrel, I felt an enormous new sense of freedom and possibility. And that's when I decided with a ferocious resolve to study every personal growth technique and modality I could get my hands on to see what really worked.

For years, I studied with the biggest motivational speakers and transformational thought leaders, like Marianne Williamson. I worked for Jim Rohn, Zig Ziglar and Brian Tracy. Piecing together what consistently worked 100% of the time from all these different sources, throwing away the fluff and combining hypnosis, psychology, neuro-linquistics, somatic psychology and body work, I developed a transformational system of my own. At that point, my income went from 10-15K a month to six figures a month — but this time, things were completely different. This time, I was living a happy, balanced life, free from the inherited patterns that had caused my previous misery.

RAPIDLY CHANGING UNWANTED CONDITIONS

The dictionary defines "conditions" as a particular mode of being of a person or thing; existing state; situation with respect to circumstances (ME, condicioun, L, condicioun). Simply put, conditions are the results that we currently have in the various areas of our lives. Our conditions can go everywhere from absolute zero all the way up to infinity as far as the gradient of how well or how bad a condition is. For example, your health is in a certain condition. Your finances are in a certain condition. Your marriage or your relationship with your primary partner is in a certain condition. Your relationship with your children or with your parents is in a certain condition. So understanding our present conditions actually gives us a scale of how we can start working on a specific area we would like to change in our lives.

So as we're looking at, for instance, our financial condition, it is on a relative scale based on our own personal financial goals. For some people, making $50,000 per year is considered a great life and a great lifestyle. For some people, that amount per year might be seen as almost living at poverty level, especially if they live in some place like New York where the cost of living is about five times higher than, let's say … Montana. So conditions are going to be relative to our personal situation and to our personal goals and outcomes.

Along with our financial condition, we also have a specific identity for ourselves – a "beingness" – and what is also called a self-image – our self-image of being a financial income earner, a businessman or businesswoman, etc. We have this specific identity attached mentally with our financial conditions in life. Our identity might be of someone that is an incredibly powerful businessperson and able to create enormous financial results. Or that identity, that beingness, that self-image might be one of someone that is always struggling to get by financially. Of course, it could also fall anywhere in between the two.

Suppose we have a financial identity, a beingness and self-image in this area, of an individual that is always struggling to get by – which we inherited as a pattern from our parents or from our role models growing up. Then no matter how much money we make, whether it be $50,000 a year or $500,000 a year, we will always unconsciously set up the conditions in our lives to fulfill that self-image!

Yes – a self-fulfilling prophecy! Our inherited financial pattern and internal wiring system will put us constantly in the condition of struggling, constantly in the condition of not having enough money. Regardless of how much money we make, we will unconsciously set things up to always "not have enough money," because that is our primary programming, our primary identity/beingness, i.e., our self-image in that area of life.

An important note is that ALL our self-images, identities and patterns are on autopilot –creating and setting up situations and circumstances through our unconscious behaviors in every area of our life, because the primary function of our unconscious programs is to help and support our survival. Yes! These programs and unconscious identities always have a positive intention automatically to help us survive better...even if they are actually creating the 180º opposite of our desired results in life!

To change an unwanted condition in our lives permanently, we must first become aware of what our specific, unproductive pattern (the cause) is for that condition, whether it's our financial life as an income earner or a relationship partner, etc. What patterns and programs do we currently have, for example, for our financial condition? ... our financial identity? ... and how do we identify them? It is really fairly easy; just take a look at our financial results as of now and the results we've been creating over the past few years. What we will usually notice is a pattern, a certain condition that we repeat over and over again.

As we become aware of our programs, we can, with a little discipline (and some personal growth tools), stop the detrimental programming and behavior that is associated with it. We can let it go and dissolve it, but the first step is always awareness. Becoming aware is immensely powerful; it's the most important part of the releasing process since, for the most part, ninety-nine percent of our programming and counterproductive identities are completely unconscious and below our level of awareness.

So take a look at the conditions in your life right now and get specific with each condition in each area of your life that you want to change. Then get even more specific with the condition and the IDENTITY that is tied to it – the condition and the identity that you have as a mother, as a father, as a business partner or an employee; the condition of your physical health as an athlete or as someone that takes care and respects themselves and their body.

As we become aware of any unwanted conditions in our lives, we can then start identifying what pattern and program is running, the limiting identity and self-image that is associated with it, and through awareness, stop it. Awareness, responsibility and discipline become powerful allies and support us in making new CHOICES. And through our own power of CHOICE, we can start CHOOSING a new pattern, a new identity, a new beingness.

So if our condition is that of being somebody who is always struggling financially, we can choose to stop that old identity and program simply through our own self-determined power of CHOICE. We can CHOOSE to be somebody instead that always has an abundance of money, a person that has financial security. Starting today, we can CHOOSE to be an affluent person. We can CHOOSE to be an individual that takes care of their health in better and better ways every day. We can CHOOSE to be a healthy athlete, a loving father, a compassionate and supportive mother. So through awareness and using a new DAILY discipline of choosing an identity, we can CHOOSE to stop the old pattern each and every day. And through the power of

CHOICE we can start daily creating a new program, a new identity, a new beingness that creates the results that we want in every area of life. Yes, all through the power of CONSCIOUS CHOICE each and every day.

ABOUT ROBERT

Robert Vitelli is a pioneer in the field of human potential as well as the author and creator of the groundbreaking new book and personal growth technology entitled **Being The Powerful You™**. Robert also recently co-authored *Fight For Your Dreams* with legendary Les Brown.

Along with his personal growth endeavors, Robert is also a millionaire entrepreneur and has traveled the globe for the past 24 years researching the most effective therapeutic and holistic modalities for creating lasting, positive change in an individual's life.

While finding value in the various therapeutic and holistic approaches available, Robert found key components missing from any one single approach that would consistently support someone in creating RAPID and PERMANENT results in ALL areas of their life.

After two decades of research, **Robert has developed a personal growth technology that consistently produces the desired results**, awareness and healing in a person's life...FAST. Robert's has a unique approach to positive and permanent change in that **it utilizes both the body as well as the brain as tools for rapid growth and increased awareness.**

To learn more about Robert and how you can receive his Free Special Report "Secrets to Realizing Your Goals & Dreams," go to: www.RobertVitelli.com or call 702-538-7650

CHAPTER 17

THE THREE "R's" FOR SUCCESS

BY DR. PAUL TOOTE

"Success is to be measured not so much by the position that one has reached in life... as by the obstacles which he has overcome while trying to succeed."

– Booker T. Washington

Pushing to the front is almost certainly not the easiest of tasks – but I do believe how you conduct yourself when you're doing that pushing ultimately determines whether you will, in fact, not only make it to the front – but also be able to remain there over the long term.

Your ability to take responsibility for your outcomes – mixed with your resilience when working towards a goal – is the major determining factor of your success. Having an understanding of this and being willing to recommit to the task at hand when setbacks arise, is a sure formula for that success.

Keeping that in mind, I believe there are three "R's" that must be mastered while on the path to achievement. Just as a child must master his or her three "R's" in school – Reading, Writing and Arithmetic (is it strange that only one of those actually does begin with an "R"?) – we adults must master our own three “R’s” to see ourselves through to our goals and our ultimate accomplishments.

So, keeping all that in mind, let’s look at those three “R’s” in more detail – and analyze why they’re so important when you’re pushing to the front.

"R" NUMBER ONE – RESPONSIBILITY

Speaking of children and adults, one of the main differences between them is that the adult has the ability to accept responsibility for his or her actions – as well as making it a vital part of the decision-making process. Now, I know many of you can point to a well-known politician or celebrity that might do the exact opposite when it comes to responsibility, but the fact is, if you don’t accept responsibility for your decisions as you move forward, you will find that you haven’t built a firm foundation for your success.

For example, Sam Walton, the man who built the Wal-Mart business empire, began his career by opening a store in 1945 and building up its annual sales from $72,000 per year to an astounding (for the time) $245,000 a year. It became so successful that the landlord refused to renew his lease, and instead gave the store to his son to run.

That didn’t discourage Walton, who said later that the landlord gave him a fair price for the inventory and the fixtures he himself had installed. Instead, Walton began running a chain of Ben Franklin stores in small towns. At the height of his success with the franchise, he had 16 stores in 16 different towns – which was, at the time, the largest independently-owned store chain in the country.

The success he achieved with Ben Franklin was due to the unique discounting strategy that he had hit upon. He asked the franchise owners to cut their margins by half so he could ramp up the policy, sure that the added sales would more than make up for the reduced margins. But the Ben Franklin people refused to do so.

Fine, said Walton. And he went down the road and opened the very first Wal-Mart in 1962. He continued to run both the Ben Franklin stores he owned as well as the new Wal-Mart chain he built for quite a few years.

And in the end, I think we all know which chain became the most successful and most enduring.

Walton's success was based on not getting discouraged when others stopped him from fulfilling his business dreams. His success was also based on taking responsibility for his own actions – and reacting positively to disappointment, by simply taking his ideas somewhere else and building on them there, rather than getting bitter and angry about the previous disappointments.

Responding to situations responsibly allows the individual to change the outcome of whatever the situation might be – and build an even brighter future from there. Life is very often a multiple choice test – and we often come to a crossroads where we have to pick answer A, B, C or D. Of course, usually only one of those answers is the right one – while many of the others can take us in very wrong directions, far away from our originally-desired destinations.

When Sam Walton came to his crossroads, he always picked the path that would enable him to take positive action and stick to what he knew were solid and successful ideas. Walt Disney was another pioneering entrepreneur who did the same.

When he was just starting out, Disney worked for the Universal movie studio, where he experienced his first success with a series of silent cartoons featuring Oswald the Lucky Rabbit. He thought he had it made – when a studio executive told him he wanted to cut his production budgets. If Disney didn't accept the diminished deal, the exec. told him he would simply create his own animation studio.

Disney did not accept and he was fired. Since he didn't own the rights to Oswald, he knew he had to create his own character that belonged solely to Disney. And that's how he ended up creating Mickey Mouse. He produced two cartoons with the mouse, but no movie studio would distribute them. Once again, he had seemed to 'hit' an immovable obstacle. Once again, inspiration would save him.

"Talking pictures" had just taken hold in Hollywood, so Disney added sound effects to the first Mickey Mouse cartoon and immediately found a distributor. The cartoon, "Steamboat Willie," was an instant sensation and launched the career of both Disney and Mickey Mouse.

As for Oswald the Rabbit? Well, the Disney studio, now owned by ABC, still hadn't forgotten about the character even after Disney himself had passed away. In 2006, they got the rights back from NBC Universal – who traded the rabbit back in exchange for sportscaster Al Michaels!

Again, Disney, just like Walton, found himself in negative situations where his best ideas had actually gotten him put out of work. Again, by taking responsibility for himself, he found a more genuine and lasting success – in Disney's case, by finding creatively satisfying solutions that would help him create his own Hollywood empire.

It's obviously more difficult to think through a real effective plan when you're down and out, instead of just reacting quickly in a self-destructive manner. Accepting responsibility, however, demands you do just that. You can make it happen if you want to make it happen – and, more importantly, you can make it happen in the right way, without 'shooting yourself in the foot' and in a manner that is actually more in your best interests. The more responsibly you handle your choices with, the better your chances of succeeding.

Those choices, however, are informed by your skill, knowledge and ability level. The more you have in those departments, the better your choices will be and the better the outcomes will be. That's why it's important to invest in your own self-improvement on a continuing basis as you proceed. The more you grow and evolve, the better equipped you are to handle a pivotal choice when you need to make it.

When it comes down to it, taking responsibility for constantly improving yourself may in fact be the greatest responsibility of them all.

"R" NUMBER TWO – RESILIENCE

I view responsibility as the vehicle that will take you where you're going – and, to continue with that analogy, resilience, to me, is the gas you put in that vehicle to *keep* it going.

That's because resilience is all about keeping yourself moving forward and not stopping – no matter what appears to be in your way. Think of the great accomplishments that were attained by people with resilience – Gandhi, Christopher Columbus, Mother Theresa and Dr. Martin Luther King Jr. These are people who risked their very lives – and in some cases, lost them – to reach goals they truly believed in.

Dr. King, for example, traveled to India to learn Gandhi's principles of nonviolent protest and it changed his life. His resilience, however, was what really enabled him to continue his mission of ending racial segregation and oppression even though he was attacked and stabbed in the chest in 1958, arrested multiple times over his career and hounded by J. Edgar Hoover and the FBI. It was only his assassination in 1968 that stopped his own personal quest – but the way he conducted his life and work continues to inspire millions to this day who continue on with his work.

Resilience is more than a mindset to me – I actually believe it's an *action* one must take, rather than a passive response to difficult circumstances. You instill resilience in yourself by making an active determination not to quit; that determination also drives you forward – it provides constant feedback and energizes you as you go.

Resilience is the difference between continually thinking you're going to quit every time the least amount of difficulty pops up on your path, and continually reaffirming your commitment to moving forward. Of course, we all have low points where giving up might seem like an attractive option – but the energy you waste on constantly wondering whether you should turn back is energy that could be used towards pushing yourself towards the finish line.

"R" NUMBER THREE – RECOMMITMENT

If responsibility is the vehicle and resilience is the gas in our previous analogy, then you should look at recommitment as the repair kit when the car comes to a crashing halt.

While resilience helps to power you through challenge after challenge, recommitment is what is needed when you need to actively renew your initial commitment to a goal or objective. In other words, you may be resilient enough to keep going, but, internally, your spirit may feel defeated and you may, in fact, just be going through the motions. What it comes down to is that you are suddenly missing the special spark that first inspired you to pursue your grand ambitions. Recommitment is all about relighting that spark and getting back your mojo.

If you remember the "Rocky" films, you remember the boxer Rocky Balboa, aka Sylvester Stallone, constantly triumphing over incredible odds in sequel after sequel. Those who might accuse Stallone of creating a false fantasy should look a little more closely at the writer-actor-director's own early struggles.

When Stallone originally wrote the script for the first Rocky, he was less than nobody in Hollywood. He had appeared in a few small roles in some minor movies and that was it. He was barely making a living and had about $100 in his bank account – he was at the crashing halt described earlier.

Then he saw a documentary about Muhammad Ali and found his recommitment. He saw the whole Rocky Balboa story – a two-bit boxer who gets the shot of a lifetime by getting a match with an Ali-like champ – and knew it could change his life. He finished the screenplay for the "Italian Stallion" in less than a week.

The studios loved the script. And they immediately wanted to pay the actor $18,000 for it. Stallone said, "Sure – but I have to play the lead." That was a deal-breaker – who was this guy? They continued to offer him more and more money just to let go of the script and let a genuine movie star play the part – he continued to refuse, even though he was on the verge of selling his beloved pet dog to get by. The studio finally gave in – and we all know what happened from there.

Steven Spielberg was another one who seemed to be denied his life's dream – to become a filmmaker. In the 60's, the ideal career path to that goal was to go to film school at USC in Los Angeles – but Spielberg ended up being turned down twice by the famous private university. That left him with nothing but his wits to make the difference.

The future legend began to sneak onto the Universal lot – until he found an empty office that he could operate out of. He made himself a part of the studio operation – and eventually talked his way into an unpaid internship. He eventually made his own short film, and convinced a high-ranking studio executive to take a look. That led to his first directing assignments at the studio.

There is another significant real-life and very American example of what recommitment is all about. As you probably know, President John

F. Kennedy committed this country to sending a man to the moon within a decade when he took office in 1961. NASA created the Apollo program to do just that.

But what you might not remember is that the first Apollo attempt ended in disaster and tragedy. During a launch pad test launch on January 27, 1967, a cabin fire broke out – the Command Module was destroyed and all three astronauts, Command Pilot Virgil "Gus" Grissom, Senior Pilot Edward H. White, and Pilot Roger B. Chaffee, were killed on that dark day.

That calamity resulted in a great deal of political pressure aimed at killing the entire space program. Then-President Johnson, however, invoked Kennedy's legacy to relight the spark and provide the necessary recommitment to keep the Apollo missions alive – and, as we all know, two and a half years later, Apollo 11 successfully made the first manned landing on the moon. *One small step for a man – One giant leap for mankind.* Imagine if we had turned back from that incredible accomplishment.

The Three R's – responsibility, resilience and recommitment – combine to help us complete the most difficult of journeys. And, as many philosophers have told us over the years, the journey is more important than the destination. How we conduct ourselves as we struggle to reach our goals ultimately defines who we are and what we're all about – and, depending on how we create that definition, we find personal success or failure. While you're pushing to the front, don't forget to make the three "R's" a vital part of your effort.

ABOUT PAUL

Dr. Paul Toote became a Doctor of Osteopathic Medicine in 2001. He graduated from Western University of Health Sciences College of Osteopathic Medicine of the Pacific, where he was both a class president as well as Graduation Class Dinner Speaker. He was certified as an Emergency Medicine Physician by the American Osteopathic Board of Emergency Medicine in 2009, and was also the recipient of the Highest Achievement Award from the Dale Carnegie Effective Communications and Human Relations Course.

While serving as an Emergency Medicine Physician at leading hospitals and medical centers in communities all across Texas, including Corpus Christi, Amarillo, San Antonio, the Dallas-Fort Worth Metroplex and Paris, Dr. Toote found he was energized by coaching trained residents and medical school students and helping them reach their professional goals.

Wishing to do more to help those with medical ambitions, he began National Premed Consulting to share his expertise and insider knowledge with those who have the necessary qualifications, capabilities and desire to successfully navigate the difficult demands of medical school.

Dr. Toote resides in McKinney, Texas and is married with two children.

CHAPTER 18

THE 5 CRITICAL INDICATORS THAT LEADERS MUST EXECUTE TO KEEP RELEVANT IN TODAY'S CHANGING ECONOMY

BY DR. JON SARVER

"When you calculate too much, you miscalculate!"
~ Tony Blair...March 2011

The truth is, if you **were there** you probably wouldn't be reading this book, so let's get to work. Just what does a leader need to not only know, but to execute, to remain relevant in today's changing economic environment?

LET'S START WITH AN ALL TOO FAMILIAR STORY...

Steve is cruising nicely in the early part of the last decade. In fact, he had started and managed several successful businesses and was able to provide very nicely for his family. Things were going well and life couldn't be better! They were rolling in money and little leadership errors here and there really didn't matter that much. It didn't for anyone back then!

Steve's mission in life was clear. He was on this planet to parlay his fortune earned from his business to a greater good. In fact, he started a non-profit foundation that was dedicated to just that goal. His passion was always part of his story. His companies reflected his passion and he always kept his mission front and center in everything he did. When asked, he was able to convey the core message of the company in thirty seconds or less. And, very well at that!

However, there was always one problem that plagued Steve and that was true accountability. He was surrounded by 'yes' people, and it often jaded his judgment.

Then there was the great economic meltdown of 2008. Steve had to confront some tough issues. Profits were falling and employee morale was low because Steve elected to cut all salaries by 10% instead of implementing immediate layoffs.

The problem: He was acting as a lone ranger and had very little support from the rank and file. His hastily gathered approach worked well for the short term, but soon mortgages were being defaulted on and employee morale hit the skids. The employees didn't know him and he most certainly did not know them.

Suddenly Steve's company was in serious jeopardy of declaring Bankruptcy-Chapter 13. The paychecks were now late and there was talk on the street that his company might go under. When Steve poured through the books, he could clearly see that profits were not matching up with expenses. He would have to make some tough cuts and he would have to make them now.

What was the best course of action to take? Steve was pondering that for a few weeks when Joe, his foreman for the major projects his company was involved with, laid it on the line. "Steve," he said, "The morale is shot around here and I have talked to three other department heads that have the answer." He went on to say, "What you need to do is fire ten employees who have not been producing anyway. The remaining employees will understand because you made the tough decisions to make it possible for all the other employees to stay with the company. It will hurt but it needs to be done!"

It was the first time Steve had really listened to an employee. Joe was a top producer and had the pedigree for credibility in Steve's eyes! "Could he be right?" Steve wondered.

Steve took a few days to reflect on that advice from a now-trusted employee. He also reflected on the purpose for his life, and concluded that the profitability of this company was paramount for his ability to serve the world for a greater good. This part was always natural for him, but took on much greater importance now.

He immediately set out to convey the central message of his company in a clear and compelling way. He understood this was the answer to rallying the troops.

He continued to master his elevator pitch and hot seated all of his employees to master it as well. They needed to do this to all be 'on message.' He had to be the pioneer of change. He had to be the one to lead it, but it was vitally important for his employees to own it. That would come next!

In two weeks time he gathered all the evidence and made a tough decision; that was to immediately fire the 10 employees who were known for not pulling their weight anyway. Immediately company morale shot up. Profits increased because of the tighter payroll and the realization that everyone needed to pitch in and pitch in now. He reviewed, listened and acted on what he knew to be true. Basic, but effective!

Two years later Steve's company has tripled in revenue, and he is well on his way to funding the foundation that reflects his passion to help others in need.

Indeed, Steve's map to success in business came back to fundamentals. In this case they are called the five indicators. These five indicators are needed to separate the big boys from the also-rans: In the business world today, you are relevant or you are dead! In Steve's case he followed a simple plan and stayed relevant.

The truth is 95% of companies never reach $1 million in annual sales and that is primarily due to the inadequacies of the CEO. Steve had grown his company to significantly over a million, which put him in the top 5% of entrepreneurs. Impressive to be sure, but why was he so frustrated over his cash flow issues? It was clear he was increasingly agitated because he was spinning fifteen different plates to keep profitable and wondering all the time, "This is just like a job" and "Why am I doing this?"

IF STEVE'S EXPERIENCE TENDS TO BE THE TRUTH IN YOUR LIFE KEEP READING....

Now for the rest of you who aren't at a million in gross sales you need to keep reading, too. First of all, don't throw in the towel because your annual sales are substantially lower than the lucky 5% who got to a million. It takes work to reach those milestones, but mastering the 5 Indicators is a great start towards mastering your business.

THE SOBERING STAT IS....

For those of you who do stumble to a million, 95% of you won't ever make it to 5 million. If you are fortunate enough to get that far, then 98% of you won't make it to 10 million. (Note: these stats were accurate before 2008. The SBA probably does not have the guts to release a new one!) Steve had bumped up and down between 2 and 3 million and his ceiling was clear. The sobering reality was that Steve was threatening to become the major constraint to the growth of the business unless HE acted!

WHICH BEGS THE QUESTION?

What was Steve thinking? What started as a great idea had become, at minimum, a nine-to-nine job and often way beyond that. There are seasons in business, and Steve had to stick to the game plan. It came down to the fundamentals. Would he or wouldn't he follow the fundamentals?

SO, WHAT ARE THOSE FIVE CRITICAL INDICATORS? AND WHAT DO THEY MEAN IN A PRACTICAL SENSE?

INDICATOR #1
THE LEADER MUST KNOW THEIR STORY!

Why is it you do what you do? If you don't know that answer right now, stop and figure it out before you waste another day. Rick Warren, Senior Pastor at Saddleback Church in Lake Forest, California and author of the phenomenal best seller ***Purpose Driven Life*** said, "We were made to have meaning. This is why so many people try dubious methods, like astrology or psychics to discover it. When life has meaning, you can bear almost anything; without meaning, nothing is bearable."

The executive with a higher meaning in life will always be the focused executive. Steve was able to regain focus because he knew his greater purpose was to parlay his fortune to help others – through channeling his purpose into compelling stories that conveyed his heart and moved his audience forward.

Peter Guber equates knowing your purpose with articulating your story. "Stories have a unique power to move people's hearts, feet, and wallet in the storyteller's intended direction." When you know your purpose in life, your story flows in a clear and cohesive way. For most leaders this is "make it" or "break it" in the battle of getting and keeping focus!

Apply it now: What is your purpose in life and how does that drive your story and subsequently your business? Steve kept moving forward towards his dream of meeting the needs of others and it drove his decision to save his business and make it profitable, no matter what.

INDICATOR #2
THE LEADER MUST HEAR THEIR EMPLOYEES!

The catch is you must know the right employees to hear and the right employees to suggest they be successful elsewhere. This is a skill that 95% of executives do not have and the lack of it can kill your business.

How do you hire your employees? What is your process? Do you really know them? It is true that even in highly successful companies only 20% of the key personnel (referred to also as "impact players"), are producing 80% of the innovations and profits. **(Many believe it is now 5% doers : 95% watchers.)** Successful companies get the market edge by identifying the positions that will create innovation… and then fill them with impact players.

Those impact players are the ones the highly attuned executive listens to at critical junctures in the life of their business. The goal of the smart executive is to surround himself or herself with as many "A plus" type executives and leaders that they can.

Chet Holmes of Business Breakthroughs International hires strictly through personality profile and interview. In fact, resumes play a minor role in the hiring of superstars for that organization. Holmes often claims with substantial proof that he has MORE "true" superstars in his company than just about any other executive training organization in the world. It was those superstars that forged the merger with Chet Holmes and Tony Robbins in 2009.

Business Breakthrough International employees have a voice in their organization because they are "A" players. Find "A" players and listen to them! Steve had "A" players he could trust. It ended up being the catalyst for real change.

Apply it now: Take your key employees through a personality profile and determine whether they are the right fit for the position. Go to www.businessbreakthroughs.com and select personality profiles for more information on how you can hire superstars. Those are the "A" players you need to listen to and release to drive your vision.

INDICATOR #3
THE LEADER MUST KNOW THEIR THIRTY-SECOND 'ELEVATOR' PITCH!

If you had thirty seconds to present a compelling case as to why your prospective client should buy from you, "What would you say?" Most business executives can't answer this question clearly and as a result their businesses die a slow death!

The 30-second pitch is designed to appeal to nine out of ten people. They may not all be buying at the time, but they will listen to what you have to say. In a traditional sales approach, 3% are buying now and another 3% are open to it. Additionally, 60% of the audience are not thinking about buying your product or just not interested. Finally, 30% could not care less about what you have to offer! Chet Holmes summarizes it in the best way possible, "A great marketing effort will appeal to the entire 90 plus percent of the audience." Then through 'education' you drive everyone to the 'buying now' category. That was clearly Steve's goal!

Apply It Now: Can you articulate your elevator pitch? Do your employees know it? If not, learn it yourself and train your employees. Steve turned his company around because he understood the central message and most importantly, stuck to it. He trained all his employees to articulate it as well and the company was primed to explode.

INDICATOR #4
THE LEADER MUST KNOW WHAT WORKS AND WHAT DOESN'T WITHIN THEIR COMPANY!

Admit it! You don't know it either and that puts you with 96% of the other company leaders in American companies. Your company dies if you don't master this skill! That's why 95% eventually die. *They are not good at this skill.*

It's not sexy and it's not particularly fun, but if you can't read a profit and loss statement then you don't know where your money is going and you will go belly up. Just recently a business owner confided to this writer that after 20 years in business he figured out he didn't really know how to analyze "the why" and "the what" of his business. He was hemorrhaging hundreds of thousands of dollars and was in danger of ignorantly running his business into the ground.

Thankfully for Steve, he saw this critical indicator and corrected his cash flow problems. He then made sure all the reporting lines in the company were clear and accountable. He got it together before his business failed.

Apply it now: Can you read a profit and now statement? Do you have a clear organizational chart and reporting lines? Does each employee possess a clear and concise position description and held accountable to it with no exceptions?

INDICATOR #5
THE LEADER MUST MAKE THE TOUGH DECISIONS NOW!

At a 2010 leadership conference in Las Vegas, 97% of the people in attendance revealed that they needed to invite one or more employees to be successful elsewhere. Tough decisions require action now. Are you up to it? It wasn't easy for Steve to reposition those employees thinking. In fact he was proud that he had never done that before, and it was killing his business.

Apply it now: Who do you need to invite to be successful with someone else? Who do you need to tune up now? John Maxwell's Law of the Lid states, "*Leadership Ability Determines a Person's Level of Effectiveness.* The lid on your leadership must be raised to increase your leadership ability and influence. One of the ways to raise the lid halting your leadership is to develop a leadership bias instead of a manager bias." In other words, lead your way out of the mess. Don't be afraid to make the tough decision based on evidence of fact. Then act on it!

CONCLUSION

In reality, Steve was truly different than most executives. He had mastered his story so much in fact, that it became the guiding light for all of his decisions. As a result, he built a funnel that resulted in hiring the right employees, making it possible to listen to the right ones when important decisions arose. Steve and his entire team were trained on how to convey their elevator pitch to any group. They became so good at it that soon they were able to divert typically tough economic situations. It also helped that he knew what was working and what wasn't working in his company. As we now know, he was willing to make the tough decisions.

If you want to learn more about the Five Critical Indicators and apply them to your business, go to www.SarverConsultingGroup.com and do something about it today!

ABOUT JON

Dr. Jon Sarver is a highly successful entrepreneur with over 25 years of experience of leadership ranging from non-profits to internet-based businesses with many having faith-based overtones. Jon has the unique ability to claim successful businesses in small rural towns and large cities alike. He has a track record of laying the groundwork for growth and vitality as several of his businesses have lasted far beyond the average, and many exist today; decades after they were founded.

He has also enjoyed a fundamental role in developing leadership education and cutting-edge mentoring in several institutions of higher education. In fact, in several cases he was called in to develop a program that was relevant to the "real" needs of the "learning" leader. All of these programs have become known for their practical application to theory and Dr. Sarver's role was to hold each leader's feet to the fire, to produce results in what was typically a non-profit environment.

Jon has been teaching and coaching the "spirit" of the 12 core business strategies for 21 years in the church, para-church and business communities.

Jon is a long time speaker and trainer in a wide variety of environments and in an even wider variety of cultures. He has coached leaders worldwide in Russia, Ukraine, Moldova, Dominican Republic and Mexico – in leadership and business principles – many times in harmony with Chet Holmes' 12 core strategies.

His clients have ranged from the largest industrial cleaning company in Los Angeles (Nancie Brown and Associates) to the Daytona Motor Speedway with many great ones in between.

Jon is an accomplished triathlete with a half-ironman finish to his credit He has also completed 21 marathons.

For more information go to: www.SarverConsultingGroup.com.

Mention **<u>Pushing to the Front</u>** and you will receive a free ONE-hour consulting call directly from Jon himself, a $1,000.00 value!

What others are saying...

DAYTONA
INTERNATIONAL SPEEDWAY

In working with Jon, I find incredible energy, a commitment to client success and an openness to listen and apply proven strategies to a sales organization. Jon has a great ability to break complex opportunities into manageable pieces. He does a wonderful job of bringing Chet's words to life.

John R. Guthrie – Vice President Business Development – Daytona International Speedway

Dr. Jon Sarver's coaching has been an invaluable addition to our executive staff. His insightfulness to our real issues, tactfulness in dealing with our issues and guidance on taking us to the next level is invaluable. I look forward to having Dr. Sarver be a part of our team for a long time.

~ Craig Rabe – President – The Computer Cafe

I have had the pleasure to have Dr. Jon Sarver as our company's management consultant. Probably the best aspect of Jon's representation has been that I have truly believed Jon has our company's best interest at heart, and he has always made time for a consultation with me and with my executive staff. His advice has been brilliant; he spent three days with our staff onsite and quickly came to understand our strengths and weaknesses and has from that time helped us build towards a more profitable, sustainable future.

~ Arthur S. Lazerow – Chairman of the Board, Alban Inspections, Inc.

Biography photo courtesy of Nancy Roux Photography .

CHAPTER 19

UNCLE FRANK'S 21 SECRETS OF CREATING A MONEY-MAKING CUSTOMER EXPERIENCE REVEALED!

BY TRACY E. MYERS, CMD

Many years ago, Uncle Frank said: "Your customer will pay almost anything if you give them an experience they will remember." He was way ahead of his time when he discovered this important golden nugget of business success.

It wasn't until the late 1990s that Joseph Pine and James Gilmore published their book *The Experience Economy.* This was one of the first books to argue that making the experience of doing business with you memorable was a way to create better – and more profitable – relationships with customers.

Just as products can become commodities, service often varies little between similar businesses. Uncle Frank's business was the car business.

It dawned on Uncle Frank all those years ago that all the car dealerships buy the same cars from the same places, pay the same for them and they all look just alike. So – if everything was the same – what could he do to set himself apart, to stand out from the others?

He wanted to be "different" – unique, noticeable and memorable. He also wanted to sell more cars. So he started to do things that made coming to our dealership an experience rather than just a trip to buy a car.

He opened a gourmet "All-You-Can-Drink" coffee bar in the car dealership. He provided a free 'new school' arcade for the kids – complete with an X-Box – and he provided an 'old school' arcade for the young-at-heart adults – complete with a Ms. Pac Man and Donkey Kong. He also added flat screen televisions featuring a FREE Family Movie Night – popcorn included for everyone, whether they bought a car from him or not.

It certainly made the dealership stand out from the competition, and it's an idea that can easily be copied by many other businesses, especially those – like retailers – that depend on building strong long-term relationships with customers.

BEING DIFFERENT

Some of the most successful businesses around today have discovered the importance of creating a great customer experience and have grown to dominant positions because of it. There are few products that are more of a commodity than a cup of coffee, so when Howard Schultz decided he wanted to open coffee shops all over the world, he knew he had to do something different.

Now, it costs about 3 cents to buy enough beans to make a cup of coffee. Maxwell House converts those commodity beans into a product and charges 20 cents for enough ground beans to make a cup of coffee. If you prefer to pay someone to brew the coffee for you, you can pick one up at your local cafe or convenience store for about $1 a cup. Yet, thanks to Howard Shultz, there's a Starbucks on virtually every corner where you pay $4 and up for a cup of coffee. And there's almost always a line of people ready to buy.

What Howard Shultz realized was that it wasn't just the coffee people wanted. They wanted an experience, and he turned Starbucks into the 'third place' after work and home – making it 'the place to be.'

One of the ultimate examples of providing memorable customer experiences is Disney theme parks. There are other theme parks and attractions all over the place – yet millions of people travel from all over the world every year to visit Disney. When you calculate time, travel expenses and the cost of tickets for the park – not to mention the gift shops that are everywhere – you pay a huge premium for the Disney experience. But the truth is, it is an experience, and Disney does it so well that many people just can't get enough of it.

Another company that has become successful by recognizing the importance of customer experience is Apple. Unless you are into all the technical details, every computer is pretty much the same – unless it's an Apple. Apple has defied the odds to not only survive, but to prosper – because they changed the whole customer experience of computers. An Apple was not the clunky gray box that you stared at all day at work. Apple enabled customers to experience a colorful machine that showed them how to "think different." It's a concept they followed through with the iPod, iPhone and iPad, which have led the way in transforming the experience of technology.

So what can you learn from these huge successful businesses? Well, they all have several points in common about the way they create a special customer experience. This not only allows them to charge more, but also helps them build a huge band of fiercely loyal customers.

If you could replicate some of that in your business, how useful would that be? Based on what I learned from Uncle Frank and my own studies of these highly successful businesses, here are my 21 tips for creating a great customer experience.

1. TELL YOUR STORY

Disney may have built an empire out of storytelling but stories are as relevant to your business as they are at Disney. Stories help people learn, build relationships and move beyond the idea of selling. *When people know your story, they start to feel part of it, so make sure you celebrate and share your heritage with your customers.*

2. CREATE CHARACTERS

You may think characters like Mickey Mouse are only relevant in theme parks. But as your business grows, it can become more faceless. *Characters give it a personality that makes it easier for people to feel they have a relationship with you.* Uncle Frank is the face of our business and is crucial to our success.

3. LEARN FROM OUTSIDE YOUR INDUSTRY

You are not going to beat your competitors by doing the same as they are. If Apple had tried to be like all the other computer manufacturers, they would not be such an icon today. *Look for ideas and inspiration everywhere, but adapt and adopt them, and make them uniquely yours.*

4. CREATE A POWERFUL CAST

It's probably not surprising that the people working at Disney are known as cast members. *They are all 'on stage' any time a customer can see or hear them.* They are 'off stage' only when they are safely out of the public's eye. But it's a concept that goes well beyond the entertainment business. For example, the book *The Experience Economy* is subtitled "Work Is Theater & Every Business a Stage".

5. FOLLOW A SCRIPT

Even the guy sweeping the streets at Disney has to follow an exact script when someone asks him for directions. *What we say to people can make a huge difference to the impression we create.* So it's worth making sure that your people know what to say at key moments. The way someone answers the phone has a big impact on how people perceive you.

6. CALL YOUR CUSTOMERS BY THEIR NAME

You know how good you feel when you walk in to a top hotel or restaurant and you're greeted by your name. It's a simple tactic but can make a big difference to the way people see you.

7. WELCOME FEEDBACK

At Starbucks, one of the principles is "Embrace Resistance." That means they welcome feedback and try to correct the situation. *Encourage your staff to respond positively to criticism and view complaints as an opportunity to strengthen relationships with customers and improve your business.*

8. MAKE IT FUN

When you go to a Disney theme park, you expect to have fun. But who'd expect to have fun in a computer store? Yet, chances are, the most crowded store in many malls will always be the Apple Store. So what can we learn from Apple? *If customers can come in and try out your products, you should let them do so.* You could copy Uncle Frank's idea and have them round to play games and watch your big TV. Even something as simple as a summer cookout could make your business seem fun.

9. PAY ATTENTION TO DETAIL

One of the guiding principles of Starbucks is that "Everything Matters". That means that all the little details in your business – the environment, your people, the background music – are crucial to the customer experience. *Often it's the small things people notice – and getting small things wrong can be a deal breaker.*

10. CHARGE PREMIUM PRICES

One thing about all three of these successful role models (Apple/Starbucks/Disney) is that they don't even try to compete on price. Indeed they often make a virtue of being more expensive. Are you trying to build a great experience on thin profit margins? *Think about how you can improve the experience to charge higher prices.*

11. HAVE A CLEAR VISION

The founders of Disney, Starbucks and Apple all had clear ideas of what they wanted their future to look like. Imagine the future of your business — think ahead 100 years and your company is still going strong. What would you like it to look like then?

12. CATER TO THE KIDS

If your business serves adults who just happen to be parents, don't forget that happy kids mean happy parents. *So it's a good idea to take account of the kids that tag along with them.* Imagine the buying experience with bored kids in tow and you will see why parents gravitate toward kid-friendly companies.

13. DEVELOP PROCESSES

Processes and standards enforce consistency. Consistency builds trust. Trust builds long-term customer relationships. There's a reason your favorite drink will taste the same at any Starbucks in the world. Starbucks prides itself on its consistent standards and processes. You can make your business work better by developing and implementing effective processes.

14. SET HIGH STANDARDS OF SERVICE

In the Disney theme parks, there is a specific procedure in which cast members are expected to interact with guests and they are candidly evaluated and graded on this regularly by their managers. *Review the key contact points in your business and draft up a standards procedure.* Then make sure it's enforced for consistency.

15. COMMUNICATE WITH YOUR TEAM

Successful businesses like Disney and Starbucks invest heavily in internal communications. They want their staff to feel part of something and to know what is going on. Yet you'll often find that smaller businesses have little formal communication and never have team meetings. *Even a few minutes at the start or end of each day or week could make a huge difference to your team.*

16. MAKE EVERYTHING EASY

Apple changed the whole way that people worked with computers by *making the process simpler, more fun and more user-friendly.* Try walking through the way customers experience your business and see what they see. Mystery shoppers and mystery videos are good ways to test it out.

17. GO THE EXTRA MILE

Every Disney World cast member knows their purpose is "to make sure that every guest who comes to the Walt Disney World Resort has the most fabulous time of his or her life." They go above and beyond what's expected. *It means if you have to bend over backwards to make a customer happy, even if you have to stay late, even if you have to call all over the world to find whatever they're looking for — do it.* Do you expect that from your team? If not, what could you do to make it reality?

18. GET PEOPLE TALKING

One of the keys behind the success of Apple was the immense loyalty they built among their customers. And few people go to a Disney resort without raving about it when they get home. *If you can get your customers talking positively about their experience with your business, they become raving fans and will be invaluable allies in marketing and growing your business.*

19. TREAT CUSTOMERS AS FRIENDS

You want people to feel that you care about them and that it's not just all about money. Little things like remembering important personal details or sending a birthday card can make all the difference.

20. ALWAYS MAKE THE CUSTOMER RIGHT

Disney cast members are taught that every customer is special and that *each interaction between a customer and staff is a link in the chain of the customer's experience.* They understand if they do something wrong, they are erasing the customer's memories of good treatment up to that moment. But if they do something right, they can undo any wrong that may have happened before.

21. MAKE A DIFFERENCE

A key principle at Starbucks is the idea that you should get the chance to "Leave Your Mark." *The idea is that we are not just in business to sell things; we should also make a difference in the world.* That may be about being socially responsible, about being involved in our communities. What is your business doing to make your community a better place? And have you told your customers?

The success of businesses like Apple, Starbucks and Disney shows that *when you create an experience around what you sell, you can charge a significant premium over the competition.* So, if you want to avoid competing in a commoditized market with thin profit margins and tough competition, create an experience for your customers to remember ... just like Uncle Frank did all those many years ago!!!

ABOUT TRACY

Tracy Myers is a car dealership owner, author, speaker and entrepreneur. He recently celebrated the opening of his newest business, The Celebrity Academy in Charlotte, NC. The Academy teaches professionals, entrepreneurs and business owners how to get noticed, gain instant credibility, make millions and dominate their competition by building their expert status.

Following these principles have helped Tracy gain enormous success at his own dealership, Frank Myers Auto Maxx. It was recently recognized as the Number One Small Business in NC by Business Leader Magazine, one of the top three dealerships to work for in the country by The Dealer Business Journal, and one of the Top 22 Independent Automotive Retailers in the United States by Auto Dealer Monthly Magazine.

Tracy Myers graduated from the Certified Master Dealer program at Northwood University and was the youngest person to receive the National Quality Dealer Of The Year award, which is the highest obtainable honor in the used car industry.

He has provided guest commentary on the FOX Business Network and has also been featured on NBC, ABC, CBS & FOX affiliates across the country. He is the author of several books, including *YOU Are The Brand, Stupid!* and the #1 best-seller *Uncle Frank Sez*.

Tracy and his wife Lorna have made their home in Lewisville, NC with their 2 children Maddie and Presley. He is a self-proclaimed Christian Business Owner whose goal is to run his business "By the Book".

Read more about Tracy at www.TracyMyers.com

CHAPTER 20

THE GOLD STANDARD OF LIFE

A SIMPLE FIVE-STEP GUIDE TO PUSHING YOURSELF TO THE FRONT OF YOUR FIELD

BY FOREST HAMILTON

"Lincoln was not great because he was born in a log cabin, but because he got out of it."

~ James Truslow Adams

Growing up in the rain shadow of the Cascade Mountains, I was the poorest kid I knew. In fact, if you ask me, Honest Abe had it easy. All the *rich* kids in *my* neighborhood had log cabins. It was the summer of 1976 and my father, a Vietnam Veteran turned mountain man, delivered me on a hot, stormy night in the rural town of Duvall, Washington. My parents raised me without running water or electricity in what we called The House-truck. It was a makeshift house built onto the back of an old broken down logging truck. My dad taught me the value of hard work on our portable sawmill and we raised chickens, rabbits, goats, and pigs. We didn't go hungry, but there was no surplus of material things or friends. I can vividly remember getting onto the school bus and all the kids moving away from me to leave a four or five seat radius between them and the smelly kid wearing moccasins and drinking goat milk. The other kids made me feel like I was worthless, but the love and kindness of my family and a few close friends got me through. All that being said, I *treasure* my childhood. Without it, I would not be who I am today and who I am striving to become tomorrow. So what happened? What changed for the poor kid that came home crying four out of five days to the rich man that comes home smiling every day?

GOOD AS GOLD

I can remember my dad singing, "I don't know but I've been told, Forest Hamilton is as good as gold". He sang it in that well known Army tune with a smile in his voice. No matter how bad things were, those words always made me feel better. I couldn't help but feel, well... as good as gold. The idea of gold as a standard for greatness in our culture is so pervasive that many of us don't even think about it. Just about everyone has longed for a gold medal, a gold coin, a gold trophy, a gold ring, or a gold star at some point in their life. Since before the times of The Bible, gold has been a means of trade and it is still accepted in any country in the world as currency. But what *is* the gold standard? As Webster's defines it, "a monetary standard under which the basic unit of currency is defined by a stated quantity of gold." Before 1933, every dollar bill could be traded in for its equal weight in physical gold. While the argument persists whether it would be sound monetary policy for The United States to return to the gold standard, I *can* say with certainty that you should immediately adopt and implement The Gold Standard of Life. These are the principles that I have adopted and applied to my life to become successful, fulfilled, and financially independent.

1. LIVE THE GOLDEN RULE: A SERVICE MINDSET

"Therefore all things whatsoever ye would that men should do to you, do ye even so to them."

Matthew 7:12 NKJV

Michael Fuljenz is the President and CEO of Universal Coin and Bullion in Beaumont, Texas. Mike and I have worked together since 1994 and I don't believe that there is a more knowledgeable, experienced, intelligent, genuine and award winning Gold Coin Expert that has ever walked the earth. Mike has taught me many lessons over the years, but none more important than his use of the Golden Rule with our customers. The importance that he places on every single client and their individual needs is beyond customer service, it is the staple of a business that I have helped grow into a 60 million dollar a year industry leader. One of the first things that I learned is that whether I am working with an investor on a 5 million dollar gold coin portfolio, a client that has yet to spend a dollar, or someone that is upset on the customer service line, I must treat them with genuine respect, care, and personal attention.

These are the three P's of Service that Mike Fuljenz has ingrained into me:

1. Preparation – The more prepared you are, the more confident you are. The more confidence you have, the clearer your mind is. When you are prepared, confident, and clear headed, you can accomplish anything in sales, customer service, *and* life.
2. Promises – If you say you are going to do something, do it. Always *under* promise and *over* perform. I have watched many sales and customer service representatives get into trouble from unnecessary promises to customers that they forget to keep or deem unimportant. People won't always remember when you keep your promises, but they *never* forget when *you* forget.
3. Practice – My uncle, Lester Henderson, used to say, "practice doesn't make perfect, perfect practice makes perfect." Don't waste your time doing things the wrong way. Do them right every time. Be fully engaged in every activity, or don't engage at all.

I have won many sales and teamwork awards in my time with Universal Coin, but I received the greatest compliment in my career on the day Mike Fuljenz asked me to be the Assistant Director of Customer Service. Why was this such a monumental honor? Because it takes a multitude of sales to keep a company moving up, but only one mismanaged customer service call to bring an entire company down.

Take Action: Do unto others as you would have done unto you. Live the Golden Rule in business and in life. As Zig Ziglar said, "you can have everything in life you want, if you will just help other people get what they want." Start using the three P's of customer service to evaluate whether you are *including* or *excluding* other people in your work and home on your way up the success ladder.

2. SILENCE IS GOLDEN: SHUT UP AND LISTEN

"You've heard it said that God gave man two ears and one mouth, and he is supposed to use them in that proportion."

~ Brian Tracy

I recently spent a weekend with Brian Tracy as a part of his Inner Circle in Santa Fe, New Mexico. The thing about Brian that stands out the most is his ability to listen intently to whoever is speaking as if what they are saying is the most amazing thing he has ever heard. He doesn't interrupt and always leaves a pause sitting in the air once you are done talking. It is like he is savoring the aftertaste of a good red wine in order to get its full flavor. He refers to listening as "white magic", because it makes the customer feel secure and comfortable. I have personally witnessed the success of this practice time and time again.

I was a *good* salesman for many years. I didn't get to the top in my field until I learned how to shut up. It turns out, I talked a lot more people *out* of buying than I did *into* buying. Once I slowed my mouth down and tuned my ears in, I was able to hear the exact things that the client needed in order to feel comfortable. I describe my early sales like a machine gun spraying facts and figures with very few hitting the mark and many sending the client running in the other direction. After attaching my "silencer," I became a highly trained sniper, listening and learning from my surroundings, before choosing my shot carefully. The reason that the shot almost always finds its mark is because it is the exact fact or feeling that the client needs in order to feel comfortable and make a decision. I am not hunting the client; I am simply shooting down the mental and emotional clutter that gets in the way of them making a sound decision. Gold and rare coins sell themselves based on history, beauty, and facts. The goal is to get the client to set their preconceived notions and fears down long enough to see the facts clearly. I have found the best way to do this is to shut up and listen.

Take Action: Practice Brian Tracy's 70/30 Rule. Make it a focus at work and at home to listen to your client or spouse 70% of the time and asking questions 30% of the time. Your sales and happiness quotient will increase immediately.

3. THE GOLDEN YEARS: PERSONAL GROWTH

"More gold has been mined from the thoughts of men than has been taken from the earth."

~ Napoleon Hill

Every time I want to learn something new, I read something old. I picked up Think and Grow Rich, by Napoleon Hill when I was 30 years old. After applying its principles directly to my life and businesses and actively watching my dreams become reality, I was shocked that more people had not found this book and its secrets. I was sitting in my study last year reading it for the tenth time and I found myself wishing that I had read it at 18. Oh, how my life would have been different! As I leaned back in my chair looking over the hundreds of books in my attitude, sales, and business library, something caught my eye. I got out of my chair, walked to the shelf, reached up and pulled an old dusty book down. Ironically, it was Think and Grow Rich, by Napoleon Hill. I opened the cover and inside were the words, "To Forest, read this! It will change your life." One of my friends and colleagues, Robert Patton, had given me this book when I was 17 years old, just days after beginning my career in the gold industry. What we don't seek, we don't find. It was right there under my nose the whole time, but I wasn't actively seeking growth and understanding, therefore I did not find it. Dr. Hill was right; you really do become what you think about. And if you think about nothing all day, that is what you will become.

Don't wait until your golden years to learn the lessons that the great minds of the world already paid a price for. 99% of the business and personal obstacles that we face have already been solved by someone else. We tend to try and reinvent the wheel over and over again instead of using the blueprints that are readily available to us.

Take Action: Choose to have a voracious appetite for learning and growing and you will be amazed at the immediate boost in confidence and results. Seek out an expert or ten in your field and learn what they have done to get from where you are to where they are. Read or listen to at least one book a month that is directly tied to your goals and dreams. Take notes, highlight important lines, and instantly apply those concepts to your world.

4. HEART OF GOLD: MANAGE YOUR EMOTIONS

"Life is about chasing your potential, not what you get from it, or whether you ever reach it."

~ Robert P. Verde

As far as I'm concerned, Robert Verde is one of the greatest humans that has ever lived. He has taught me more about my mind, my emotions, my process and myself than all of the Napoleon Hills, Earl Nightingales, Brian Tracys, and Albert Einsteins put together. He is the General Manager at Universal Coin and Bullion, but he is much more than my boss. I have remarked for years that he has more common sense than anyone I have ever met. But it is more than common sense. It is as if he has a thousand cameras on every situation, giving him perfect perspective and a simple and clear path to what he calls "solution mode." Through extensive research and daily clinical trials in our offices for 15 years, I have finally figured it out. I would venture to guarantee that his E.I. (Emotional Intelligence) is off the charts. One definition of E.I. is "the ability to perceive emotion, integrate emotion to facilitate thought, understand emotions and to regulate emotions to promote personal growth." As early as 1920, Edward Thorndike used the term social intelligence to describe the *skill* of understanding and managing other people.

There are four types of E.I. *abilities* that I watch Robert Verde use on a daily basis to change people's lives:

1. Perceiving Emotions – the ability to detect and decipher emotions including the ability to identify one's own emotions.
2. Using Emotions – the ability to harness emotions to facilitate various cognitive activities, such as thinking and problem solving. The emotionally intelligent person can capitalize fully upon his or her changing moods in order to best fit the task at hand.
3. Understanding Emotions – the ability to comprehend emotion language and to appreciate complicated relationships among emotions.
4. Managing Emotions – the ability to regulate emotions in both

ourselves and in others. Therefore, the emotionally intelligent person can harness emotions, even negative ones, and manage them to achieve intended goals.

What is the common denominator in all of these definitions? The word *ability*. It is not a gift – it is a learned skill that is a direct result of your motivations and your discipline. Robert Verde's motivation is clear, and if you were to ask anyone that has ever met him, they would testify to the fact that he has a heart of gold. Because of this desire to help others, he exchanged his learning *disabilities* for life-changing *abilities*. The majority of communication breakdowns in life are a mismanagement or misinterpretation of emotions either in yourself or in others.

Take Action: Evaluate your ability to perceive, use, understand, and manage your emotions and you too can find the missing link to successful relationships.

5. GO FOR THE GOLD: TAKE ACTION

"You will be held accountable for your actions. Your dreams will be held accountable for your inactions."

~ Forest Hamilton

Jared Hanley is a principal of Brereton, Hanley & Co, a successful private investment banking firm that handles $200 million dollar mergers and acquisitions. Before that he was a graduate of Yale University with a B.A. in Economics and Cognitive Science. Before that he founded a successful SAT tutoring program. Before that he scored 1590 on his SAT in high school (when 1600 was perfect). Before that he was just my best friend. We were inseparable from the day we met on the school bus. You see, he didn't care if I smelled bad. He was the first kid on the bus to ever sit next to me without a malicious intent. He sat down, asked me if I wanted to play a game, and we've been playing the Game of Life together ever since. His decisive action in the face of peer disapproval was a defining moment in both of our lives. We live by Gretzky's Law, "you miss 100% of the shots you don't take." Jared and I recently formed Poor Kid Enterprises, LP along with our partners Ryland Aldrich and Jensen Millar. All of us started with nothing (or less) and now run successful businesses and lead fulfilled lives. Ryland, who will always be my little brother, grew up on the same property as I did and is now a screenwriter in Hollywood living his dream. Jensen, the brother of Red Sox World Series Legend Kevin Millar, owns Synthetic Turf Solutions with his loving wife, Elaine.

POOR KIDS, RICH MEN

We turned from poor kids to rich men in an instant. Don't get me wrong, there was, is, and always will be a lot of hard work, dedication, self-discipline, and failure in reaching and surpassing our goals. However, once we stopped filtering everything through the lenses of generational poverty and environmental circumstance, we were able to focus our entire vision on a reality that had only been in our dreams. Once I stopped the record that was on repeat in my head – that was saying, "Forest, you aren't good enough and you will always be poor," I could hear my mom's voice clearly saying, "You can be anything and do anything that you set your mind to." She was right. I am happier, wealthier, and more fulfilled than I ever dreamed possible. I look forward to every day and every challenge because I am equipped to handle whatever comes my way, good or bad. I am not special, I have simply adopted the time tested and proven principles and disciplines that I have discussed here. They will work for you just as they have for me. Make a choice to push yourself to the front of *your* field and then be committed to the discipline and effort that it takes to accomplish that goal.

"For anything worth having one must pay the price; and the price is always work, patience, love, self-sacrifice – no paper currency, no promises to pay, but the gold of real service."

~John Burroughs

Bibliography

Miriam-Webster online dictionary for definition of gold standard.

Wikipedia for definitions of Emotional Intelligence and Social Intelligence, as well as the quote by Edward Thorndike.

All other quotes were given with permission or gleaned from books and internet with appropriate credit given.

ABOUT FOREST

Forest Hamilton was literally delivered into his father's hands. When the midwife was late in arriving, David Hamilton had to find a way to bring his boy into this world. Through fear, uncertainty, and an umbilical cord wrapped around his son's neck, he found a way. Raised without running water or electricity into his teens, Forest followed his father's example and continued to persevere. His father taught him to be the hardest worker on the farm, the most competitive athlete on the field, and the most dedicated student in the classroom. This work ethic, coupled with his mother's consistently encouraging ways, helped him find his way to Texas to pursue his dreams at an early age.

Forest Hamilton is now an Assistant Director of Universal Coin and Bullion, Ltd. in Beaumont, Texas. He has held many positions in his nearly 15-year career with UCB, one of the world's largest gold, silver, and rare coin investment firms. Beginning his career at UCB as a teenager, Forest has been awarded numerous honors for sales, teamwork, and customer service on his way to becoming an invaluable resource in every department. He has trained well over a hundred salesmen, customer service representatives, and managers – helping propel his company from a five million dollar a year business into a multi-national, award winning, sixty million dollar a year industry leader.

Forest is also a partner and co-founder of David Hamilton Winery, LLC in Mt. Vernon, Oregon. This family-run winery specializes in organic fruit wines of the Northwest. He truly enjoys working with his family in the acquisition, production, distribution, marketing and drinking of their unique wines.

Forest and the love of his life, Stormy, have two beautiful daughters, Taylin and Tinsley. He is a dedicated husband and father and applies the same passion to his personal life that he does in his business life.

Forest is an accomplished author, speaker, and life/business coach. He is known to many as a "Perpetual Positive Emotion Machine." His goal is to help others realize that happiness and success are direct results of choices, not chances. He considers sales, communication, and coaching to be the three greatest arts in human nature and is constantly striving to master each of them in an effort to better himself, his family, his businesses, and those that come to him to be mentored.

If you are interested in having Forest Hamilton help YOU find a way in life, business, or wealth preservation and diversification in Gold and Silver, please visit: universalcoin.com. You can also call 800-248-2223 or email Forest directly at: foresthamilton@universalcoin.com

If you are interested in learning more about organically grown fruit wines with no added sulfites, visit davidhamiltonwinery.com or call 541-932-4567.

CHAPTER 21

ENJOY THE GOOD LIFE:

THE GUIDE TO HAVING IT ALL

BY ALAN & BONNIE CASHMAN

Some people will tell you that success in business is all about timing, luck, and innovation. Yet in the same conversation, they may warn you that there is a cost to success. That in return for freedom and monetary gain, your relationships and health may suffer.

But this has not been our experience. While timing and innovation are important ingredients to our recipe for success, we can proudly say that we have created incredible success in our life without a cost. Not everything we have tried has been a success, but we have accomplished every major goal, seen our dreams come to fruition, and we have done this hand in hand, together, throughout our thirty-nine years of marriage.

Our answers to success are quite simple. Incorporate them into your life and decision-making will become clear. You will be healthy, focused, and happy in your personal life and in business.

OUR STORY

We are Alan and Bonnie Cashman, two Seattle natives who were born into middle class families with no special talents, privileges, or connections. Our adventure together started as a chance meeting in college forty years ago. And like most young couples, our first years were spent developing our professional careers. Having ignored his parents' request to become an attorney, Alan dove into life insurance sales and quickly realized that finding a narrow niche market would boost his career. In his search for the right focus, he found an angle with retirement planning and, within a year and a half, became one of the youngest sales managers within his large company. Shortly thereafter, he was made partner at one of the leading general agents in the city.

His progress did not slow down. At the time, insurance sales involved individual meetings with prospects in person three times. Most agents were focusing their sales efforts on high wealth individuals seeking a larger commission. But this was a competitive market, and Alan recognized that there was an opportunity with less competition. Furthermore, he realized that selling insurance one policy at a time was less effective than selling to groups.

So as his competition went right, Alan turned left. He developed a process to sell to the masses and to help the middle class. The Balanced Program, Inc. (BPI) was born, and so was the opportunity for the Cashmans to work together. Bonnie came on board.

BPI grew quickly and it became clear that administration was very important to our success and to many companies like ours. Contemporary administrative processes were a hassle for agents and were not providing the best customer service to our clients. Our frustration with the system led us to a perfect opportunity. We answered these problems by developing an administrative system from scratch. This system handled everything from billing and customer service to commission accounting and policy issuance. And while it was complicated, it solved a problem in our industry and created a better experience for everyone involved. Our second company, Administrative Systems, Inc. (ASI), was built around this asset and was founded in 1990 – less than ten years after establishing our first company. And in January 2003, both companies were purchased by a company listed on the New York Stock Exchange.

LOOK FOR THE RIGHT OPPORTUNITY

As our story illustrates, our success came not only because we were in the right place at the right time, but also because our eyes were looking for the right opportunities to take us to the next level. We saw challenges or problems within our industry, and in finding the answers, we found great opportunities that we were ready and able to take advantage of.

Finding the right opportunity is the key to achieving financial independence and success. Whether you are trying to think of an idea to take to market or ready to grow your business, remember these five things:

1. **Do what you are passionate about.** Business is what intrigues and interests Alan most, but what if he had followed his parents' guidance and became an attorney? Would he have found the same level of success and happiness? Alan is a self-disciplined achiever and would have been successful at whatever he attempted, but in finding an industry that he was passionate about, he was more engaged and therefore more aware of opportunity.

   There is a correlation between success and the number of hours you work at a particular skill or in a specific field. The more time you put in, the better and more successful you will be. So you should enjoy it!

2. **Look for trends.** There are trends in every industry, culture, and geographic region. Think of the direction your market is taking and embrace it. Consider who the industry has yet to serve, and build a solution that suits the needs and desires of this demographic. In realizing that there was another way to serve the middle class and their need for life insurance, Alan and Bonnie sold ten times the volume of other agents PER DAY.

3. **Look for problems that need solving.** When you are focusing and working within a particular industry, you may notice inefficiencies or unfulfilled markets. Explore the gap and figure out why it remains unserved. You may find a perfect opportunity in doing so.

4. **Evaluate the opportunity.** Before diving into a new business

or project, consider the potential upside of the opportunity. How will it impact your life? Is it the right time in the market? For you personally? What risk is involved and what is the financial commitment? Make sure all sides of the equation make sense for your life and for your business.

5. **Find customers immediately.** In most of our business endeavors, we have started with a potential client. This has rationalized the risk, given us a point of valuable feedback as we build a business, and started us off on the right foot. There is no greater risk than building a business without making sure that there are potential customers. Give yourself peace of mind and the right start by finding a customer immediately!

AFFIRMATIONS WORK

Finding the right opportunities came naturally to us as we focused on a particular industry throughout our career and aligned our growth through observation and need. However, starting businesses and seeking these opportunities took courage, energy, and skill, and in order to do this well, we had to be focused, aware, and confident. Early in our careers, we spent our free time listening to training tapes, attending seminars and workshops, and reading books on sales and marketing. Throughout our professional career we have practiced ways to harness our thoughts and to understand how our thinking influences our success.

In 1978, we were introduced to affirmations, and they hugely influenced our lives. What is an affirmation? It is a declaration that is focused on a positive outcome or attitude. For example, Alan has used affirmations like, "I am an excellent speaker, well prepared, logical and completely at ease before any group" to give himself a boost for public speaking, and "I especially love, cherish and enjoy Bonnie" to maintain a special and endearing attitude toward his wife.

Use affirmations to build your confidence, to help you accomplish goals in your life, and to become the person you want to be. Every affirmation is a reflection of your subconscious and inner truths and helps you realize your goals. In order to succeed in business, it is important to be confident and positive. Negative thinking will only hinder your growth.

Observing your thoughts is not a common or easy activity, but it is an incredibly valuable tool. We encourage you to listen to yourself, to think positively, and to embrace the power of affirmations. Please read and follow these:

SIX TIPS TO INCORPORATE AFFIRMATIONS INTO YOUR LIFE:

1. **Make positive statements.** Your affirmations should be positive and about you. They work when you address goals and attitudes for which you have full control. (Making a statement wishing that someone else will do something for you or that something will happen to you is not an affirmation.) An example that works is "I enjoy being economically self-sufficient."

2. **Use the present tense.** Affirmations should always be in the present. For example, say: "I am very successful at sales" instead of "I want to be very successful at sales." Own the statement as if you are there now.

3. **Consider your lifestyle and goals.** Affirmations help you feel confident and able to reach goals you are working toward actively. Make sure they fit your lifestyle and goals. To quote George Lucas, "*you can't do it unless you can imagine it.*"

4. **Write them down.** Write your affirmations down on 3 x 5 note cards and keep them with you. Add them to Post-it® notes and stick them to your bathroom mirror or to the dashboard of your car. You want them to stay present in your mind and reminders help.

5. **Repeat them over and over.** We recommend saying your affirmations about ten times twice a day. Get in the routine of saying them first thing in the morning and last thing at night before bed.

6. **Visualize your affirmation – as it is accomplished.** Picture yourself having achieved the goal of your affirmation. Think of how you will feel, how you will look, and what it will be like.

And remember this quote from the clergyman, Norman Vincent Peale, "When you affirm big, believe big and pray big, putting faith into action, big things happen." We look at our list of affirmations today and all of them have been accomplished!

YOUR HEALTH IS MOST IMPORTANT

Being a business owner and working toward ambitious professional goals adds a lot of responsibility to your life. It is easy to put off exercise and eating healthy meals when you are busy managing projects and people. But at the end of the day, can you be your best if you are not taking care of yourself and maintaining healthy habits?

We don't think so. In fact, we believe that taking the time to be healthy makes you more productive and focused.

After retiring from the insurance business, we started living part time in both Seattle and Palm Springs. Alan started working out more than he ever had. He was playing golf, doing Pilates five times a week, and walking many miles a day. But, strangely, he was not losing weight. At the suggestion of a well-known cardiologist, Alan changed his diet and started staying away from sugar. He lost 30 pounds in 90 days and got his blood pressure issue under control without medication for the first time in 15 years.

Bonnie had a similar experience with lifestyle changes. In 2008, she developed areas of skin cancer and had 22 operations over the next eleven months. In early 2010, Bonnie followed the advice of Alan's cardiologist and removed sugar from her diet. It worked! The cardiologist suggested that cancer cannot live without sugar, and the Seattle doctors were amazed.

After having these experiences, we now believe that many of the causes of weight and health issues facing Americans are related to sugar. We believe that everyone needs to understand some basics about eating, fitness, and health to enjoy the good life! And we have created a business around it. Our book titled *The Cashman Lifestyle* explains how to live a healthy and wealthy life, and our website keeps you up to date on ways to incorporate "the good life" and to become as successful and healthy as you can be.

We firmly believe that learning some basic principles and incorporating these habits into your lifestyle will give you what you need to be at your best. Here is an important list for you:

THE TOP TEN THINGS BUSINESS OWNERS CAN DO TO STAY HEALTHY:

1. **Get plenty of sleep.** Plan your day to allow for an hour of relaxation time before bed and 8 hours of sleep at night.

2. **Limit your sugar intake.** Plan your meals and snacks to incorporate natural whole foods such as meat, fruit, and vegetables. If the food comes from this earth and not a factory, you can eat it! Prepare your meals in advance to make this easier, and if you find yourself craving sugar, try adding more protein to your diet. It should help.

3. **Eating on the Go.** Make sure you eat three meals a day and prepare before attending lunch meetings. Review the restaurant menu online to find healthy options before heading out the door. Find healthy restaurants near your office and suggest them when you are planning a meeting.

4. **Exercise at least 30 minutes per day.** If you are just starting out with exercise, make small changes first. Take the stairs instead of the elevator. Take the parking space furthest from the entrance and walk. Get out of your chair and stretch several times a day. Eventually have the goal of walking at least 30 minutes a day.

5. **Learn how to use supplements.** Supplements can help you gain energy. They can protect and help heal your body, but it is important to understand how to best use them. Ask your physician or read more of our insights on this topic on our website.

6. **Deal with burnout before it happens.** It happens to the best of us. You have a big project or goal, and you put all of your resources toward it. You start losing your normal routine and working longer. If you are not careful, anxiety and fatigue will step in. Be sure to stop burnout before it happens. If things start feeling too intense, take at least half a day off to recalibrate. You will be much more productive when you return.

7. **Be open to change.** It is important to be flexible in business and to adapt to changes as best as you can. Change is inevitable and the longer you resist it, the more difficult it will be to control stress and maintain your healthy routines. Find ways to help yourself through a change. Read books, find a mentor, or think of ways to benefit from the new environment.

8. **Prepare, prepare, prepare.** And then prepare some more! The more prepared you feel for a project or task, the better you feel about your performance. It also helps to control anxiety and negative feelings that work against you.

9. **Never stop learning.** Learning strengthens the mind and makes us feel more secure and confident. It makes us better at what we do. There are audio books on many areas of business and self-help that will improve your skills. Take advantage of your commute to work and meetings. Plug in your iPod or audio discs. We recommend starting with Brian Tracy's programs.

10. **Take care of your relationships.** Business and life are all about relationships – spouses, family members, customers, vendors, managers, consultants, etc. It is important to communicate your needs clearly and directly and to know when to listen. Take care of your relationships and keep your communication skills sharp. It will eliminate a lot of stress in your life.

As a business owner, you are stretched thin. You manage many tasks and relationships each day, and we truly empathize with the pressure and energy this takes. We are not painting a portrait of perfection or holding you to unrealistic goals. But we have spent most of our lives learning how to think about things, educating ourselves to find success in all areas of our lives. And we hope that you will start incorporating these valuable tools into your everyday life.

Look for the right opportunities in life, affirm big, and stay healthy. Enjoy your journey, as we have, and the best is still yet to come! Keep up with The Cashmans.

All our best of success to you. Enjoy the good life!

~ Alan and Bonnie Cashman

ABOUT ALAN AND BONNIE

For Alan and Bonnie Cashman, life is about building sturdy foundations – for their marriage (40 years and counting), for their successful businesses and for better health through diet, fitness and positive thinking. Cashman Lifestyle is their way of passing along the personal and professional lessons they've learned to others so they too can "enjoy the good life."

The Cashman's unique partnership began when they met while both were attending Seattle University. They would spend the better part of the next four decades married and working together to establish not one, but two successful companies; the Balanced Program Institute (BPI), one of the premier employee benefit firms in the Pacific Northwest, and Administrative Systems, Inc. (ASI), a top provider of office systems/support to insurance companies. As founder of both companies, Alan acquired valuable experience in key areas of financial services, including employee benefits, wealth management, retirement planning and individual/corporate life insurance. Bonnie was BPI's president while also establishing herself as a sales leader, building relationships with more than 1,000 employer groups in the Seattle area. She also is a sought-after speaker for her experience in worksite marketing and in 1999 was inducted into the National Association of Professional Enrollment Specialists Hall of Fame.

In 2003, the Cashmans sold both BPI and ASI to a New York Stock Exchange company, giving them the financial freedom to build a private art collection and search for new challenges. Although both had more time to exercise, Alan continued to struggle with weight and blood pressure and Bonnie developed a form of skin cancer. But the Cashmans brought the same work ethic and research to their health that they had brought to bear on the business world. They learned of dietary secrets that did away with sugar and set them on the road to wellness – so much so that Seattle doctors were surprised that Alan had quickly turned around his vital signs and Bonnie ended her skin cancer issues.

The Cashmans have opened an innovative multi-discipline fitness center, Lab5 Fitness, in Seattle's Capitol Hill, and have started Cashman Lifestyle as a way to share their expertise in helping others live healthier, wealthier lives. The Cashmans "enjoy the good life." Now their mission is to teach others how to do the same.

Learn more at www.CashmanLifestyle.com.

Website: http://cashmanlifestyle.com/
Facebook: http://www.facebook.com/pages/Cashman-Lifestyle
Twitter: www.twitter.com/cashmanlife

CHAPTER 22

CHANGE YOUR SALES RESULTS FROM GOOD TO GREAT!!!

BY CHUCK MITCHELL

Over the past 30 years I have had the pleasure to meet and talk to thousands of business owners about their businesses and more specifically, their sales teams. While most realize that sales is critical to their success, unless they have a strong sales background, a high percentage view sales people as a necessary evil. Some of the more frequent comments I have heard are:

- My sales people are not closing well enough.
- Our activity level is too low; not enough cold calls.
- My sales people just don't get it!
- I need my sales reps to be hungrier.
- I can't get my reps to sell the right products.
- Sales people make too much money!
- I can't seem to motivate my reps to .....
- My reps just don't work hard enough.

If you are a business owner and/or sales manager that have uttered or even thought something similar, then this chapter is for you. In the next few pages I will provide an overview of **Six Steps** to **Change Your Sales Results from Good to Great!!!** This is a process that I have personally implemented on numerous occasions to build award-winning sales teams, and I continue to utilize it successfully with my clients today. It is simple to understand, easy to implement, and most importantly IT GETS RESULTS!

STEP 1 : CLARIFY YOUR MARKETING MESSAGE

The majority of business owners I have met over the years want to improve their sales results. In fact, I believe it may be one of the greatest challenges facing small and medium-sized businesses (SMBs).

Question: **Why is it so hard to improve sales results?**

The answers to this question could fill several books but since I have one chapter, my focus will be on the tendency of many business owners to fix the symptoms rather than digging deeper to understand the fundamental problems that are causing poor sales performance.

Business owners are understandably looking for a quick fix and there is no shortage of so-called experts more than willing to provide solutions. These 'magic pills' may work on occasion, however, the most effective way to ensure sustainable long-term improvement is to take a more diagnostic approach.

Nowhere is this more important than in developing an effective marketing message, since it is the base on which all of your sales success is built.

The key is **CLARITY**. A business owner can perform the necessary diagnostics by working through this series of clarifying questions with their team:

1. What business are you in?
2. Who is your ideal customer?
3. Why does your ideal customer buy your product?
4. Why would your ideal customer buy from your competitor?
5. What are your unique marketing/selling messages?

While these questions may sound straightforward, this should not be a five-minute exercise. It is one that should be given serious consideration and be vetted over several weeks with the whole team and key customers, if possible. When you have some answers to the fifth question, put them through the SW/WIIFM filter by imagining your customers asking the following two questions about your unique marketing/selling messages:

5a) So what? (SW)
5b) What's in it for me? (WIIFM)

Keep re-working your answers to question 5 until you get solid messages that focus on benefits your customers receive from your products and services, rather than the features that your products and services deliver.

It is vital to your sales success and therefore to your company's success to focus your key marketing messages around the customer. With information readily available online and through social media, all businesses must establish clear and consistent positioning and messaging in every form of communication, PR, marketing and sales materials. Getting this right is an important first step to improving your sales results.

STEP 2: BUILD A "GOLD MEDAL" TEAM

Now that you have solidified your key marketing messages, you need to ensure you have the right people delivering them to your clients.

There are two pivotal elements to building a strong and effective sales group for your company. First, leverage the knowledge of a Sales Expert and second, establish clear accountabilities/deliverables for your sales people.

1) **Leverage a Sales Expert**: unless someone in your company has a strong sales management background, HIRE AN EXPERT. Options include hiring a business coach, a sales coach, or search online for a virtual sales manager; find someone who can offer sales management services to your firm.

Many business owners try setting up their own sales teams or delegate the task to someone with little or no sales experience. They feel that sales people should be easy to find. In fact they are correct, sales people are easy to find; GREAT SALES PEOPLE however, not so easy. In addition business owners may believe the popular myth that great sales people are born, not made. While I agree that it is true some individuals have behavioural styles that appear to make them sales naturals, effective selling in today's marketplace requires so much more.

2) **Establish Clear Accountabilities/Deliverables**: the second critical element of building a strong sales team is to develop a thorough list of activities your salespeople need to accomplish in order to be successful. Focus on the job itself rather than the individual that may currently be in the role.

Ask yourself:

1. ***What are the most important things I need my sales person to accomplish that will significantly grow my business?***
2. ***Do I need my reps focused on nurturing and growing the business from existing clients or is the focus on new client acquisition?***
3. ***Is the salesperson responsible for creating leads (marketing), selling and closing prospects, after sales service?***

   Develop an exhaustive list then select the 5 most important activities.

Now it is time to review your current staff and make sure that they meet all of your criteria. If yes, fantastic you have some STARS; if not its time to make a change.

When hiring sales people, I strongly recommend using behavioural assessment tools (such as D.I.S.C. or P.I.A.V.[1]) to assist in your analysis of candidates. Focus on individuals that have demonstrated high levels of achievement and commitment to excellence. Look for applicants that demonstrate strong sales skills during the interview. They **Develop Trust**, they ask **Great Questions**, they **Listen** well, they **Uncover Needs**, they **Provide a Solution** and they **Ask** for the job. Always check references! This extra work is well worth it.

1. D.I.S.C. is an assessment that classifies four aspects of behaviour, "How You Act"
   P.I.A.V is an assessment that explores your passions, "Why You Act"

Note: A critical interview question I would ask any potential sales rep is "What sales book or audio are you currently reading/listening to?" ask for some details and how they are using this to get better results. If the candidate does not provide quality answers it is my recommendation that they do not get hired. Clearly they are not committed to excellence!

STEP 3: TEACH AND EMBED KNOWLEDGE AND SKILLS

Now that you have hired your Gold Medal sales team, as a business owner it is critical to equip each of your sales reps with the tools necessary for success. If you are following the steps outlined, you have used a sales expert to help build your sales team. It is now time to leverage that expert to train your sales people not only how to sell your products/services but also to ensure they have sufficient product knowledge to provide the expected level of expertise to the marketplace.

All too often in small or medium-sized businesses, newly-hired sales people are given a few brochures, a crash course of product knowledge, then sent out to make cold calls. It is often assumed that an experienced sales person has been trained how to sell effectively, however that is frequently not the case. In a couple of months, sales are well below the expected targets and we find ourselves back at page one of this chapter with a frustrated owner.

My experience has shown me that to develop top salespeople you have to help them establish a strong belief in their products and services, their company and most importantly themselves. By dedicating time upfront with new hires to ensure that they have sufficient product knowledge and thorough training on how to sell, the more likely it is they will achieve sales excellence. Do not take short cuts; invest the time in your salespeople.

The final piece to this puzzle is that the sales rep must be committed to continuous learning and improvement. While no one can be forced to improve, it is very important that a culture is established where sales people take responsibility for their own self-improvement. By setting an expectation that all sales people should be reading books on selling, listening to audios in their car and constantly trying to improve their selling skills your sales team will develop a superior level of performance.

STEP 4:
UNLEASH THE "INNER ENTREPRENEUR" OF YOUR SALES PEOPLE

Top sales people are generally motivated by money and recognition. The ability of the SMB owner to leverage these two motivating factors effectively will be the key to successful sales results.

Brian Tracy in his book "Be a Sales Superstar" states:

"the highest paid sales professionals in every field accept 100% responsibility for results…they see themselves as the president of their own professional sales corporation. They view themselves as self-employed."

This concept presented by Brian Tracy might be difficult for some business owners to accept. It can be contrary to their natural or understandable desire to have control over all aspects of their business. This need for control is often the cause for capped compensation plans, salaried sales positions, and the treatment of the sales position as an assembly line job.

Again I am strongly recommending the business owner leverage the experience and knowledge of the sales expert they have engaged in Steps 2 & 3. Have this individual:

1. Clearly communicate the accountabilities/deliverables developed in Step 2 to each sales person.
2. Establish compensation plans that align with the values of your company but also allows the sales people to treat this as their own business. The more they put into it, the more they get out. That's good for them and good for your company.

Avoid the trap I have often seen, which are compensation plans that cater to average performance because there is little incentive to excel! Never, ever be shy about incentivising your sales people to strive for excellence.

STEP 5: EFFECTIVE MEASUREMENT AND MANAGEMENT

In the previous section, I talked about the need for business owners to release some control to unleash the inner entrepreneur of their sales people. Also mentioned was the importance of clearly communicating the expectations of the job.

Sales is about performance and as the age-old saying goes "what gets measured, gets done" so it is necessary to develop Key Result Indicators. KRI's allow a business to track results in key areas considered critical for measuring the success of the business.

These metrics will provide the business owner, sales manager and salesperson with the ability to monitor performance, make adjustments to strategy, and ensure the established sales goals and targets will not only be achieved but exceeded.

Utilize your Sales Expert, plus Finance, Marketing and Operations people (I recognize this may be one person!) to determine the key metrics that need to be measured to insure that the sales performance of your team is meeting the requirements of the company.

STEP 6: CELEBRATE THE WINS!

One of the realities of business today is that everyone is stretched for time. As a result many businesses take very little time, if any, to celebrate the wins. While this chapter is focused on sales teams, this principle applies to all departments or groups. As a business coach, I encourage all of my clients to have company-wide and where applicable, departmental S.M.A.R.T. Goals (Specific, Measurable, Aligned, Realistic, Time activated). In all cases, it is truly worthwhile to take time to celebrate the achievement of those goals.

This process of celebration and recognition for a job well done provides motivation and increased focus on the achievement of future goals. As stated earlier sales people are motivated by money and recognition. An effective compensation plan takes care of the money; celebration provides the recognition. The type of celebration can take many forms but most importantly the people it is recognizing should view it as meaningful.

How can you do create meaningful celebrations? Ask your sales people upfront when goals have been established; "How shall we celebrate when you achieve these goals?" Quality celebrations should make your sales people eager to take on and surpass the next challenge!

SUMMARY: CHANGING YOUR SALES RESULTS FROM GOOD TO GREAT!!!

One of the top business coaches in the world Dan Creed of Phoenix, Arizona reminded me recently that all great performance starts with Clarity.

My Goal for this chapter was to provide **CLARITY** to SMB owners about how to dramatically improve their sales results by establishing a highly skilled and motivated sales team.

A common theme throughout the **6 STEPS** has been to leverage the knowledge and expertise of a sales expert. Do not underestimate this suggestion, as I believe it is a key to your success. I also recommend to all business owners to commit to learning more about effective selling by reading at least one book in the next 12 months. Three recommendations are: *SPIN Selling* by Neil Rackham; *The Psychology of Selling* by Brian Tracy; and *Book Yourself Solid* by Michael Port.

Thank you for taking time to read this Chapter and I welcome anyone that has questions, comments, requires additional insight or would like additional reading recommendations to email me at cmitchell@focalpointcoaching.com.

In addition I would love to hear from business owners about your success after using the **6 STEPS**.

GREAT SELLING!!!

ABOUT CHUCK

Business Coach Chuck Mitchell is One of Canada's Leading Experts at Helping Business Owners, Executives and Sales Teams Change Their Results From Good to GREAT!!!

Chuck has been hooked on out-of-the box thinking and inspiring exceptional performance since he completed his first business plan while still at University of Toronto. That first plan changed his career path and lead to a 35-year career of leading, coaching and empowering award-winning teams in some of Canada's largest and most successful corporations as well as a handful of SMB companies.

Now Chuck is leveraging his focus on results to assist SMB owners reach their full potential and to get everything out of their business that they deserve. To each project Chuck brings an extensive wealth of experience and expertise in Sales, Sales Management, Marketing, Operations and Human Resources. He is passionate about the success of every one of his clients and uses a customized, structured approach that utilizes content from Brian Tracy and is targeted at the exact needs of each business.

Business Coach Chuck Mitchell's FocalPoint Coaching practice is located in Markham, Ontario, Canada and he serves clients face-to-face in the Greater Toronto Area and by phone & online throughout North America.

To learn more about Chuck Mitchell and how you can receive a free 45-Minute Business Coaching session visit www.businesscoachchuckmitchell.com , or contact me directly at cmitchell@focalpointcoaching.com or 905.477.1551.

CHAPTER 23

WISDOM FOR PUSHING YOU TO THE FRONT

BY DR. EMMA JEAN THOMPSON

My friend, perhaps you have had a situation where you faced a serious challenge in your life that in order to get success, you would have to "really push --- really push to the front" to get the success you wanted.

There is a story that many people have told me that inspired them to "push forward" – that is, not give up on their dream or goal but rather keep their dream alive. These people are of different backgrounds, financial status and both young and old alike, who share with me, that after reading or hearing this story, instead of giving up in defeat, they find themselves "pushing to the front in victory."

So here's the story that many say should be my "signature" story that I should share with everyone. After you read my story, I will share some "tips" of wisdom that will help you to "push to the front" as well.

What has been your dream, your goal – the thing that you really wanted?

Well, I really wanted and deeply desired to have a baby. After twelve years of marriage and believing God, the big "push" that I wanted was on the way – I was finally pregnant.

Our family, friends, and various ones around the country and abroad who knew that my husband and I were 'believing' to have a baby – were excited for us. When we gave the announcement at our church, the people jumped up out of their seats, grabbed one another with hugs and exuberant joy, as they praised God for our prayers – and their prayers for us – being answered. My heart was filled with gratefulness to God and thankfulness for the wonderful people who had stood in faith with me.

Then, just a few weeks later, my joy was shattered. Late one night in October, when I was about eleven weeks pregnant, I began bleeding. The bleeding was steady and profuse. The sight of it all scared me. As my husband and I were rushing to drive to the hospital, I called our Church family, who would alert other designated ones to also pray for us.

"You have to have a 'D and C' right now", the doctor told me, coldly. He did not examine me nor did he ask questions of me or of the nurse. He only knew that I was bleeding profusely.

"D and C?" I quickly asked. "What is that?"

"It's a procedure to scrape out your womb," he answered.

"But what will that do to my baby?" I asked with great concern.

"Baby?" he responded.

"Well, you know that I'm pregnant, don't you?" I answered.

"You passed tissue." He answered roughly.

"Passed 'tissue'?" I asked. I did not understand.

"You passed tissue. You lost the baby and your life will be in jeopardy if I don't do a 'D and C' procedure immediately. "

As I hesitated, I could see him getting angrier and more impatient.

"You have to do this now," he said.

"But," I shared, "Myra…the nurse said that my cervix is still closed."

"So," he retorted, "We'll just go in and open it."

"But isn't there something I can do to save my baby's life?" I pleaded with the doctor. "Isn't there some test…or…or something I can take to show me whether my baby is still alive?" I asked.

He was leaning over me. The veins stood out on his neck as his face was filled with annoyance, impatience and anger. As he leaned over, his name badge hovered in front of me like a huge billboard, displaying his name – which consisted of two "first names" that I will always remember. He had burst into the room without introduction. So now I put a name to this doctor who was seemingly forcing me to make this decision without giving my baby a chance.

"No! There is no test you can take. It's too early in your pregnancy. You have to do this *now* – otherwise you could walk out into that hallway and drop dead."

My husband and I had been married for twelve years, and we were waiting to have a child. In my ministry, I had prayed for many women who had been told that they could not conceive. I'd seen miracle after miracle occur as they got pregnant and gave birth. It had not yet happened for me. But the Lord had told me that I too would conceive and have a child one day, and I trusted in His message and had looked forward to it for all these years. When we discovered that I was finally pregnant, we were overjoyed.

"Doctor, we've been married twelve years and are really wanting to have this baby," I said, hoping for some understanding and compassion.

The doctor did not want to hear my story. He abruptly answered, "You'll just have to start all over again," he shot back. In frustration, he stalked out of the room.

My husband and I held hands and prayed. He immediately said "This is a decision that you have to make. It's your body …and it's your life that's on the line, Sweetheart."

I was drawing on what I learned as a little girl that has always helped me to "push to the front" regardless of how difficult or painful the situation. When I heard and read in the Bible that Solomon made God's heart happy when he asked God for wisdom, I wanted to make God's heart happy and began praying every day for God to give me wisdom to bless and lead people.

On an Easter Sunday morning long ago, when I was but ten years old, my father abandoned our family. That day, I had a revelation – and wisdom – from the Lord, that although my earthly father had left me, my Heavenly Father, God, would never leave nor forsake me. Since then, my whole life, I have trusted in the wisdom and guidance of the Lord.

For years I had been used by God prophetically to minister to others and to give them messages from the Lord. And I also helped them to know how to hear God for themselves. Now, as I always did, I listened for the voice of the Lord to lead me in making my decision.

I clearly heard, sensed and understood God saying to me, "Do not let that doctor touch you."

The doctor returned in a huff saying "Let's get you ready for the procedure," as if I had no say so in the matter.

"I understand what you're advising, but I'm going to wait and see another doctor and see if there is any possibility to get some kind of test. I want to at least give my baby any possibility to live."

He went into a flurry of anger at the thought that I would question what he told me to do – as if I was his "property."

Before I knew it, he had a clipboard in his hand and shoved it at me saying, "You have to sign this document that I warned you that you are putting your life in jeopardy by your refusal to have this procedure."

Skimming over it quickly, the words "own life in jeopardy" seemed to stand out big on the paper. Yet, without hesitation or doubt, I signed it and he virtually snatched it from me.

"You can *leave now!*" he said, and stormed out of the room.

My husband went to pull our car up to the hospital entrance, and since I was weak and still bleeding heavily, the nurse, Myra – may God forever bless Myra – helped me get dressed and gave me hope.

"You go home and rest," she said, kindly. "Doctors are not God," she whispered in my ear so that the doctor who had returned could not hear.

The doctor made sure I got no help at all as I walked out of the room. As I walked down that long corridor by myself, I felt the warmth of the heavily oozing blood and remembering what the doctor said, "you could walk out into that hallway and drop dead."

Yet I chose to dwell on the fact that I knew that I had heard God speak to me, and I was giving my baby the chance to "live" – to "push to the front" and for me to "push to the front," and not "lose" this precious gift.

It was a long, long drive home from the hospital that night. As my husband and I drove along the dark winding, lonely streets of Prince George's County, my body feeling the effects of the amount of blood I had lost yet we held hands declaring the faithfulness of God. I held back the hot, stinging tears that welled up and demanded to be released.

My mind began to race with thoughts of the words that doctor, the "expert" had spewed out of his mouth, "You are putting your life in jeopardy if you walk out of here without this procedure!" I felt my husband's hand grasp mine even tighter and again decreed, "God is faithful. God is worthy to be praised." I washed the words that had been spoken by that doctor out of my heart with God's word. I reflected on the Friday Night Praise Service we attended the night before. I thought about the tithe and the offering I had given during the Service. "I gave my tithe, Lord," I said, "I gave an offering to you, Jesus." It was my custom to give my tithes and offerings at our Sunday Worship Services. At our Services during the week, I would give an offering however the tithe I presented to my Heavenly Father on Sundays. This Friday service was different. I was impressed to give my tithes that Friday night at church service. Even though I did not understand why, I believed that it was the Holy Spirit leading me – and the Holy Spirit leads and guides in all truth and wisdom – I obeyed that leading.

As I reflected on the paying of my tithe, the many promises about the tithe and the power of the tithe filled my mind and heart.

> *"Bring the whole tithe into the storehouse, that there may be food in my house. Test me in this," says the LORD Almighty, "and see if I will not throw open the floodgates of heaven and pour out so much*

blessing that there will not be room enough to store it."

Malachi 3:10, New International Version, Holy Bible

So many thoughts were coming to my mind, and in order to stay on the "faith track," I had to respond to each negative thought with a faith-filled response.

Early the next morning, I visited a new doctor. "You're still bleeding," he told me after the examination, "but your uterus is thick, which is a good sign. And your cervix is closed which is also a good sign. We'll do a sonogram and lab tests. I have a wedding to attend. You go home and rest, and I'll call you later today with the test results."

When the doctor called back, he said, "I want to tell you that you are carrying a very viable eleven-week old baby. We don't know why you're bleeding, but we can't find anything wrong and the baby is fine."

We thanked the doctor and hung up the phone praising the Lord, and so elated that God had shone His favor upon us. We called our Prayer Support to alert everyone with the good news.

Later in his office, the new doctor asked "Why did you to resist having the "D and C" when the doctor tried to get you to have it?"

"The Lord spoke to me and told me not to have it," I answered.

Shaking his head in amazement, he said, "It's a good thing you did not have that procedure – otherwise you would have been scraping out a living baby."

Throughout my pregnancy, there were other difficult "episodes," yet there was caring, loving encouragement from my husband, our relatives, our Prayer Support, our church family, and our loved ones in America and abroad. Most importantly, I am grateful for the wisdom of the Lord through His Holy Spirit and His Holy Word and for those who believed with me.

At last, after two and half hours of labor, our precious baby was being born. Oh! …the magnificent joy of holding this beautiful bundle of blessings in my arms. How wonderful to see her, to hold her, to kiss her, to lay my cheek against her little cheek.

She was not just our "child"; she was a "representation" of God's faithfulness. Even if she had not lived, I would have still praised God. But what a blessing that she was alive and that God had caused me/us to "Push to the Front" with my faith and His wonderful wisdom.

That "baby" that the "expert" doctor at the emergency examining room did his best to get me to give up on is now, as of this writing, our 25 year old beautiful daughter, Sherah Danielle Thompson, who was born in perfect health on May 1, 1986 – and she is our only natural child. Her names are from the Holy Bible. Sherah means "Builder for God," and Danielle (named after Daniel of the Holy Bible), who was "beloved of God" and who had "wisdom of God." Sherah is known as the young lady who encourages people and builds them up with inspiration, and who asks them "Has anyone reminded you today that Jesus loves you?"

After graduating from Howard University's John H. Johnson School of Communications – Annenberg Honors Program, with a degree in Film, Radio and TV, Sherah Danielle is presently a graduate student at Regent University obtaining a MFA in Film Directing. Already her writing, directing and production projects have won awards – two of her projects were selected and shown to over 30 million households.

My friend, you may have a dream, a goal – something precious – that you are carrying in the "womb" of your heart. If you don't have such a goal at this time, more than likely you will in the future.

Would you like to know how to "Push to the Front?"

From my many personal experiences and my numerous experiences helping others to "Push to the Front," here are the tips I promised earlier:

SEVEN TIPS ON HOW YOU CAN PUSH TO THE FRONT WITH WISDOM

1. Know that wisdom is "the principle and supreme thing" that you should have to protect, bless and enrich you and your loved ones.

   The beginning of Wisdom is: get Wisdom (skillful and godly Wisdom)! [For skillful and godly Wisdom is the principal thing.] And with all you have gotten, get understanding (discernment, comprehension, and interpretation).

Proverbs 4:7 AMP Holy Bible

2. Know that wisdom is available to you.

 "[5] If any of you lacks wisdom, you should ask God, who gives generously to all without finding fault, and it will be given to you. [6] But when you ask, you must believe and not doubt, because the one who doubts is like a wave of the sea, blown and tossed by the wind. [7] That person should not expect to receive anything from the Lord. [8] Such a person is double-minded and unstable in all they do. James 1:5-8 NIV Holy Bible

3. Recognize the difference between faith (and belief) over presumption and foolishness.

 And without faith it is impossible to please God, because anyone who comes to him must believe that he exists and that he rewards those who earnestly seek him. Hebrews 11:6 NIV

4. Be prepared to handle risks, obstacles and criticism of your decisions.

 [2] Consider it pure joy, my brothers and sisters, whenever you face trials of many kinds, [3] because you know that the testing of your faith produces perseverance. [4] Let perseverance finish its work so that you may be mature and complete, not lacking anything. James 1:2-4 NIV

5. You can receive heavenly guidance and direction so that you make decisions that cause you to "Push to the Front."

 [4] So shall you find favor, good understanding, and high esteem in the sight [or judgment] of God and man. 5Lean on, trust in, and be confident in the Lord with all your heart and mind and do not rely on your own insight or understanding. 6In all your ways know, recognize, and acknowledge Him, and He will direct and make straight and plain your paths. Proverbs 3:4-6

6. Make Room for Jesus in your everyday life so that it is easier for you to make all kinds and sizes of decisions.

But seek (aim at and strive after) first of all His kingdom and His righteousness (His way of doing and being right), and then all these things taken together will be given you besides. Matthew 6:33 AMP

7. Prayer and a prayer covering are important to help you to know how to reap the benefits for you, your loved ones, your situations and your future.

   I do not cease to give thanks for you, making mention of you in my prayers, Ephesians 1:16 AMP

   Now to Him Who, by (in consequence of) the [action of His] power that is at work within us, is able to [carry out His purpose and] do superabundantly, far over and above all that we [dare] ask or think [infinitely beyond our highest prayers, desires, thoughts, hopes, or dreams] Ephesians 3:20 AMP

   6Do not fret or have any anxiety about anything, but in every circumstance and in everything, by prayer and petition (definite requests), with thanksgiving, continue to make your wants known to God. Philippians 4:6 AMP

To learn more about the importance of prayer and a prayer covering, please contact me at info@MakeRoom4Jesus.com for your free CD.

It is my joy to have shared with you one of my many experiences of how these principles and prayer – operate and bless my life and enable me to daily "push to the front" of any circumstance and situation I may encounter.

You can receive your **FREE** video and audio on "God's Wisdom Success Principles" that give you greater and deeper insight on how to use these lessons and principles to "push to the front" in your life situations.

Please visit: http://www.MakeRoom4Jesus.com.

ABOUT EMMA JEAN

Dr. Emma Jean Thompson is internationally esteemed as a speaker, #1 Bestselling Author, motion picture producer and trusted advisor serving leaders in Ministry, Business, Education, Entertainment and other arenas.

Passionate about empowering women and men in business and in life, Dr. Thompson's powerful and proprietary **"God's Wisdom Success Principles™"** have guided thousands of people worldwide to achieve business breakthroughs and personal transformation. With audiences praising her work as "miraculous" and "inspirational", media including CNN, CSPAN, Time Magazine,USA Today, Fox TV, Christianity Today Magazine (twice on the front cover), BET, Jet Magazine, Time Magazine, and Miami Herald have already featured Dr. Thompson and her team. Other TV and media appearances include "The Brian Tracy Show," "The Michael Gerber Show" and "Success and Hope for You".

As an end-time Prophet and Apostle of God and Jesus Christ, Dr. Emma Jean will help **you** to profit and prosper. Building on timeless biblical principles, Dr. Thompson uses documented success stories and case studies to create step-by-step blueprints for her audience on how to more than double their income and their free time at the same time, enjoy rock-solid, meaningful relationships, and thrive in complete health (III John 2 Bible). Guiding men and women to joyfully discover and fulfill their God-given purpose, all while keeping "Make Room for Jesus™" in their everyday life their priority and foundation, is the compelling message that Dr. Emma Jean Thompson feeds her hungry crowds, leaving them filled with valuable insights, yet always eager for more.

Her husband, Dr. James J. Thompson Jr., along with the leadership and congregation of Integrity Church International, which is headquartered in Landover, Maryland, joyfully acknowledge Apostle Dr. Emma Jean Thompson as the lead Pastor and InternationalOverseer of their churches, missions and outreaches which include Ghana, West Africa, India and Jamaica.

Their daughter, Sherah Danielle, who at the time of this writing is a Masters of Fine Arts Graduate Film Directing Student at Regent University and also received her Bachelor of Fine Arts at Howard University. Sherah is also a #1 Bestselling Author.

Dr. Emma Jean Thompson is the Founder and CEO of **"MakeRoom4Jesus.com"** of which the December 2009 Dedication Celebration was sponsored and hosted by dear family friends **Dr. Nido R. and Mariana Qubein** at **High Point University in High Point, North Carolina.**

For the past 18 of her 33 years of ministry, Dr. Emma Jean has been in a time of intense prayer, preparation and research documenting that individuals, churches, businesses, schools, and any organizations that are experiencing significant success are using **"God's Wisdom Success Principles™"**- even if they are not aware.

Her "Purpose Passion" is to *"cause young people and adults to be blessed in every way in this earthly life AND to be ready for the coming of Jesus Christ and Judgment Day.*

You may contact Dr. Emma Jean at Info@DrEmmaJean.com or DrEmmaJean@MakeRoom4Jesus.com.

CHAPTER 24

CLEARING A TRAIL FOR SALES SUCCESS

BY DAVID DOMOS

Right now, there is probably a Sales Manager or company President somewhere uttering the words… "nothing happens until something is sold." I have heard this phrase in one form or another countless times over my career. Sales are an important function whether you are a small, independently-owned company or a large Fortune 500 company. Someone has to buy your product or service for your company to exist.

You're probably thinking that's obvious! With that being said, then why do a majority of the small businesses I have worked with over the years not given the support their sales staff needs to excel at their primary function – selling. Don't get me wrong, it's not just the small companies that pull their sales teams away from their core purpose, I have seen industry leaders have their staff spend countless hours performing tasks that do not increase sales for the company.

So, as a sales manager or business owner, you should be looking at ways to get your sales team spending the majority of its time selling. Like the early settlers who headed west in search of gold and riches, the first to make the trek helped clear the trail for future settlers. With every tree that was cleared along the trail, with every hole that was filled, with every bridge that was built, ...each increased the success rate of future settlers. If you want to find your gold and riches, you, as a leader in your organization, need to clear the way for your sales team to go out and find the gold, your clients.

Let's break down the issues that exist within many small and large companies separately. With small companies, it is usually a lack of resources or perceived lack of resources, while the bigger companies tend to overcomplicate the sales process. In reality, you need to create a hybrid of both to truly get the most out of your sales team.

First, let us take a look at the smaller organization. I have spent the last 17 years helping over 700 small, medium and large-sized business owners across the United States grow their sales. It is interesting to see the similarities and the differences among these organizations. Since they are independently owned, each one has its own business model. Even though each organization has their own model, there are two primary schools of thought on how they handle their sales professionals.

The first school of thought is a model that does not support their sales people in the most effective way. They have their sales people handling every aspect of customer interaction, whether it's a true sales function or not. Many small business owners have their sales people filling every role you would expect a large company to have. Here is a sampling of the roles many small business salespeople fill – in addition to the traditional sales function. They act as customer service, order entry, technical support, repair person, accounts receivable, inventory control, warehouse support and logistics. As you can see, many of the items take time away from finding the next customer. Many of these small business owners are very successful, but not to the degree of the second group of business owners. This first model can limit the financial success of an organization. With today's economic conditions, I have seen many of these companies close their doors or lay off most of their staff, because their revenue can no longer cover the overhead they amassed during the recent economic boom in the 2000's. If they had cleared the trail for their sales staff, many more of these businesses could have made it through these turbulent times.

The second school of thought is made up of more sophisticated business owners. They have taken the time to determine best practices for their organization. They have also formalized policies and procedures. This group of business owners has focused on ways to get more productivity out of each individual sales person. They focus on removing the time obstacles that are present in the first group. They hire non-sales staff to handle the non-traditional sales functions performed by the sales people in group one. This leads to their sales teams being much more productive.

Here is a real world example of the difference between the two groups. I worked with two companies in the Boston area with the same product offerings and very similar sales levels. The main difference between the two organizations was that one had 7 full-time sales people handling most of the roles listed in group one. The second company had 2 full-time and 1 part-time sales people, with an expediter who focused on the nontraditional sales activities. The second company was able to produce just as much in sales as the first company and was more profitable since they had lower sales overhead. This is just one of many examples that clearly show that more time selling equates to greater sales and profitability.

Now let's focus on the larger organizations. My 15 plus years in a sales leadership role for a Fortune 500 industry leader taught me a lot about what to do, as well as what not to do. It is amazing to me how similar the stories are from sales professionals working with other Fortune 500 companies. It seems that many management teams have the same mindset. The result is a sales team that has very little time to sell.

One of the main challenges sales professionals face within large organizations is the proverbial 'fire drill.' This is where management feels they need instant gratification. Yes, this happens in organizations all around the world. It might be a survey, a report or task that must be completed within a short time frame. Many managers look for satisfactory completion of the activity by close of business the same day it was requested. The problem with this management approach is that they do not pause to think of what each of the representatives already have scheduled that day. Do they have visits scheduled with one of their key customers or the A+ prospect they have been trying to close for months? If the managers would only pause to think what the impact of missed or delayed appointments with these customers could have on the future success of the organization, they may have acted differently.

Sales representatives complain about the proverbial 'fire drill.' "Don't they respect our time?"... or "Do they think we are sitting around waiting for something to do?"… or "I guess I'm really not a sales person?" If sales representatives feel undervalued or unappreciated it is only a matter of time before they start a job search looking for a company that appreciates what they have to offer.

Here is an example of a 'fire drill' a sales representative recently shared with me. The entire sales force was contacted and instructed that they had to go into their CRM system and review and update every contact, and it had to be completed the day of the request. In the case of this sales representative, he had over 850 contacts to review and update for the accounts that were assigned to him. Now let's do the math, if he had completed the review of one contact per minute it would have taken him over 14 hours to complete the request. This representative had to cancel all his appointments for that day to give it the attention that was requested by that company's management team. Based on the limited time frame, he did not give it the detailed review it deserved.

To avoid the problems associated with the 'fire drill,' ask yourself if this really needs to be completed today or tomorrow? If not, slow down long enough to give your sales team a week or more to complete a new task. This gives your sales representatives the ability to adjust their schedules in a way that will not have a negative impact on your business. Experience has shown me that the data you receive from your sales force will be more precise when they have been given enough time to complete a task. If you insist on a reply the same day, you may not get the information that you really need. Ask yourself: is it more important in your decision-making process to have the data now or to have it right? If you are like most managers, you want truly accurate information.

In addition to 'fire drills,' many organizations will schedule a conference call or a web meeting on short notice. Even those who schedule these meetings a week or two in advance don't think about the time they hold these meetings. The location of the management team tends to drive which half of the country ends up having to sit in a home office waiting for the meeting to begin. Yes they can be doing paperwork, but in many cases they had already scheduled meetings with current customers or prospects. East Coast organizations will often hold meetings at 11:00am EST or 4:00pm EST, which has either the East Coast Representatives sitting around or the West Coast Representatives sitting around. It's not always possible, but many organizations attempt to hold two different meetings, one at 8:00am Eastern then another at 8:00am Western. The people in the other time zones will select between the two options. I have seen web meetings that have 2 or 3 people sitting in a meeting room at a corporate office force 150 sales representatives to block off a half-a-day for one of these meetings. So, much of the sales force has to block-off three additional hours to accommodate the schedule of 2 or 3 people back at corporate. In many cases, it might be better for those 2 or 3 people to do the meeting twice and give the affected sales staff those 3 hours back. In this scenario, the office personnel would sacrifice an additional hour each versus 50 to 75 sales representatives sacrificing 2 to 3 hours each. It may not always be possible to conduct a web meeting twice, but you, as managers, should at least look at the best way to allocate your resources.

Another time waster in large organizations is reporting that is not read. You should occasionally review all the reporting that your sales representatives are required to submit. You may find that some reports lose their usefulness over time. There was one report that our sales representatives were filling out every week that was not reviewed or used by anyone in the organization, in fact they had not been used for 4 or 5 years. The person they were sending them into would just file them away and after they had enough of them they would throw out the older ones. When questioned, that person said, "When I got this job no one told me what to do with this report." Needless to say, that report was no longer completed by the sales representatives. In this case there were 40 people, each spending roughly 30 minutes a week to complete this useless report. Each representative spent an additional 26 hours per year to fill out this report.

I have heard countless examples of required reporting that sales representatives are required to complete, but never receive feedback on. I have also heard from many sales managers of reports they require, but never utilize. If a report is not being read or not bringing value to the organization it should no longer exist.

Reporting can be of incredible value to your organization, you just want to be sure you are only getting the reporting you need. A good alternative to traditional reports is implementation of a Customer Relationship Management system, or CRM. This is something that both large and small companies will benefit from. They can manage schedules, follow up activities, leads, sales cycles, potential value by stage, determine closing ratio's, lead sources, along with countless other items you will want to track. If developed properly, these systems can handle most of your sales management reporting needs. In just a few clicks you can gather information about trends and make projections to make informed decisions. CRM systems let you and your sales representatives better manage the entire sales process. With proper training and a commitment to fully implement, your sales team will save time and be more responsive to your customers. One word of caution is to be careful not to go overboard and overcomplicate your CRM system. There are many cloud-based versions available that fit into any budget. Try it; you will be glad you did.

In summary be sure to formalize your policies and procedures. If you want to run an efficient sales team, don't count on tribal knowledge. Everyone needs to be on the same page on how a process should flow. These formalized policies and procedures make it easier for employees and ensure a level of consistency. Building formalized policies and procedures is the foundation of a good sales force.

As you can see, the best practice should be somewhere in the middle between what small organizations are doing versus large organizations. Small organizations need to provide more sales support, while large organizations need to simplify the sales process.

Here are the 10 critical 'to do's' that are the foundation for clearing a trail for sales success:

1. Review all sales activities
2. Remove any activities that do not enhance the sales process
3. Simplify the sales process
4. Hire support staff for non-sales activities
5. Avoid 'fire drills' by providing sufficient time to complete new projects and reports
6. Provide ample time to plan for phone and web meetings

7. Make sure all paperwork is necessary
8. Implement a CRM system as main reporting tool
9. Formalize your policies and procedures
10. Make sure your representatives are in front of your customers and prospects

Both large and small organizations need to focus their sales team's time on selling. They must avoid unneeded and unnecessary involvement in non-sales activities that take time away from your current and future customers. The battle for customers is won face-to-face, and one thing that has become evident to me over the years is that people tend to buy from the sales representatives they see or hear from most. Think on this truth, if your sales people are not in front of your customers, someone else will be.

Commit to clearing a trail for sales success!

ABOUT DAVID

David Domos is the National Sales Manager for Custom Cupboards, Inc. They are a company that specializes in bringing exceptional value and style to consumers looking to purchase custom Kitchen and Bathroom cabinetry. David continues to focus on simplifying the sales process. He has created easy-to-follow, real-world-tested programs and templates that provide measurable results focused on improved performance at both the field and management levels.

Prior to his current role, David was a Director of Sales for a billion-dollar Division of a Fortune 500 company. This manufacturer had the largest volume and highest brand recognition in the industry. In this role he was responsible for the sales operations of its independent dealer base. During his 15 plus years with that company, he received several promotions with increasing responsibility in its sales division, and was a significant contributor to its growth.

David is a member of the Sales Management Association. He graduated from Indiana Wesleyan University with a Bachelor's degree in Business Administration, and Kent State University with an Associate's Degree in Technical Studies. He also graduated with distinction from the Masco Leadership Program – an award winning co-operative between the Masco Corporation and Michigan State University, which certifies graduates in Operations Management. Only 30 managers were selected to attend the program out of its 40,000 employees that year. David's leadership ability was key to his being named as one of the programs distinguished alumni and his participation in this book is yet another step towards his goal of self-actualization.

David is still deeply in love with his wife of over 20 years, Pamela. He is also the proud father of three children, Jenna, Delaney and Dylan.

CHAPTER 25

THE ONLY GAME IN TOWN:

4 POWERFUL SECRETS TO BUILDING YOUR UNIQUE AND EXCLUSIVE MARKETING PLATFORM

BY JW DICKS, ESQ., NICK NANTON, ESQ., AND LINDSAY DICKS

"Your brand had better be delivering something special, or it's not going to get the business."

~ Warren Buffet

If you're a business owner, professional or entrepreneur in today's economy, you know it's much more of a struggle for market share than ever before. The bad news is that your main competition is no longer limited to your neighborhood. The good news is that, for the time being, it's still limited to this planet.

It used to be simple to build a successful business. Many times, it was just a matter of getting a great location on the corner of the busiest street in town, joining the local chamber of commerce, and building a solid and trustworthy reputation along with a healthy client base.

Then the internet came along. In the early days it was easy to nab a great domain name that was guaranteed to get you traffic. Cars.com, Pets.com, Lawyer.com…as long as you had something simple and straight to the point, you were set. Now, it's a matter of making endless lists of words that are relevant to your business, until you finally manage to put a few of them together to create a domain name that's available but barely makes sense.

On a larger scale, online marketing is something everyone is now doing on some level – whether it's just Facebook posts or full-blown cross-platform campaigns. Since the great recession hit, there have been more businesses fighting over less dollars, making it harder and harder to stand out from the pack – especially when you're caught between the giant companies that can crush you with their marketing budgets, and the one-man bands that are lucky enough to come up with a genius viral campaign that blows you away.

That means having an awesome product or service just isn't enough – you have to have a distinctive and memorable marketing niche to go along with it, if you truly want to "push to the front." It's a challenge we face every day at our Celebrity Branding® Agency whenever we go to work with our clients. In this chapter, we'll share some of our secrets of how we meet that challenge and how you can create your own unique and exclusive marketing platform.

SECRET #1: MAKE THEM JOIN *YOUR* CLUB

When you control the conversation, you've put yourself in the driver's seat when it comes to success. There's a reason they say the President always has "the bully pulpit," when it comes to setting agendas and political dialogue; he's the head of the free world and the person we expect to set the tone for our country.

How do you build that kind of bully pulpit for yourself in *your* business sector? Well, the law itself gives you certain tools you can use to keep away the competition and to make you and your product or service more valuable. Yes, two out of three of us are lawyers, so we understand how to make those tools work both for our own businesses as well as our clients' (and there's a reason you see that little "®" or

"TM" on many of our company names and titles).

Those tools include legally defining associations, franchises, area exclusives, as well as trademarks and patents on your systems and processes, so that nobody can take your ideas and make them their own. And people have to come to *you* to avail themselves of those ideas.

We utilized many of those tools, including name trademark, association structure and certification, to form an entire network of industry experts under our America's PremierExperts® banner. If you want to be an official PremierExpert® or CelebrityExpert® and get all the perks of that status, only we can make that happen. That not only allows us to control the standards and quality of this membership, but it also helps identify ourselves as leaders in the branding industry.

And there's absolutely no reason you can't do the same in your industry, whatever it might be. A client of ours, Lisa Miller, spent a decade building her company whose emphasis is on helping hospitals cut costs – definitely a necessary business in this day and age. Now, she's expanding her expertise into other areas, and to that end, we helped her form the National Association of Expense Reduction Professionals using the legal tools we discussed earlier. She will train and certify others in her specialty, making her the *de facto* leader in a new and very in-demand field.

Creating your own coaching and mastermind groups is another popular way to position yourself as the expert in your field and share your knowledge. For example, Ben Glass, a very successful attorney in the Washington, DC area, has created his own organization for attorneys under the banner of Great Legal Marketing. Ben coaches and trains these attorneys how to use his own successful brand of marketing to bring in more businesses for their legal practice. He has built into his training: seminars, newsletters, mastermind group training and private coaching – all targeted to his niche field. This same business model has been successfully done in almost all other industries and the expansion possibilities are endless.

You can also create special events within your core client-base that helps bond them to your business. In the past year, we've combined specialized training programs with "can't miss" events such as **The**

Kentucky Derby and **The Grammys** that everyone wants to be a part of. Integrating high profile, fun and even glamorous events with your business adds an extra enjoyment factor that can't be beat – and creates another unique and high-powered reason to work with you.

SECRET #2:
CREATE NEW METHODS OF OPERATION

In 2005, Amazon.com, the biggest online retailer, introduced Amazon Prime – now, for a flat yearly fee, Amazon shoppers would get unlimited and no-cost two-day shipping when buying Amazon products. Regular Amazon customers loved the idea.

Wall Street, however, hated it.

The program was instantly deemed an unprofitable disaster by most financial analysts; it would be costly and drag down profits. And, as a matter of fact, both the stock and profits were negatively affected at first. But Jeff Bezos, the Amazon CEO, held firm and said the program would end up paying off. Within a couple of years, it had. Amazon Prime upped customer loyalty to Amazon, so that sales consistently rose – after all, if you were guaranteed two day free shipping by one shopping site, that would be the first place you'd go to buy something, right? Profits followed along, jumping a whopping 257% from 2006 to 2007.

Even now, however, Amazon continues to be questioned by financial analysts for focusing too much on infrastructure that will generate big-time future benefits. Bezos doesn't care, because he wants Amazon to be a very far-sighted company, continuing to risk short-term loss for long-term gain. That vision accounts for a lot of its singular success today; it's also garnered them tremendous repeat business and locked their customers in for the long run. It's perceived as *an exclusive business like no other.*

This is a strategy that can pay off with how you run your business internally as well.

For example, Google has a program it calls "Innovation Time Off," where Google engineers are allowed to spend as much as 20% of their company time pursuing projects that interest them, but aren't officially endorsed or initiated by management itself. They're kind of off the clock while they're still on the clock.

Now, throwing away a fifth of the cost of highly-paid tech teams in order to allow them to work on whatever they feel like working on might seem like company suicide. However, Marissa Mayer, Google's Vice President of Search Products and User Experience, says that half of all new product launches in recent years have originated from the Innovation Time Off program. Those new products include such now-iconic features as Google Gmail, Google News and AdSense.

These products not only have helped build Google's brand and online dominance, they've also enhanced Google's cutting-edge reputation as a company that encourages and creates innovation. Again, it's viewed as a company like no other – an "exclusive" brand that no one else can touch.

SECRET #3: BUILD A BETTER MOUSETRAP

Often, how you set up your payment and fulfillment systems can dramatically differentiate you from your competition – especially if you take aim at a common customer complaint about your industry.

Take the simple act of calling a plumber. How many times after you set up an appointment, do you end up sitting around the house, waiting for him to show up – or any kind of service person for that matter? Their excuse is always that they're running late due to previous appointments – and all it does is make you feel like their time is worth more than yours, even though you're the customer. It's frustrating, especially when, in today's world, we're overscheduled as it is.

Well, The Ben Franklin Plumbing franchise makes it a point to *guarantee* they will show up for a service appointment on time – or it's money out of *their* pocket. They say, "Any delay and we pay" – and they mean it, offering $5 for every minute they're late, up to a maximum of $300. In other words, they've now reversed the situation entirely – these are people with whom you set up appointments and then you start *hoping* they're late. And it works for them – every year, they move up the All-Star Franchise list.

Zappos.com is another company renowned as much for its customer service as its actual products. There was a time that buying shoes online – especially dress shoes – would have seemed crazy. You can't see how they look on your feet or fit – and then you have to pay to send them back again if they're not right?

Well, Zappos also reversed the situation – they offered two-way free shipping (in other words, if you wanted to send the shoes back, it cost you nothing), which encouraged customers to order different styles, sizes and colors, try them on in the comfort of their own homes, and then send back the ones that you don't want for a fast no-hassle (and no-cost) refund. By creating this kind of service-driven system, they create an exclusive platform for themselves just as Ben Franklin Plumbing did.

Another example. The timeshare vacation is one that has been plagued by cons and scams over the years. The Disney corporation, however, applied its own squeaky-clean brand to the industry to create the Disney Vacation Club (…see? They formed their own club too!), with a special menu of extra guest benefits and points systems that make their customers feel appreciated and rewarded for their investments. And, of course, the Disney name instantly makes families feel comfortable with them.

Now, exclusive systems can also be formulated to actually make a customer want to pay *more* than they ever would have normally – and, simultaneously, make the business seem more exclusive and unique than ever before.

Our case in point here is a restaurant in Chicago named "Next," a new eatery opened by a famous local chef. Don't bother to call and try to get a reservation the next time you're in the Windy City – you can't. Instead, potential diners have to buy online, all-inclusive (drinks, main course, dessert, tip, etc.) "meal tickets" that begin at the $45 to $75 range.

We say "begin" at, because restaurants have one big problem – everyone wants to eat there at the same peak times and nights. That increased demand for those times, however, does not usually result in an increased profit from the individual customers who dine at those times. Next solves that problem – because the meal tickets for dining at high demand times cost substantially *more.*

Of course, it helps that this restaurant is currently a hot commodity and everyone is desperate to eat there. But, on the other hand, the online system causes even *more* demand – meal tickets are being resold on sites like eBay for as much as $3000 to desperate diners anxious to get in at the time of their choosing.

Not only that, but the Next system solves another big restaurant economic problem – no-shows. When people make a reservation and don't come, the restaurant loses that potential money. When it sells a ticket in advance, however, and nobody comes, it's the person who bought the ticket who's out of luck, not the restaurant.

In all of the above examples, the company's customer systems actually help define the business itself to consumers. When they think of Next, they think of the online reservation system; when they think of Ben Franklin (the plumbing company, not the founding father), they think of their "punctual promise." When a system is effective and high profile enough, it becomes an integral brand differentiator – in effect, your USP (Unique Selling Proposition): *This is how we sell – and nobody else does this.*

SECRET #4:
SELL IT WITH A STAR

How many of you out there have heard of Michael Boehm?

No clue? Well, that's the point of this section, because Boehm created one of the most famous and successful products of the last two decades – but his name isn't the one you think of when it comes to this particular item. And even though the product was an obvious winner, when Boehm had it ready to go to market, he couldn't find a corporate backer to help him put up the money and marketing to make it happen.

That's when he decided he needed some star power. His invention was a portable contact grill that cooks food items faster and more healthfully – and he knew boxer George Foreman ate two burgers before every fight and that he and his two sons loved to cook meat. He approached Foreman's management, and all agreed that the product and the star were an amazing fit.

Once Foreman was on board, Boehm had the credibility to get the corporate backing he needed – and to ultimately sell over a 100 million George Foreman Grills.

Sometimes a Boehm has to find a Foreman to achieve his entrepreneurial dreams – because a unique testimonial or endorsement is yet another way to create a special position for your business or product. Celebrities and notables help you cut through the clutter in an entirely different way to help get you noticed by potential customers.

The pitfalls here, of course, are obvious: just ask the companies Tiger Woods had endorsement deals with before his extracurricular activities came to light. You have to make sure the celebrity you approach makes sense for your brand and your base, and is also an ethical person that you can feel comfortable having a long-term relationship with (especially if you're going to put the person's name on your product or service).

Of course, the other way to work this is to make *yourself* the star and the unique brand. This, of course, helps if you have a certain level of star power, savvy and charisma. People like Richard Branson and Donald Trump know how to capture the spotlight and keep it firmly trained on them – they're experts on how to build their names to the point where they can slap it on anything and easily make a few million.

Along the same lines, and a method we use successfully for our clients, is to establish *you* as the *expert* in your field, through authoring books, doing TV interviews on ABC, NBC, CBS, and FOX, getting press in "USA Today," "The New York Times" and other local and national publications, and creating regular, authoritative online content under your name. We provide the coaching and training, as well as the opportunities, for entrepreneurs to effectively 'pull off' all of the above. That's because we know that this is the *most* important element of creating a unique and exclusive marketing platform.

Why? Because when *you* become the face of your own business and its most powerful selling tool, *nobody* can take that away (unless you have a twin!). Once you've built your own personal brand, you've created the ultimate in exclusivity, so that potential clients don't go looking for just *anyone* who does what you do – instead, they believe they have to have YOU and no one else.

These are just a few of the most powerful and effective ways you can push your business or enterprise to the front by making it one-of-a-kind. When you create a unique and exclusive marketing platform, you make yourself the *only* choice in your business category – and that means you become the only game in town.

And when you're the only game in town… you generally win at it!

ABOUT JW

JW Dicks, Esq. is America's foremost authority on using personal branding for business development. He has created some of the most successful brand and marketing campaigns for business and professional clients to make them the Credible Celebrity Expert in their field and build multi-million dollar businesses using their recognized status.

JW Dicks has started, bought, built, and sold a large number of businesses over his 39 year career and developed a loyal international following as a business attorney, author, speaker, consultant, and business expert's coach. He not only practices what he preaches by using his strategies to build his own businesses he also applies those same concepts to help clients grow their business or professional practice the ways he does.

JW has been extensively quoted in such national media as USA Today, The Wall Street Journal, Newsweek, Inc. Magazine, Forbes.com, CNBC.Com, and Fortune Small business. His television appearances include ABC, NBC, CBS and FOX affiliate stations around the country. He is the resident branding expert for Fast Company's internationally syndicated blog and is the publisher of Celebrity Expert Insider, a monthly newsletter targeting business and brand building strategies.

JW has written over 22 books, including numerous best sellers, and has been inducted into the National Academy of Best Selling Authors. He is also an Emmy nominated Executive Producer.

JW is married to Linda, his wife of 38 years and they have two daughters, a granddaughter and two Yorkies. JW is a 6th generation Floridian and splits time between his home in Orlando and beach house on the Florida west coast.

ABOUT NICK

An Emmy Award Winning Director and Producer, Nick Nanton, Esq., is known as The Celebrity Lawyer and Agent to top Celebrity Experts for his role in developing and marketing business and professional experts, through personal branding, media, marketing and PR to help them gain credibility and recognition for their accomplishments. Nick is recognized as the nation's leading expert on personal branding as Fast Company Magazine's Expert Blogger on the subject and lectures regularly on the topic at the University of Central Florida. His book *Celebrity Branding You®* has been selected as the textbook on personal branding at the University.

The CEO of The Dicks + Nanton Celebrity Branding Agency, Nick is an award winning director, producer and songwriter who has worked on everything from large scale events to television shows with the likes of Bill Cosby, President George H.W. Bush, **Brian Tracy**, Michael Gerber and many more.

Nick is recognized as one of the top thought-leaders in the business world and has co-authored 10 best-selling books, including the breakthrough hit ***Celebrity Branding You!®***.

Nick serves as publisher of Celebrity Press™, a publishing company that produces and releases books by top Business Experts. CelebrityPress has published books by Brian Tracy, **Mari Smith**, Ron Legrand and many other celebrity experts and Nick has led the marketing and PR campaigns that have driven more than 300 authors to Best-Seller status. Nick has been seen in USA Today, The Wall St. Journal, Newsweek, Inc. Magazine, The New York Times, Entrepreneur® Magazine, **FastCompany.com** and has appeared on ABC, NBC, CBS, and FOX television affiliates around the country speaking on subjects ranging from branding, marketing and law, to American Idol.

Nick is a member of the Florida Bar, holds a JD from the University of Florida Levin College of Law, as well as a BSBA in Finance from the University of Florida's Warrington College of Business. Nick is a voting member of The National Academy of Recording Arts & Sciences (NARAS, Home to The GRAMMYs), a member of The National Academy of Television Arts & Sciences (Home to the Emmy Awards) co-founder of the National Academy of Best-Selling Authors, a 6-time Telly Award winner, and spends his spare time working with Young Life, Downtown Credo Orlando, Florida Hospital and rooting for the Florida Gators with his wife Kristina and their three children, Brock, Bowen and Addison..

ABOUT LINDSAY

Lindsay Dicks helps her clients tell their stories in the online world. Being brought up around a family of marketers, but a product of Generation Y, Lindsay naturally gravitated to the new world of online marketing. Lindsay began freelance writing in 2000 and soon after launched her own PR firm that thrived by offering an in-your-face "Guaranteed PR" that was one of the first of its type in the nation.

Lindsay's new media career is centered on her philosophy that "people buy people." Her goal is to help her clients build a relationship with their prospects and customers. Once that relationship is built and they learn to trust them as the expert in their field then they will do business with them. Lindsay also built a patent-pending process called "circular marketing" that utilizes social media marketing, content marketing and search engine optimization to create online "buzz" for her clients that helps them to convey their business and personal story. Lindsay's clientele span the entire business map and range from doctors and small business owners to Inc 500 CEOs.

Lindsay is a graduate of the University of Florida. She is the CEO of CelebritySites™, an online marketing company specializing in social media and online personal branding. Lindsay is also a multi-best-selling author including the best-selling book "Power Principles for Success" which she co-authored with Brian Tracy. She was also selected as one of America's PremierExperts™ and has been quoted in Newsweek, the Wall Street Journal, USA Today, Inc Magazine as well as featured on NBC, ABC, and CBS television affiliates speaking on social media, search engine optimization and making more money online. Lindsay was also recently brought on FOX 35 News as their Online Marketing Expert.

Lindsay, a national speaker, has shared the stage with some of the top speakers in the world such as Brian Tracy, Lee Milteer, Ron LeGrand, Arielle Ford, David Bullock, Brian Horn, Peter Shankman and many others. Lindsay was also a Producer on the Emmy nominated film Jacob's Turn.

You can connect with Lindsay at:

Lindsay@CelebritySites.com
www.twitter.com/LindsayMDicks
www.facebook.com/LindsayDicks

CHAPTER 26

7 TIPS ON GOAL ACHIEVEMENT

BY TARIK ALSHARAFI

Wouldn't you want to simply achieve any goal and any plan you set for yourself, effortlessly and without burden? I have worked with sales goals, business plans, work plans, personal task lists, small and large projects for the past ten years. I have built my own CODE of how to manage my emotions while I am pursuing my success. This CODE is simply a set of techniques that I revert back to when I have certain emotions or feelings that stand between me and my goals. These techniques help me quickly pinpoint where the problem is, and help realign my energy towards keeping on track.

The following Tips are the result of improving and testing the CODE in many different ways. I don't have as much emotional fight with myself anymore because I use these tips and techniques. I hope you will be able to benefit from them in pursuing your success.

HOW IT ALL STARTED, A $100,000 PROJECT TO TEACH ME A LESSON...

When I started my first business, my partner and I had a goal to make the first sale at any cost. We worked hard for the first few days with our staff to get the first deal. Finally our break came, we made a website for our next-door business for $120. We celebrated for months. One year later, we were frustrated and we wanted to become rich quickly. We were working hard, but we were spending all that came in.

With luck and hard work, we were able to land a deal to make 20,000 T-Shirts for a large company in less than a month. This was a $100,000 deal. We worked for 10-12 hours a day and our staff increased from 5 to 30 working on 24-hour shifts. We achieved the project and delivered on-time. We received our payments, calculated our profits and started spending. We paid off some debt, paid rent for 6 months, and had payroll for 6 months as well. No money was left for luxury or personal satisfaction. We were frustrated, angry, and resented all that wasted energy.

What happened? Why did a goal of $120 make us happy and a goal of $100,000 make us feel like quitting? It was the focus of our goals which had changed over time. The goal changed from building and growing our business to becoming rich. We moved our focus from a goal outside of ourselves, to a goal focused on us and our personal satisfaction.

Now I delicately monitor my emotions and my focus to simplify my goals, simplify the process of achieving them and celebrate small successes every day. Below are the **Top Seven** techniques that I use to be and feel wealthy every day of the goal-achieving process. I have also built a website to share these techniques and others on: www.IAmWealthyToday.com

1. REMOVE YOU FROM YOUR GOALS!

To be able to enjoy the process of achieving your goals, you have to remove yourself from them. What this means is that you should do what you do either because you enjoy it or because you want someone else to enjoy the outcome of your work. If you are working towards a financial goal that you feel you will enjoy spending once reached, then let me tell you that you will want more once you get there. You will always feel dissatisfied about achieving any financial goal. This doesn't mean you shouldn't have financial goals. You can have financial goals, but for the right reasons.

Make your goals in a way so as to share the benefit from achieving them with others. For example, you can have a financial goal to improve the livelihood of your family (you included). You can have another financial goal to grow your business and benefit your staff, partners and customers. You can also have a financial or a business goal to benefit your children. In my country, Yemen, we have a saying, "when you build, you always build for your grandchildren." Your financial goal can be focused on benefiting your family, friends, partners, neighbors, city, country, mankind, etc.

This goal-setting method helps disassociate greed and ego from pursuing financial goals. It helps focus your attention on higher-than-self objectives in your life. It has helped me feel great every day of pursuing my goals – not only when I achieve them.

"To get the full value of a joy, you must have somebody to divide it with."

~ Mark Twain, Writer

2. TURN FINANCIAL GOALS INTO HOURS

All my business and professional goals (including financial) are translated into controllable, actionable objectives and tasks. For example, if I have a sales target to achieve $10,000 in sales, then I turn that into 20 cold calls, 3 calls to old customers and 5 hours of research and development. All of them are in my control and I can measure if I did them or not. If I don't achieve the $10,000, then I simply change/improve the tasks above to something that will get me closer to my target of $10,000. This allows me to focus on what I can control and achieve (given my time, energy and resources) rather than a purely financial goal which I cannot control, and one that is out of my hands (maybe in my boss' or customer's hands) and will leave me frustrated if not achieved. Your energy should be directed to tasks that you can do and be challenged with, and results will follow.

"Success is not to be pursued; it is to be attracted by the person you become."

~ Jim Rohn, Author

3. PRIORITIZE YOUR ATTENTION!

Have you ever just felt like quitting everything? Wanted to just stop working, thinking about business, and money issues, and family issues, etc.? Did you feel like turning off your phone and just staring at the TV for countless hours to distract yourself from the way you feel – then went to bed really exhausted? You might be overwhelmed.

To deal with the 'overwhelm' factor, you need to prioritize your life. I prioritize my businesses and functions, depending on how much I enjoy each one and the consequences each one poses. For example, I have found that if I have an issue in my real estate business, I wouldn't be able to do any other work until I resolve that issue. This is because I have most of my net worth in that business, and I need to ensure that it is working 100% before I can work on anything else. I have now prioritized all my businesses, job, family, friends, fun activities …etc. I enjoy my work better now and I can shift gears quickly to where my attention is required.

So, when you feel overwhelmed, ask yourself what is the most *critical* thing right now that is bothering you – and schedule time to work on that before anything else. If you cannot find an answer to that question, ask yourself what is the most *enjoyable* thing you could work on right now – and schedule time to go and do that right away.

"The key is not to prioritize what is on the schedule, but to schedule your priorities."

~ Stephen Covey, Author and Speaker

4. GIVE YOUR GOALS A SCORE! NO MORE PASS OR FAIL

During our schooling we get a score for courses, and if it is below a certain point, we fail that course. However in business and in real life, there is no fail. There is only learning from mistakes. If you make a goal, and you don't achieve it, then you already have made progress in your life by thinking of the goal, and by thinking of how to achieve it. Making the goal in itself means you already passed; now, depending on how much you work, you get a score of A, B, C, ...etc.

For example, if you make a goal to increase your salary by $1,000, then you should rate your progress towards that goal appropriately. For example: A – if you achieve it all, B – if you achieve 66% of it, and C – if you achieve 33% of it – or any similar combination (maybe a D for no achievement). Remember you should already be happy you made the goal – which is already "progress". This reduces negative feelings of low achievement and helps us to do better by tracking goal achievements.

"Failure should be our teacher, not our undertaker. Failure is delay not defeat. It is a temporary detour, not a dead end."

~ Denis Waitley

5. GIVE YOUR GOALS CLARITY AND ENJOYMENT

I use visualization to see my goals as "already achieved" and enjoy the feelings associated with that. Sometimes, when I feel down or have too many things to do, I have to use detailed visualization for the next action, the reward, and the achievement.

Here is an example, if you have a goal to write a one-page report today and you can't 'get your head around it,' you can use this technique. First, you reduce it to a smaller-sized objective, for example, the first paragraph. Visualize that you already have done a perfect first paragraph. Then visualize giving yourself a small reward for achieving that small paragraph. Now keep visualizing how you would feel after having the reward and achieving that small but important objective.

Now open your eyes and go write that paragraph. It will be ten times easier once you have internalized it's achievement in your head. If you still feel you cannot get your head around starting, reduce the objective to one sentence, one word, just opening the file, ... etc.

"Visualize this thing that you want, see it, feel it, believe in it. Make your mental blue print, and begin to build."

~ Robert Collier

6. CONNECT THE ELECTRICITY

How much energy do you have during the day? It's good to keep track of your energy on a scale of 1-10 on daily basis and see what activities increase your energy and what decreases it. 10 is your best, most energetic, smartest day and 1 is when you are good only for breathing and watching TV. Here are three tips I use to try to be a 7-8 most of my days:

First – I must get 9-10 hours of sleep. Sorry, the standard 7-8 hours doesn't work for me. I live in Sanaa city, which is around 2500 meters above sea level, which I think contributes to a requirement for longer sleep. Measure your sleeping need.

Second – I must walk/sprint for 15-20 minutes every day. For example, early in the morning, I would walk 5 minutes, sprint for 5 and walk again for 5 (I do it at home either on the treadmill or in the garden). This keeps me alert and energetic most of the day. Note: If I can't reach a 7 with this exercise especially when I have a large task to complete, I increase the exercise period to 45 minutes. It works wonders.

Third – I try to the greatest extent possible to follow Brian Tracy's advice to avoid the three white poisons: Sugar, Salt and Flour. I try to focus my diet on high protein and greens, eat less than I feel I need and only eat when I get hungry. I stay alert, awake and never sluggish like I do after a large meal.

Consider the above three recommendations to be similar to the three pins of a 220V electric plug, if you have only one or two pins working, you might not function at your best ☺.

"You have to gather your energy together...conserving it and insulating it from dissipation in every direction other than that of your purpose."

~ Walter Russell

7. ASK FOR DIRECTIONS!

If you don't know how to start a project or a business, just start doing it, and ask for directions along the way. You learn how to manage a business while you are managing a business. You learn how to write while you are writing. Writing guides can help you improve, but they can never make you a good writer. I enjoy writing, so I started writing two years ago (just on my laptop, in MS Word documents). Then I felt ready for the next step, I researched for the best way to share my knowledge. I recently started my blog site and Newsletter and started sharing my writings with others.

If you have similar passions and enjoy writing and would like to start your own blog website, I can help you – with everything from the domain registration and hosting to blog setup – in no time. Just go to my site: www.iamwealthytoday.com/blogoffer and get a special 50% discount. Use the discount code "pushingtothefront".

"Skill to do comes of doing."

~ Ralph Waldo Emerson, Poet

CONCLUSION – BE WEALTHY TODAY.

My focus is different now, I still have yearly, monthly and weekly goals, some of which are financial, but my ultimate purpose in life is the daily achievement of personal excellence and happiness. Once I changed my focus from yearly financial goals to daily fulfillment of my life's time on earth, I have become happier, healthier and more appreciated by people around me. I still have negative emotions, but I use the CODE to implement techniques that have worked in similar situations or make new ones. I have selected above what I feel are the Top Seven tips to make you feel wealthy every day while pursuing your goals. I hope you make use of them like I do. If you'd like to learn more, you can sign up for my free Newsletter at: www.iamwealthytoday.com

"Set peace of mind as your highest goal, and organize your life around it."

~ Brian Tracy, Speaker, Author, Consultant

ABOUT TARIK

Tarik Alsharafi, MBA, CMQ/OE, PMP, CCNP, CCDP is the founder of IamWealthyToday.com where he shares how to be wealthy and successful every day of your life. Tarik has over 10 years of experience working in many areas ranging from Administration and Operations to Quality and Change Management. He has managed large and complex projects from increasing business efficiency and effectiveness to real estate development to country wide IT networks.

Tarik has founded and co-founded several businesses in Information Technology, Design & Printing, Real Estate Development and FMCG. He has worked with International Organizations – including the United Nations, Oil Companies, Government Entities, Private Sector Companies, Consulting & Auditing Firms and Training Institutes.

From his experience, he believes success and wealth building are an everyday process. They can be achieved by changing our daily habits to wealthy ones, removing emotional barriers from one's mind, and allowing wealth and success to manifest themselves easily and smoothly.

IamWealthyToday.com provides both personal and business advice. The website is like a giant user guide with tips and techniques on how to be wealthy and live life to its fullest.

To be all you can be, visit IamWealthyToday.com and …

"Become Wealthy & Successful Everyday"

CHAPTER 27

GOALS:

THE 11 VITAL STEPS TO ACHIEVING EXTRAORDINARY RESULTS

BY MELISSA D. WHITAKER

"Whatever man can conceive and believe he can achieve."

~ Napoleon Hill

Throughout my life I have been asked the question, how did you do it? How did you buy your first two-story single family home by the age of 26? How did you become the Vice President of Sales & Operations of a small company by the age of 27? How did you start your own successful business at the age of 35? My answer to every person is simple: it is by setting goals, developing a plan, and taking action by implementing that plan. That combination along with a charismatic, positive attitude can only equal success.

It all started when I was ten years old. I had worked very hard to sell enough wrapping paper, Christmas cards and various other items to win one of the highest point items in the rewards book – a trampoline. I was so excited when it came in the mail that every day when I came home from school I jumped on it for hours. The trampoline was made with an inflated inner tube on the inside and the strong material on the top and bottom were held together with straps around the inner tube. Unfortunately, I jumped on it so much that one day the inner tube popped – I was devastated. I went to my father and asked him if he would buy me a new inner tube to fix the trampoline that I had worked so hard for. He said, "I don't have the money, get a job and pay for it yourself." I do not know why I was different than most children that I now see throwing tantrums when they want something and do not get their way. I did not even think about throwing a tantrum; I just took my dad's challenge to heart.

All I could think about for the next couple of days was what kind of job could I get, at the age of ten, to buy a new inner tube. Within a few days I figured it out. I walked one block away from my house to the newspaper press that printed and delivered the Northwest Herald in my hometown, Woodstock, Illinois. I walked in the front door and the old lady at the front desk, smoking a cigarette, asked me what I wanted. I told her I need a job. She of course asked me if my parents knew where I was since I was by myself and was so little that I looked much younger than even ten years old. I said, "Look at me lady, I'm only ten years old, of course my parents know where I'm at." The reality was my parents had no idea where I was or what I was up to. So the lady gave me the paperwork I needed to start a paper route, and she told me that I needed to have my parents sign the paperwork before returning it. Then I went home, figured out how to fill out the required paperwork and gave it to my dad at dinner to sign. My dad was shocked. He, of course, was somewhat kidding when he told me to "get a job," but I had no idea. I just had a goal in mind and NOTHING was going to stop me.

Needless to say, my dad signed the document and I started my route. When I started training with the junior high boy who currently had the route, the newspaper bag (you know the ones that have the bright orange shoulder straps) dragged on the ground since I was so little. The junior high boy thought I was crazy, and said "Are you sure you want to do this? Maybe you should wait until you are older." I said, "No way, tie up the shoulder strap for me and let's get going." You see, at that time, most of the people that had paper routes were boys and they did not start until they were in junior high. I did not care; I was determined to make this work so I could buy that new inner tube. After I collected money for the first time since I started my paper route, I went straight to the store and bought a new inner tube. I was elated. I did it!

That was just the beginning of my drive and persistence in achieving my goals in life. As I got older I applied the same mentality to everything I did and achieved amazing results at very young ages. So I started analyzing what steps I had taken throughout my life to achieve these types of results. What made my experiences different than others I know who set goals, but do not seem to achieve them? I am not referring to setting New Year Resolutions, but clear concrete goals. What I found is that by implementing the following **11 key steps**, extraordinary results are possible:

1. **Set Goals:** Most people have no idea what they want or where they are going in life. I am sure you have heard the saying, "*if you do not know where you are going, you usually end up somewhere else.*" It seems like such a simple and obvious step, but apparently not to everyone. Some people wander through life without much direction or desire, and then wonder why life just *happens* to them. This is the first step toward taking control of your destiny. Be clear in what you want.

2. **Be Specific:** The more specific and detailed you can describe what you want, the better your chances will be for achieving it. Here are a few examples. The first one is if you want to buy a new house, be clear on every detail. Do not just say, "I want to buy a house." Decide and visualize the following: What square footage do you want? How many bedrooms do you want? How many bathrooms do you want? Do you want the outside to be brick, siding, or something else? What color do you want the outside of the house to be? What City and State do you want your house to be located in? Consider another example. If you want to buy a car, what make and model do you want? Brand new? Used? Classic car? What color is the exterior? What color is the interior? What options do you want the car to come with: sunroof, convertible, leather, etc? The most common example is the goal of losing weight. Be specific on *how much* weight you want to lose rather than making the blanket statement "I want to lose weight."

3. **Determine Timeframe:** That takes us to the next step of making sure you put a timeframe to each goal you want to achieve so you can track your progress and push yourself to stay on task. Hold yourself accountable to meeting your goal with a sense of urgency.

4. **Measure Progress:** By being specific and setting a timeframe, you can then measure your progress. You must know the benchmark of where you are today and the goal of where you want to be tomorrow, to know if you are succeeding. Take the example we last spoke about: losing weight. If you are specific and say, "I want to lose 15 lbs. within the next 6 months," then you can measure and track your progress toward your desired outcome much easier and usually within a faster timeframe.

5. **Make it Achievable**: It is vital that you are realistic with the goals you set. It is human nature that when we see positive results, no matter how small they are, we get motivated to do more. An example would be as simple as making a "To-Do List" or what some people call their "Daily Task List." As we mark off each item we accomplish we feel good, motivated to do more, and successful. That trickle effect builds momentum and you will be amazed at what you can accomplish. However, it is very important that you do not set your goals so out of reach that you are setting yourself up for failure. I like to tell people, "Shoot for the stars and you will fall somewhere in between." Set your goals high enough that it stretches you, but not so high that it is impossible to reach. To achieve great things in life, we must strive to overachieve and not just meet the minimums.

6. **Know the WHY:** Define and know WHY you want to achieve a goal. This is one area that I find most people do not define, which leads to a failure to meet their goals. The BIGGER your reasons and convictions are for accomplishing a goal, the better chance you have to achieve it. Studies show that it is human nature to gravitate towards what brings us pleasure and resist anything that gives us pain. Just take a look at the show "The Biggest Loser." The winners on that show are at their last straw. They win, or some people say succeed, because the

pleasure of the outcome outweighs the pain of the process. Many people however, set a New Year's Resolution to lose weight. They join a gym in January and start working out, but that soon fizzles because they associate more with the pain of the process than the pleasure of the outcome. If you track the goals you've achieved, you will find that your priorities tend to fall where you feel the most conviction, and your WHY (reason) for accomplishing the goal is bigger.

7. **Put Goals in Writing:** I come across many people in life who tell me that they have goals that are clearly laid out in their head, but they do not believe in writing them down. However, I will tell you based on my personal experience and the experiences of many others, successful results of people who write their goals down far outweigh those who do not. When we write goals down and look at them frequently, our subconscious starts working with us in many ways. You will be amazed how people will come into your life, and/or unexpected situations happen that help you achieve your desired results.

8. **Have a Plan:** Unfortunately life happens so fast today that most of us try to "wing it," because who has the time to plan? Well, make some time. Even if you can only find 15 minutes here and there, take the time. People who plan can anticipate obstacles that might get in their way, and are more proactive than reactive in finding ways to still accomplish their goal(s).

9. **Positive Attitude matters:** Take a look at some of the most successful people around you. I guarantee you that those people most likely have a charismatic, positive attitude. Every day we wake up, we get to choose what attitude we are going to attack life with. People are attracted to those who have a positive attitude, and people want to work with people who are likeable and positive. Do not underestimate the power of "Attitude."

10. **Take Action!:** A good idea without action is just a "wish." Do not let fear prevent you from taking action. I am not saying that things will always go your way. However, remember it is the times when we feel the pain of situations that we

grow the most in life. Along those same lines, ideas with a well-thought-out plan usually leads to success. I find that getting started is half the battle, and the people that will not implement step one usually will not implement step two. Anything is possible, you just have to take some action and put it in motion.

11. **Visualize the Outcome:** It is psychologically vital to visually see yourself already achieving your goal. Some of the most amazing athletes in the world have said they achieved record-breaking results by visualizing their success before it happened.

So my question to you is: What is **your** next "inner tube"? What is your plan to achieve it? Do not wait, take ACTION NOW! Follow the 11 steps above, and experience extraordinary results in your life.

ABOUT MELISSA

Melissa D. Whitaker is a sales and management expert, business consultant and published author who helps executives and their teams achieve alignment and drive profitable sales. After 14 years of proven sales and management results with leading organizations – Impact Networking, Toshiba America Business Solutions and Chicago Office Technology Group (COTG/GISX/XEROX), Melissa founded Melissa Whitaker International.

Prior to founding Melissa Whitaker International (MWI), Melissa was the Director of Professional Development & Managed Print Services for a $40 million dollar technology company. Also prior to that, as a Global Relationship Manager and Business Analyst for a $54.3 billion dollar international organization, she helped 55 different companies gain market share within their respective industries – by focusing on identifying and developing business opportunities with enterprise-wide cost reduction strategies.

Utilizing superior consultative approaches and talk tracks, she has successfully trained over 400 sales representatives to maximize their sales and develop long-lasting, stronger client relationships. A dynamic and passionate leader, Melissa has helped over 60 companies run more effective Sales Departments by increasing sales revenue, gross profit and company morale.

Melissa's high-performance, customized training consultations and proven selling system help you drive performance, generate new prospects, improve negotiation skills and ultimately win more sales.

To learn more about Melissa D. Whitaker (Melissa Whitaker International) and how your business and team can increase revenue, profits, commissions and market share, visit: www.melissawhitakerintl.com or call 1.847.845.4922.

CHAPTER 28

HOW IMPORTANT IS CUSTOMER SERVICE?

BY DULCEE LOEHN

Everyone who knows me knows that my dogs are my kids. Having two of them, I find myself at the veterinary clinic often. We arrive at the clinic, and the dogs, who are so thrilled about going anywhere with me, are excitedly poised waiting for me to open the door. Due to the fact that my kids have some interesting issues, handling them, my purse, and my keys can be a challenge. So, I request assistance. In just a few moments, someone comes out and helps me get my family into the clinic. We enter, and the receptionist greets me by name. She efficiently checks me in and offers me something to drink while I wait. We chat about what is new in my life. Within just a few minutes, I am ushered into an exam room where we can relax and wait in private.

After another few minutes, our doctor comes in, greets us, and shakes my hand. We exchange some pleasantries and discuss what has been going on in our lives since my last visit. He also talks to the dogs and offers them treats, which, of course, they are too nervous and excited to eat. With the help of a very knowledgeable and friendly technician, they methodically and thoroughly examine each patient. All the while, they talk to and comfort them. We talk in detail about everything that is going on with each dog. The doctor takes plenty of time to answer my questions and explains all the necessary information to me.

Once the exam is complete, I am told when I need to come back and am given all necessary medications and paperwork. I walk up to the check out area to find my file waiting for me. I make my next appointment and pay my bill. After being asked if I need assistance once again, I am cheerfully wished a great day.

My veterinarian is almost an hour away from my home. A couple of years ago, I decided to try another veterinarian who was located much closer. After that experience, I went back to making the long trek whenever my dogs need medical attention. Why? My customer service experience could not compare to what I had grown accustomed to. My veterinarian understands that they don't have clients; they have parents and extended family members. They recognize that the customer experience must inspire confidence, security, safety and trust in order to get and keep clients.

All businesses need to create a strong customer service philosophy that permeates all members of their team. Unfortunately, business owners often focus on all other aspects of the business, putting customer service on autopilot. They believe that if they provide the product or service at a fair price, it will be enough to keep the clients coming back. However, today's consumer is very savvy and has high expectations. It takes more than a smile and a sales receipt. Our customer service process must touch our customers on an emotional level. Every customer wants to feel special. This requires a deeper, more sophisticated delivery. And it is not difficult or expensive to create this type of experience.

In order to 'knock the socks off' your clients, here are twelve basic steps to follow:

THE 12 STEPS TO OUTSTANDING CUSTOMER SERVICE:

1. KNOW THE REASON "WHY"

We all have a purpose for doing what we choose to do. Providing your product or service satisfies something in you, a deeper, more emotional outcome. How do you feel when you create a very satisfied customer? Why do you feel that way? Take some time to discover your reason *why* and write it down. Post it where you will see it everyday. It is easy during the day-to-day hustle and bustle to forget the beliefs and emotions that make us enthusiastic about our work. Without this guidepost, we lose focus on the conduit that enables us to live our *why* – our customers.

2. HAVE A MISSION

As Brian Tracy tells us, leaders are intensely future-oriented. They have a vision of what their business looks like three to five years down the road. He describes your mission as what you and your team must do every day in order to achieve the vision. Having a strong, specific Mission Statement clarifies for everyone how we must treat each customer every hour of every day.

3. CHOOSE VALUES AND CHARACTER

When hiring, skills and experience are important, however, not as important as the beliefs and characteristics that drive that person's behavior. Technical skills and knowledge can be taught. However, the beliefs, values, and characteristics that guide how a person treats others are anchored within that individual and very often cannot be altered. Take your time when hiring, interview thoroughly, and ask questions that will cause the candidate to articulate thoughts and experiences about the characteristics you seek. Hire a person for their values and character and teach them the rest.

4. FOLLOW THE GOLDEN RULE

We all know the Golden Rule, but very few people or businesses follow it. I hear story after story about very disappointing customer service experiences. Think about your customer service process. Consider the experience that your customers undergo. Then, put yourself in their shoes at each step in the process. Is this the experience you would want for yourself? Ask yourself, "What do I need to see, touch, and feel to return as a customer over and over again?" Following the Golden Rule is a simple thing that can set you apart from your competition and transform your business.

5. KNOW AND TEACH YOUR PROCESS

Your customer service philosophy and the corresponding process should be written down so that everyone on the team can learn and follow it. Every customer should have the same outstanding experience – regardless of the time of day, day of the week, or team member that serves them. Lay your customer service process out in vivid detail and instruct every new team member how to perform it flawlessly.

6. DELEGATE EFFECTIVELY

Once you have documented your process and trained your team members, you must observe your team and ensure they are performing the process and getting the results you desire for your customers. Business owners are busy people, and often make the mistake of instructing team members once, and then are surprised and disappointed to discover that the team is not performing the tasks as expected. The truth is, most people need more than one explanation. They need to be educated, observed, given constructive feedback, and mentored. Observe your team and continue to coach and provide feedback to them until you get what you expect. Yes, all this takes time. However, as I tell my clients, it is short-term pain for long-term gain.

7. ASK YOUR CUSTOMERS

The best way to find out why your customers buy from you, or why they don't buy, is to ask them. Implement a customer survey process that will provide periodic feedback on what your customers think about you and, more importantly, how their tastes and expectations are changing over time. Customers can be quite fickle these days. What they desire or how they want to receive it can change very quickly. It is your job to keep up with your evolving market. Your customers are critical to the survival of your business. Don't guess. Guessing is like playing darts in the dark. Make sure you know what your customers are feeling and thinking. Ask for their feedback on how you can improve their experience. Then, act on their feedback.

8. TOUCH THEM DEEPLY

Your customer service process is about creating an experience that moves your customer on an emotional level. It unmistakably tells your customer that you truly care about them. As a result, they feel like they are your only customer. They feel valued and special. These are the events and experiences that drive a customer to come back again and again. When you reach this level of customer service, the price of your product or service becomes of little importance to your customer. They buy because of the feeling they get.

We have all seen new businesses that have some kind of original, fun experience for their customers. When the business first opens, they are packed with people! But, over a short period of time, sometimes only a few weeks or months, their customers stop coming back. Why? Because they didn't touch their customers on a deep, emotional level. Make sure your customer service experience is a robust one and not just a "fad", wearing off and losing its appeal in the hearts and minds of your customers.

9. DO THE WORK

Your customers are critical to your success and the longevity of your business. One common mistake is to focus on the internal elements of the business and forget about the external customers and their needs. We put our customer service process on autopilot and hope for the best. I have already asked you to spend some time putting yourself in your customer's shoes. Be honest with yourself, and determine exactly what you would want your experience to be like as your customer. After this analysis, it is not surprising to find that as a customer, you are picky too! You may realize that it will take some work to deliver the experience you would expect. Remember, you did this analysis for a reason. Consider the old adage, "if it were easy, everybody would do it."

10. SHEPHERD YOUR CUSTOMERS

For some businesses, the customer service experience can be short. For others, the process can be long and require many steps and handoffs. It is important to make sure that someone is accompanying your customers through every step of the process, until the last service is performed. Make sure your process describes the details and requirements of each handoff and that they are performed consistently and flawlessly. There is no greater frustration than to execute almost all of the experience perfectly, and lose the customer because of one minor misstep or missed commitment.

11. ADDRESS ALL ISSUES AS OPPORTUNITIES

Remember, a complaining customer is giving you a chance to keep them as a customer. They could just choose to quietly never return to your business. When they raise an issue, they are giving you the opportunity to not only correct that specific problem, but they can cause you to look at the big picture, and make lasting, significant improvements in your business. When a customer complains, you are getting a rare look into their heart and mind. You are given the gift of seeing your business from their perspective.

Have you ever been a customer and been told something by the customer service representative that seemed really important to them, but from your perspective, was of little or no importance? The customer service representative spends several minutes telling you all the internal reasons why he cannot help you. You find yourself getting bored, frustrated, and promising yourself never to return.

Because we are internally focused when it comes to our businesses, we often create customer service experiences in a vacuum. We may think their experience is exemplary, but from their perspective, it is only mediocre. When a customer complains, pay attention! You have been given a gift, a chance to see your business through their eyes.

12. REWARD FOR EXEMPLARY SERVICE

We all say we want our staff to go above and beyond to take care of our customers. Then, when they do, we often reprimand them for giving a discount, or taking too long with a customer. It is true we want our team members to be fiscally smart and productive, but we also want to celebrate their dedication to providing first-class service.

First, we need to appreciate their attitude and dedication to our customers. Once again, these are qualities that are very difficult to teach and should be celebrated.

Second, we must consider the true value of the time they spend with a customer. After receiving service beyond compare, that customer will come back again and again. In addition, they will tell others about their experience and refer other people to your business. Based on how long that customer remains your customer, and the amount that they spend, ask yourself, "What is the true, long-term value of that customer?" In most cases, we realize that the extra time or effort we spend to create a unique customer experience is well worth it.

OUTSTANDING CUSTOMER SERVICE IS VITAL AND BENEFITS EVERYONE

Our customers are the lifeblood of our business. Their experience with us largely determines our success or failure. Business owners regularly spend a tremendous amount of time and money acquiring new customers. With an impactful customer service experience, we can create long-term customers and amass many more new customers through referrals. As a result, superb customer service has the added benefit of reduced costs and improved profitability.

ABOUT DULCEE

Dulcee Loehn is a FocalPoint Certified Business Coach and the owner of FocalPoint Business Performance of Tampa Bay, Inc. Dulcee partners with her clients, and together they improve all areas of the business, maximizing revenue, profitability, and return on investment. Using the FocalPoint system, powered by Brian Tracy, Dulcee introduces business concepts and then works with her clients to unearth effective ideas to apply those concepts to the business. This step by step process produces continuous improvement to the business. Her clients begin to realize the goals and aspirations for their business, many for the first time. Dulcee's passion for what she does comes through to everyone she touches because through coaching, she can live her purpose of improving the professional and personal lives of business owners to new levels of success, prosperity and fulfillment.

Dulcee founded FocalPoint Business Performance of Tampa Bay in 2007, but has been a coach for over 10 years. She brings to her clients extensive experience in all aspects of business management, organizational effectiveness and leadership. This, coupled with the FocalPoint system, equips her with the foundation and robust tools to deliver huge value to her clients.

What excites Dulcee the most about being a FocalPoint Business Coach, is the measured, tangible results enjoyed by her clients. Through working with her, the clients put methods in place to measure and track the key data that drives the business. Her clients know the exact value, monetarily and otherwise, they are getting for every dollar they spend in the business. They know their return on investment for their efforts and money. The clients make smart, strategic decisions that transform the business toward their vision.

In addition to being a coach for business owners and executives, Dulcee is also an experienced and sought after speaker and trainer. She also works with incoming FocalPoint coaches, assisting them to build healthy and profitable coaching practices. She is a FocalPoint Certified Trainer, participating in the education and certification of incoming coaches.

To learn more about Dulcee Loehn and FocalPoint Business Performance of Tampa Bay, and receive a free coaching session, visit www.yourbusinesscoachisin.com or call #813-469-0012.

CHAPTER 29

CONQUERING COMPLACENCY

BY DIANE CIOTTA

Do you ever feel like you're in physical checkmate or mental grid-lock? Perhaps you frequently suffer from *analysis paralysis* or are just plain frozen with the fear of failure.

When we allow ourselves the luxury of being stagnant, we become more accepting of things as they are. Often we even justify our lack of motivation through an unfair comparison of ourselves to others less fortunate than we are. To *rationalize* in this way is detrimental to our personal growth. It's actually like telling ourselves *rational-lies*.

Complacency is similar to a disease that debilitates our thoughts and activities. The good news is that just as a well-balanced diet and exercise can reduce our health risks, …there are seven behaviors that can increase our resistance to becoming complacent, provided we make a conscious effort to focus on them constantly. As the following actions and attitudes are outlined as a prescription for conquering complacency, consider how many doses you would be willing to consume on a daily basis.

1. DETERMINE YOUR DESIRES

What are the things you'd like to have, see or do? Make a list...*a Dreams List*!

The act of writing down desires versus just thinking about them makes each one more tangible, and makes us more focused on acquiring them. It's easy to stop thinking about something that seems too unrealistic to attain. On the other hand, physically erasing a want from a written list is more difficult – because it feels like a non-verbal submission of defeat. Written goals encourage a greater, long-term commitment to achievement while eliminating any lure of complacency.

Can you imagine waiting over 30 years for a dream to come to fruition? I can, ...because I have! ...and it was worth every day that went by for that hope to become a reality. Having hope is when we grab onto nothing and hang on to it until it becomes something!

You are the author of your Dreams List and you are not soliciting any readers. You're just seeking opportunities that move you closer to your goals. This focus on the possibilities will keep you in a positive mindset and deny the temptation to become complacent. If your want is big enough – the facts won't matter!

We're never too old to make a Dreams List...because making dreams come true never gets old!

2. ANTICIPATE DREAM STEALERS

Put one crab in a pail and you'll need a lid to keep it from crawling out. Put two crabs in a pail and no lid is necessary. Why? Because when one begins making its escape, the other will pull it back down. This is true of crabs, and sadly, not so unlike human nature.

Dream Stealers are those who find the negative in other people's aspirations. Very often their comments have less to do with their opinion of the person's goal and more to do with their own need not to feel outdone by someone else's motivation. Digesting the poisonous viewpoints of others can dilute our desires and eventually result in them being deleted from our menu of wants.

Beware that some Dream Stealers are less obvious and can be disguised behind legitimate concern for your best interests. Family members are a common example, as their guidance is heartfelt. They lack the same passion for your dream, so their input is based on their perspective – not yours. Their vantage point is ordinary while yours is extraordinary!

Complacency is contagious! It's imperative to ignore negativity and when possible, avoid it. While it is easier to retain the *status quo,* …it's much more rewarding to strive to improve and ultimately exhilarating to achieve a self-established goal.

A dream strived for, but not achieved, is still more fulfilling than making no attempt to attain it.

3. EMBRACE CHALLENGES

Hey, nobody said success would come easy! How many times have you heard that line? Well, unfortunately, it's true. Challenges are part of the package for conquering complacency.

It's been said that challenges build character. I've personally been through some times that were so trying, it felt like I wasn't just *building* character, …but actually *becoming* one!

This may come as a surprise, but not all obstacles can be overcome. There are two types of road blocks: ones that we can get around, over or through, and ones we can't. For the barricades with a green light: step on it! On the other hand, use caution with the ones that stop us in our tracks as they are there for a reason.

Sometimes there is a lesson to be learned in our need to think or act differently than we normally would have, had we not been redirected. Have you ever taken a detour off a common route and then realized that it was a more efficient way to go? It's the same principle.

Other times, a challenge *has* to happen in order for the next opportunity to become apparent. Isn't it awesome when we can clearly see the good that comes from something that we previously wished had never happened? It's funny how hindsight always has perfect vision.

The road to success is paved with obstacles. Don't let them cause you to make a U-turn or pull over and put up a white flag! Stay the course... the finish line is worth crossing!

4. ASSOCIATE WITH SUCCESS

As children, our parents ensured that we had quality friends because they knew we would be influenced by them. So, at what point do we grow out of being impressionable? Never! Even as adults, we are who we associate with.

In our commitment to conquering complacency, we can enhance our motivation level through interaction with people who already have acquired the things that we are in the hunt for. When we search for a hand-up, NOT a hand-out, we position ourselves right on target to learn as we grow. This first-hand experience enables repetition of productive behaviors and avoidance of unproductive ones.

Finding a mentor begins with humbling ourselves to become a student in our areas of interest. It's been said, 'when the student is ready…the teacher will appear.' In other words, when we are willing to admit that *we don't know what we don't know*, we'll be less intimidated by successful people and more open-minded to gaining their wisdom.

Mentors are the greatest tools on our workbench as we build personal success. A lot can be learned from their successes, and even more from the mistakes they made during their own construction period. In the same way that a sturdy structure stands on a solid foundation, we must start from the base and use positive association for support as we create our own skyscrapers.

5. INITIATE RESULTS

Does this sound like an oxymoron or what? As deemed by the Thesaurus, to **initiate** is to *start, begin* or *commence,* while **results** is synonymous with *outcome, end* and *solution.* That's exactly the point! We must start the outcome, begin the end and commence the solution.

In this case, the concept is the activity. To initiate is to be in control of your own actions. Taking the initiative will guard you against being robbed of your potential, because procrastination is the thief of productivity and complacency is its ready accomplice.

Your security lies in depending on the only person passionate enough to commit to engaging in your progress…you! There is more promise in making a wrong move than not making a move at all. Passion fuels activity and momentum creates results.

The fall from taking action is much less painful than the danger of inactivity. Movement is essential to ensuring that you never feel like your *get-up-and-go* just *got-up-and-left*! There are those people that make things happen, some that watch things happen and still others that wonder what happened? Which one are you?

Leaders lead. Do something. You can always clean up the mess later. Stand on principle, walk in confidence, run on adrenaline and think outside the box! Get ready...Get set...Go!

6. EXUDE ENERGY

Enthusiasm is internally uplifting and externally appealing. It actually takes fewer muscles to smile than it does to frown! No matter how good-looking somebody may be, …they're even more attractive with a "shot" of charisma! Granted, it's not always easy to be upbeat all the time – but it beats the alternative!

THINK in the *when* versus *if* tense, anticipating that great things will happen, SPEAK in positive phrases; for example, "the good thing is…" or "this is great because…", and MOVE at a pace faster than complacency can catch you.

It's my opinion that too much sleep makes us tired! I'd rather go to bed late, wake up early and catch-up on all that missed sleep when I'm permanently laid to rest. After all, what else will there be to do at "six feet under?"

Energy is the gear that turns a bicycle into a motorcycle. Being vivacious fuels our dream, "tunes up" our attitude, jump-starts our actions and ultimately drives our accomplishments. Many years ago, someone rudely asked me, "Doesn't your bubble ever burst?" I was so hurt by such a malicious comment until I realized that it was actually a huge compliment! So Steve, if I didn't say it before, "...thank you!"

A personal objective of mine is to make *others* feel better about themselves *after* I've spoken with them. I believe that people don't care how much we know until they know how much we care, AND, that when we genuinely care – it makes a bigger impact than we know.

7. ENGAGE IN RISKS

If you were accused of being a risk-taker, would you be convicted? *For the sake of success, being overly cautious can be the culprit of missed opportunity, while it locks us in a cell of complacent mentality.* On the contrary, 'gut-feel' and natural instinct are often the most valuable traits in the mindset of an achiever.

It's true that a blind man can have better vision than a man with sight. The question "What if…?" can only be answered by taking chances when the outcome is unclear at the time of the commitment. The past tense of 'possibility' is *would have*, *should have* and *could have…* words that are best deleted from our vocabulary. Risk is the potential to return greater reward.

When others question our actions while we are engaged in the process of moving forward, it's a good indication that we are on the right track. Running into the wind or swimming against the tide enhances a workout and returns better results, sooner. Don't be concerned when you see significantly more people heading in the opposite direction. Rather, consider it advantageous that the lane to success is less congested than the mainstream – as it's shared only by other achievers.

It's by choice that I live on the edge... and feel that those that don't are taking up too much space!

In summary, if the thought "Lucky 7" has run through your mind as you shuffled through these pages…think again! You won't need luck if you are willing to modify some behaviors and keep an optimistic attitude. No lottery ticket or slot machine can offer a better pay-off than your bet being on you.

So, here's the deal, ...'ante up' to writing down your Dreams List and anticipate the need to discard those people who try to steal those desires from you. 'Up' your bet by recognizing that challenges are just jokers in the deck of success, and draw on the fact that mentorship opportunities are like being dealt an ace. Hold yourself accountable to your own hand by initiating results, and replace your poker face with exuberant energy, as you confidently take each hit while you engage in risks.

In the game of life, …this is your future. The jackpot is big and it's your turn!

Make a mental move, …then *get out of your own way*!

ABOUT "DI"

With an enthusiasm for selling at an early age, Diane Ciotta dedicated nine years to a Manhattan-based retailer, becoming the youngest store manager in the history of the 50-year company. Being a go-getter, she eventually decided to pursue an outside sales position, where she could more fervently initiate her opportunities for new clients.

Diane propelled herself to become a top-selling representative with a respected publishing company, and enjoyed a successful 10-year career that included territory sales, sales management and sales coaching. As a result of her personal experiences, Diane's passionate commitment to the widespread need for more integrity-based selling inspired her entrepreneurial 'leap of faith' to start **Training Classics** in 1989.

For 22 years, Diane has effectively motivated sales consultants around the country to focus on their customers' needs vs. wants through dynamic skills-enhancement seminars. She concentrates on increasing participant's confidence and uses Jersey sarcasm to emphasize the thrill of being in control of driving incremental revenue. Her specialty in the advertising industry has been with an incomparable ability to relate to her participants, and her resume includes publishing a children's educational newspaper.

Determined to intensify the results of her positive impact, Diane diversified her focus and is stimulating audiences as a presenter at major speaking engagements, doing business as The Keynote Effect. With a strong message addressing her perspective on our "national complacency crisis" and the necessary attitudes and actions to successfully conquer it, she is responsible for many life-changing decisions.

Diane Ciotta is a professional member of the National Speakers Association.

Di has two sons, Brian 26 & Kevin 25, and one soul mate – the love of her life, Tom.

Contact Info:

www.thekeynoteeffect.com
di@thekeynoteeffect.com
diane@trainingclassics.com
Cell: 732.672.7942
Toll Free: 1.866.301.9455

CHAPTER 30

14 SECONDS

BY DOMINIC KNIGHT

"So many of our dreams at first seem Impossible, then they seem Improbable, and then when we summon the will, they soon become Inevitable."

~ Christopher Reeve

14 seconds can literally change your life. I've seen it happen time and time again. And I've been lucky enough to be in a position to prompt that change. One of my primary goals is to make those 14 seconds happen with everyone I see. Behind those 14 seconds, however, is a great deal of training and study, as well as eternal secrets and the teachers who were willing to share the knowledge *behind* those secrets.

But let's start with a story.

...The young man had spent hours trying to decipher the hidden message, a message that the majority of readers never could understand. But he finally did.

Looking in the mirror he stared deep into his eyes; they began to dart left and right. He then honed in on his left eye which, as legend tells us, is the gateway to the subconscious mind. He continuously reaffirmed the same message with so much emotional intensity that the protective veneer of self-doubt began to slowly crack as he gained access and control of his very mind. His heart was pounding faster as a metamorphosis was taking place; the caterpillar was turning into a butterfly and the hero potential that runs through all mankind was revealing itself through him.

This was greater than any premonition; it was reality forming in front of his very eyes. 14 seconds later, the creative motion of the universe was underway, resonating throughout all time and space, the universe organizing itself to fit the image projected from his mind's eye; people, places, circumstances were being orchestrated to realize his dreams in perfect order like a flawless symphony.

Who was he?

He was a young Chinese immigrant who had found himself on the shores of the U.S. As a child growing up in China, he had wished to become the greatest master of the martial arts on the planet just as so many others did. Now in America, immersed in the culture of watching movies, a desire was welling up inside of him, dreams of fame and wealth, maybe one day becoming a world famous Hollywood star...

But, at the time, ethnic minorities just didn't become movie stars in America. Anyone he would have shared his dreams with would have told him he was crazy. Even he thought he was totally deluded – but these insane ambitions wouldn't let go of him – the more he tried to resist, the greater the desire grew.

To prove the power destiny sometimes has over our lives, he stumbled upon a book written in 1937 – a book that detailed the amazing workings of the subconscious mind and the secrets to planting powerful seeds within it. The author, interestingly enough, planted his own powerful seed in the book – a secret indirectly contained in the writing over a hundred times in the book.

That secret was 'a law of laws' that has been used knowingly or unknowingly by every incredibly successful person throughout history. And, the author promised to any reader that discovered the secret planted in the book, that practicing this method would allow a person to literally achieve anything they wanted.

He took out a clean sheet of paper. At the very top of the page, he wrote "SECRET." Then he followed the instructions by writing his life's definite major purpose in a way that would influence his subconscious mind...

"I, Bruce Lee, will be the highest paid Oriental superstar in the United States. In return, I will give the most exciting performances and render the best quality in the capacity of an actor. Starting in 1970, I will achieve world fame and from then onward till the end of 1989 I will have in my possession $10,000,000. Then I will live the way I please and achieve inner harmony and happiness."

Although his life was tragically cut short, Bruce Lee attained all his unlikely goals – and his legend still reverberates to this very day. And this story teaches us a profound lesson – it's what goes on inside the part of the mind that we're not fully conscious of, ...which affects our life in the most impactful way.

PUSHING YOURSELF TO THE FRONT

As you know, the theme of this book is "Pushing to the Front." All of us have at least casual daydreams about achieving amazing things – and most likely, you read this book to pursue large ambitions. What stops you from actually transforming those dreams into reality? What is the absolute root cause of your roadblocks? What must be addressed before any other issue in your life?

It's your Mind.

As a decidedly unconventional therapist, I've devoted my professional life to employing the secrets of the subconscious mind, those same secrets that Bruce Lee once tapped into, and using those methods to cure my patients quickly and permanently – often in one single session. They don't spend years on a couch revealing every last emotional scar from their childhoods.

They don't have to. Let me share a few examples...

- A paralyzed girl came into my office in a wheelchair. She began moving her legs during the session. By the time she made it home, she could walk again.

- A man with no background in sales joined the UK's second-largest real estate agency – after working with me, he broke a 19 year-old sales record within 6 months.
- Another man about to do trials for a professional rowing team became the world's fastest rower that year– after just one session.

I can't take credit for these amazing stories – I just showed them how to release what was already inside of them.

My unique blend of hypnotherapy and other subconscious disciplines such as NLP (Neuro-Linguistic Programming) and TFT (Thought Field Therapy) allows me to zero in on the subconscious issue and fix it – just as easily as Lasik eye surgery can correct someone's vision.

That, in turn, has enabled me to help people from all walks of life – everyone from company CEOs and Hollywood personalities to everyday people. You can be at the highest level or lowest level of society – and still endure fears and phobias that continually prevent you from having a full and happy life. It's really all about removing what currently holds you back and developing a belief system that you will succeed.

I am fortunate enough to have developed my expertise over the past decade to the point where I have one of the highest success rates in the world when it comes to my working with people. Fears that we have learned throughout life are all developed relatively quickly– but they can be equally as fast to overcome with the right methods.

As a matter of fact, it can be as fast as...14 seconds.

THE SECRET TECHNIQUE THAT CHANGES LIVES

How does someone who thinks they can't walk suddenly get on their feet? How does someone who has never sold before suddenly break records with their salesmanship?

The answer – it can take only 14 seconds of a concentrated emotion to be the catalyst to change or develop any desired behavior – this took me over a decade to discover!

When I first started studying personal development, I decided to learn directly under Dr. Richard Bandler, co-creator of NLP. My studies continued through a decade of research, distilling the wisdom of over 500 books on the topic of success, as well as dissecting the knowledge of the world's leading thinkers past and present, I found the same message, the same golden thread running through every book on success. It was simply one message; it's all in the mind and the mind is the only thing that we have 100% control over if we know how.

To learn more about the workings of the subconscious mind, I dived into the works of Dr. Milton Erickson, the forefather of clinical hypnotherapy. Erickson excelled at the power of indirect suggestion – and through this technique, he would cure the so-called "incurable." On a smaller scale, he could cause people to pass him the salt at the dinner table without even asking for it – or cause people to arrive at his house at a designated time, again, without him specifically instructing them.

Erickson never documented this technique – instead it was observed and loosely written about by students of Erickson. I learned it, tried it, and, to my astonishment – it worked!

But at this stage I needed more, I wanted to learn how to powerfully influence my own mind and push myself to the front as a way of realizing my own dreams. Whilst on a seminar in Switzerland; the leader of our group mentioned that he had uncovered in the unpublished manuscripts of the late Napoleon Hill the following passage; *"14 seconds of concentrated thought is the equivalent of 2000 hours of work."* – meaning that if you can focus on a desire for those 14 seconds in a uniquely concentrated manner, the frequency of that concentrated thought will continue to vibrate even when you are distracted by other things in your life.

Now that may sound esoteric – but modern science has shown us today that 5 minutes of a heightened emotion can reside in your nervous system for up to 6 hours. So could it not be true that a concentrated thought imbued with positive emotion would continue to reside within you, even after you've resumed your normal day-to-day life? I began to test this to see if it would actually work, to put all this knowledge together and work on improving every one of my techniques.

Things began to look more like wizardry than science – and the astonishing came to seem like the norm.

The techniques I have now developed involve a four-dimensional visualization tool that takes you directly to where you store your belief systems in your subconscious mind. Which means you have direct access to the "script" that literally runs the way you think.

Much like altering the code of a computer, this allows you to make incredible changes to the way you approach your everyday life – and, as a therapist, it gives me the ability to influence the minds of others, through indirect suggestion, in a manner that they can't detect.

Three more examples…

- A professional fighter trapped in bed, due to severe internal damage to his legs, was told he would never be able to do anything athletic again. Within 3 months, he became a national martial arts champion.
- An eating disorder that plagued a woman for over 35 years suddenly vanished.
- A woman who couldn't leave the house without severe panic attacks now comes and goes with ease.

These aren't extraordinary people that experience these miracles. Whatever you personally feel is holding you back from ultimate success can also be vanquished. The resources are already within you for positive transformation – they just need to be unleashed and harnessed to take you to great heights. Every one of us can experience this growth and ultimately change the course of this planet, one person at a time. It all starts with belief and knowledge.

OVERCOMING "NO"

What is it that causes people to approach life in a negative and fearful way?

Well, think back to when you were six years old and try to remember what that felt like. You probably thought you could be anything you wanted to be – an astronaut, a pop star, even the President. Nothing felt out of reach. But, as you continued on your life journey, suddenly you regularly heard phrases that cut you off from that feeling of absolute freedom; phrases like, …"No, you can't," …"Be realistic," and …"You'll never be able to do that."

In fact, some studies have shown that by the time you reach 18, you've been told NO over 180,000 times. Now *that's* powerful conditioning – and it's a big reason that only 5% of people really make it financially and emotionally in life.

We all need to learn to reverse those "No's" – and lose our fear of failure.

Think back again to when you were a child – and the times you were afraid of imaginary monsters or other scary things that weren't real. At some point, as you were growing up, you trained your mind to realize these things weren't real and you didn't need to be scared of them. That's the *exact same mechanism* that can still be utilized as an adult.

Unfortunately, as already noted, we can also be trained to think *negatively* as we attain adulthood. If you grow up in a state of freeform anxiety and depression, you will likely carry that with you no matter how wonderful your external circumstances might be. For example, a research study looked at people who were big lottery winners. Those that were depressed and anxious were briefly happy after winning the money, ...and then simply returned to their previous negative state.

This is because the brain has an incredible ability to ruminate, to hold on to emotions and to familiar patterns of thinking. It's not that naturally happy people don't get depressed – it's just that they don't hold on to it. They shorten its duration as much as they can, then they go back to pursuing happiness. That's how their mind is *trained.*

Unhappy people go through much the opposite; they've taught their brains to react negatively to life and happiness for them is always very fleeting. As I already noted, science now shows us that a person who is in a state of extreme emotion for just 5 minutes will keep that emotion in their nervous system for *over 6 hours.*

But that ability to "train your brain" and hold on to emotions, can also be worked to your advantage. If you can prolong a thought long enough and infuse it with intense positive feelings, the emotion will continue to reside in your central-nervous system long after you have thought about it. If you do this consistently enough it becomes automatic. Essentially you will be broadcasting to the universe your desires of what you want to manifest in your life and how you want to be. The amazing thing is that what you think about most of the time you become- and that's the secret behind my 14 second approach.

In the years of working with patients harbouring anxieties, fears and phobias, as well as those who wanted to enhance their ability to perform, *every single time without exception* I have discovered that their difficulties stem from a behavior which the individuals themselves have reinforced. They simply tell themselves the same story over and over. When that story finally changes, and is reinforced into something positive, then the internal as well as external behavior changes very quickly.

PUTTING YOUR MIND POWER TO WORK FOR YOU

Learning how to influence yourself to take action in your life may just be the single most important skill that there is. It's the starting point for any sort of accomplishment in your personal or professional life.

Imagine if you could triumph over everything that makes you hesitate or stop along the road to success. You could possibly develop the body of your dreams, create an empire, have the most incredible relationships, exude confidence and instill it in others and learn virtually anything you wanted to.

It's not just a matter of knowing what has to be done to create those kinds of changes in your life. That knowledge is all out there and easily obtainable. You can go online and literally access any of it.

No, the stumbling block is in the lack of ability to *apply* that knowledge. The critical fact to know about yourself – about *any* of us – is that 95% of our behavior is subconscious. That means you are using the other conscious 5% of your willpower to override that other 95%. Obviously, the odds are incredibly stacked against you if your subconscious balks at something your conscious mind thinks it wants to achieve.

What I have discovered is that there are very real ways of entering the doorway to the unlimited potential of your subconscious mind. When you step through that gateway – you can make things happen!

While there is hardly enough room here to fully explain how you can change your subconscious programming, I can offer four important steps towards finding the change you desire in your life.

1. **Begin by fully understanding your past and releasing it.** Forgive anyone that has ever harmed you and most

importantly, forgive and love yourself. Close the door tightly on the past and only revisit it to gain insights and lessons. If you do not learn from past errors, those cycles will continue in your life until you do learn and apply the lessons from them.

2. **Focus on the things you are most grateful for in your life.** Concentrate on your happiest moments, amplify them by making the pictures bigger and brighter in your mind's eye and relive the experiences. Have "present moment awareness" and enjoy every precious second of life, and be grateful for the wonderful future that awaits you.

3. **Change your story into a story of success.** When you constantly transmit thoughts of happiness, you will see evidence of it all around you and your mind will only look for the positive in every scenario. Then, as your nervous system is bathed in love and happiness, within a very short period of time this will become the dominant pathway of your mind and body; your mind will automatically generate the chemicals that will produce within you generalized feelings of well-being.

4. **Transmit thoughts about your goals and future in a duration of concentrated thought for 14 seconds;** *Concentrated thought* means literally 'hallucinating' the outcome you wish to achieve and engaging all your senses in a spirit of harmony. You must then move these positive images to the location of where your beliefs are stored (we all store images in different geographical locations). Now the key is to hold on to that feeling and transmit it until it becomes a belief. Your mind will continue to work through this process if you keep doing this. Eventually, you will not even have to think about the goal – your mind will be transmitting this frequency automatically!

You may not be able to attain the rapid and amazing results I do in my practice right away – and it will definitely take you more than 14 seconds to learn – but when you begin to incorporate and learn these methods, you too will begin to use them successfully in your life.

Just know that there is often a very good reason the rich keep getting richer and the poor keep getting poorer. It has to do with what we've been trained to believe and to do (or to *not* do).

Overcoming that training is the ultimate game-changer – and an objective that I am excited to be able to accomplish. As I progress with my practice, I hope to reveal much more of what I have learned through my journey and share it with everyone all over the world. It's the kind of knowledge that the world urgently needs.

For now, I hope that *your* journey is one that you can enjoy with a sense of adventure and excitement. Without a doubt, people only ever excel at something that is in their hearts. Bill Gates loves computers; Mohammed Ali loved boxing – look at the common denominator – *love.*

Love is the most powerful creative force in this universe. Elvis Presley, Michael Jackson and Bruce Lee, all legends in their own time, all reached the pinnacles of their success in the areas that they loved.

Use it wisely and you can't help but *push yourself to the front.*

ABOUT DOMINIC

Celebrity Therapist Dominic Knight is one of the UK's most recognised and highly credited Clinical Hypnotherapists and NLP Master Practitioners, providing relief to those suffering from life-altering conditions. Knight has devised The Knight System a breakthrough method of influencing and re-programming the subconscious mind in record time while generating automatic behavioral change.

Knight's famous Harley Street clinic has treated a vast number of extreme phobias to crippling addictions. He has helped hundreds of people each year to put their lives back on track and return to the normality that so many take for granted.

With a career that continues to grow, Dominic's achievements have earned him coveted appearances on FOX, CBS as well as ABC and national press coverage in The Times & The Gaurdian. Knight has also assisted Channel 4's BAFTA award winning ***Embarrassing Bodies***team, curing a chronic agoraphobic woman of her life consuming fear.

Aside from his achievements within the world of media, Knight is heavily involved with the performance enhancement of professional athletes and executives inside of The Metropolitan Police, IBM, JP Morgan, HSBC, Royal Bank of Scotland, The Royal College of Surgeons, and key individuals inside the entertainment industry.

Determined to work to the best of his ability, Dominic has read over four hundred books and studies continuously to expand his knowledge of how to remove fears and addictions and also the art of getting the best out of people, helping them to realize their innate potential.

Whether his challenge is to cure panic attacks, fear of public speaking, eating disorders or simply enhance human potential, Dominic offers the highest level of help and understanding possible, providing a cure to some of the most complex and unimaginable psychological conditions.

Dominic's Achievements: Licensed Master Practitioner of NLP and Hypnotherapy, Licensed Trainer of NLP and Hypnotherapy, Recognized by The General Hypnotherapy Register (GHR), Validated by The General Hypnotherapy Standards Council (GHSC)

Interesting cases, in record time after a 1hr 30min session:

1. Turned a former anorexic to catwalk model
2. A young man with no sales background breaks a 19-year record inside of 6 months
3. A rower becomes the worlds fastest rower that year, after only one session

4. Chronic agoraphobic of 30 years cured
5. Theatrical Actress lands lead role
6. An Injured martial artist becomes a champion when 3 months earlier doctors said he would never be able to train again.
7. Paralyzed from the waist down for the past 6 months a girl comes in a wheel chair, during the session her leg begins to move, by the time she reaches home she is walking.
8. 7 year old boy overcomes fear of flying

CHAPTER 31

THE INNATE POTENCY OF THE CRY FOR HELP

BY MFON EKPO

When she finished reading the letter, her mouth was agape. After a short spell of silence she said, "Did you really send that?" … and without waiting for a response added, "that was a pretty audacious and somewhat ridiculous letter." Ridiculous maybe, but as I prepared to recount to my protégée the events that had led to the letter and how everything pretty much changed after that, all I could say to her was, "Well…it worked."

The events began to unfold after I read an article about a young entrepreneur. And though I tried to ignore it, the more I read the more uncomfortable I got, and there were many reasons for that. The subject of my attention was about the same age as I was, in his mid-twenties and in the same career I was in, and as I read about him I thought, "Wow! He is just like me." However there was one major difference, he was succeeding in a particular area of business I had not yet discovered how to be successful in. So while reading up more on him, my thoughts changed from "Wow! He is just like me!" to "What on earth is he doing that I am not?" This was not a sarcastic question, I really did want to know and wished I could somehow ask him, but I did not know him personally and my research findings did not reveal any book in which he had outlined his strategies to demystify the tricky aspect of our common trade.

Then an idea occurred to me, …write to him. Write to him? In this day and age? I laughed incredulously as I gave myself a million-and-one reasons why I dared not attempt it. He was a busy person; even if he did get the letter he probably would not even respond. I did not have his mailing address, why would he tell a complete stranger his success secrets – he did not even live on the same continent as I did, what if he turned out to be arrogant and pompous? On and on, I gave myself one reason after another why I could not venture down this ridicule-ridden path. However, one niggling reason why I should kept popping up, "What if he does respond?" It would make a world of difference. It was a quick decision, I would write him. I really had nothing to lose save the fear of rejection. Since I did not have his mailing address, I turned to what I did have, Facebook. He was on facebook and seemed to be quite active there, whether he administered his facebook page himself or if a member of his staff did it for him, I was not certain, but since that was the only means of contact I had, I was going to use it.

However the question then became, what would I write? From reading about him I had garnered that he was very successful and quite busy but he was also young, very human and liked to have a good laugh. From my own entrepreneurial experience, I also knew he would have loads of people asking for his help. So I knew I needed to write something that would capture his attention yet show him I did not intend to waste his time or freeload, but that I was worth the investment of time and was willing to learn. So I sent a cry to heaven for help, opened my laptop and proceeded to write the most outrageous letter I had written to anyone in my life, which I titled "Desperation in Action".

Hi John,

My name is Mfon and I am a lawyer resident in the UK. The reason I chose to write you is because I really want to get the kind of results you are getting in (I gave him details about the areas I was struggling with), but I don't know how. So I said, "Why don't I eat the humble pie and ask John, he should know because he is involved in the same field and must have encountered the same issues." So here I am gorging down

the humble pie as fast as I can, falling at your feet with tears streaming down my eyes (Ok, John, well…that's obviously a tad bit too dramatic, I'm just staring at my laptop and typing a letter, but I did vividly imagine the former "movie – worthy" scenario) and asking "how?" How did you do it? I would really appreciate your help. You can use this letter much later in life when I become very famous to get me to return the favor, but for now I'm unashamedly asking for your help. I do hope you reply as I'm keeping my fingers crossed, praying and fasting and covering my self with the proverbial sackcloth and ashes…(alright again, not so dramatic, I'll just be checking my mail every other hour).
I anticipate your response.
I anticipate your response
I anticipate your response
I anticipate your response (oh, have I said that 3 times already?).

Kind regards,

Mfon

Now you might realize why my protégée's jaw dropped after she read the letter, but I was serious and I must have done some thing right because less than a week later he replied and his mail began with the words…

"Your letter was so funny…"

That was the beginning of one of the most fruitful business relationships I have ever had. He did not however leave all his work to focus on me. No, I had to study his itinerary, endure months of silence, and spend money traveling to meetings he taught at; but I was not one to give up, not when I had come this close. Finally his itinerary brought him to my town and we finally met and clicked. After that he gave me tasks and showed me a number of things to implement, which I did conscientiously.

One day, out of the blue, he called and said 'I have a project to do, I can't do it due to the time structure, I need some one who can work on it with the same level of excellence I would have …can you do it?" My day was made, of course I could. It turned out to be more work than I anticipated and some days I lost track of time as evening turned to morning, other days I did not remember to eat because I was so caught up in work as I was determined to prove that he had not wasted his time and I had indeed learnt. On the final day of the deadline as I looked at my work, I realized working under his instructions had stretched my capacity to think and create in ways I would not have done on my own. He was a man of a few words and high standards, so I cautioned myself against expecting glowing praise after he had seen my work. Four days later, I got a mail from him that said,

"Hi Mfon,

How are you? This is excellent work. I am so proud of you! It was worth the wait and I can see the hard work."

I let out a sigh I must have been unconsciously holding in for a long while. I had done it. I had proved I was worth the investment of time.

From then on, it became commonplace for us to work together on projects. He called me up for projects and taught me things from his business I didn't know. I taught him things from mine he didn't know. It became like a partnership, a practical proof of the truth emphasized by Ralph Waldo Emerson that one of the most beautiful compensations of life is that no man can sincerely try to help another without helping himself.

When the time came for him to nominate someone for a major project that involved major corporations and institutions, he said the only person that he and his partners unanimously agreed on nominating was me, and all this happened because I chose to ask for help.

I have deliberately chosen not to go into the details of what I needed help with so as not to lose the essence of the underlying lesson, or have it associated with any particular field because the potency of the cry for help is universal, irrespective of what field of business or aspect of life you require help with.

That singular event in my life taught me the following invaluable lessons about business success that I now pass on to others.

1. BE HONEST ABOUT WHERE YOU ARE

You can only reach for help if you honestly appraise yourself or your business and come to terms with the level you are on and the fact that you need help to go further. Being ignorant does no good and research has shown that even ostriches do not hide their heads in the sand. Hence, in business as in life, truth is best known – no matter how painful it is.

2. ASK THE RIGHT PERSON

When faced with a dilemma, don't just ask anyone. Ask for help from someone in a position to help. If you had to pull up to a curb due to a flat tire, would you rather ask for help from someone who pulled up at that same curb with two flat tires or from a mechanic with all the right tools? Ask help from someone who has succeeded at what you are attempting to achieve, and it does not have to be as dramatic as my story. There are many other ways in which you can ask for help and that includes simply reading books or attending courses.

3. ASK AGAIN AND AGAIN

There is nothing wrong with not knowing, what is not right is staying ignorant after discovering you do not know. In my earlier years, my father continually told me to never be afraid of asking questions no matter how silly they sounded to others. He said the worst thing that could happen after I asked was that people would laugh, but even their laughter would contribute to the learning process because the ridicule also meant I would never forget the answer.

5. TAKE RESPONSIBILITY

Remember the Spiderman catch-phrase "With great power comes great responsibility." Well, the same applies to asking for help, as the answers you get after asking will come with its demands. It may be demands on your time, demands on your ability to change, demands to give as good as you get or demands to undertake projects you never would have thought of doing. In my case, I had to meet all these demands and it turned my business around. Life is not a stroll in the park, so do not expect help to come cheap and fit into your old way of doing things. Get ready to be flexible, get ready to change, get ready to work at it, get ready to do what it takes to make the most of the help you have been given.

6. GET INTERESTED IN THE PERSON YOU ARE ASKING FOR HELP

Finding out what makes someone tick might go a long way in determining how much you get out of the person. People are appreciable assets and the more you pay attention to them, the more you are likely to receive from them. The type of letter I wrote would definitely not work for everybody, but I had studied the intended recipient of my letter and knew what would work with him. Everyone has something that makes them tick – study them and find it.

7. LEARN BALANCE

Do not give up, but do not turn yourself into a pest either. Help comes mostly to those who seek it with dignified humility. I have asked for help from many other people and in many other ways and I have not always gotten a 'yes'. To enjoy business success, you have to be able to pick up the pieces and try again. Mary Anne Radmacher's quote captures this succinctly, 'Courage does not always roar, sometimes courage is the quiet voice at the end of the day saying…I will try again.'

8. HELP OTHERS TOO

Do not forget that someone took the time to answer your cry for help. Today, I take the time to teach others how to succeed because I do not forget that someone took the time to teach me. Take out time to answer somebody else's cry for help.

Asking for help takes a certain amount of courage, everyone can but not everyone will, and that is what separates the successful from the failures in business and in life. I have often heard that when the student is ready the teacher will appear, but most times in life when the student is ready, the student has to go in search of the teacher. Do not sit idly by waiting for help to locate you, go after it and never underestimate the innate potency of the cry for help.

None of us has gotten where we are solely by pulling ourselves up by our own bootstraps. We got here because somebody bent down and helped us.

~ Thurgood Marshall

ABOUT MFON

Mfon Ekpo is a lawyer and an entrepreneur who also juggles multiple roles as professional negotiator, writer, speaker, coach, singer and songwriter. She is the founder of Premier Pioneers Network (http://www.premierpioneers.org), training people in the art of public speaking, writing, negotiation, and ideas generation and implementation since 2006.

A staunch advocate of personal development and a firm believer in the limitless possibilities of the human capacity, she is a founding partner of the John Maxwell Team and a Member of the British Institute of International and Comparative Law. She is currently the Director of Strategy at Red Media (http://www.rednigeria.com), a leading Media and Communications Development Company, and trains young people on humanitarian issues as a school speaker for the British Red Cross.

As a teacher, she enjoys expounding life lessons to her readers on her blog, ...The School Called Life. (https://theschoolcalledlife.wordpress.com/)

CHAPTER 32

THE SECRET TO LUCK!

BY PHAP TRINH

I was born into a poor family– a really poor one. My father went to sell lottery on the streets to earn money for our whole family, therefore, I don't have money to buy things which I like very much, not even just a pencil or an eraser.

Not a lot of people play with me in school. They looked at me as a poor child and most of them thought "He is unlucky to be born into a poor family."

I started my job as a temporary dishwasher in two different restaurants: one fast food chain and one local restaurant. After one year: I had achieved Employee of the Month AND Crew Person of the Quarter Award (remember, I am just a *temporary* staff).

In the local restaurant, from a dishwasher, I was promoted to waiter and then to team leader within the same year. I am 19 at this time. At that same time, I got my Higher School Certificate and qualified to go to University, but my father's business went bankrupt, and I had to stop my education. People said that: "He is unlucky again."

One year later, I applied for position of Assistant Restaurant Manager, pass, get the chance to learn in Thailand for two months, and became

Restaurant General Manager when I was only 22. Now, people say, "He is lucky!"

However, after four years working, my life was changing. When I decided to stop working for the restaurant and wanted to find a job that takes me to a higher level of manager, I learned that, unfortunately, with no university degree and with my experience only in restaurant management – this does not fit requirements for high level of manager job in an office. Therefore, I could not find a suitable job for the next two years. Then, I had to restart and work as a sales consultant for my father's business – in fact, Sales Consultant = Salesman.

Once again, people said "He is unlucky to have made the wrong decision to quit his current job; and now he cannot study in University and cannot find a better job."

In 2003, I got a new job with the position of Field Force Manager which I have never done before, as well as I have no idea how to control the staff which always works in the field. However, my General Manager thinks that if I can be good in controlling restaurant staff, I also can be good in controlling the staff that works in the field.

One month later, my direct boss, the Project Manager, and two other important people; the finance manager and the human resources manager, all quit at the same time. The reason: the general manager is not good, they are working long hours, they have too many things to do and they receive late salary payments, etc. I just ask myself: "Am I choosing the right company or not? All high-positioned people are leaving and the reasons they gave are all reasonable. Am I unlucky (again) to join this company?"

Within only six months working there, I was promoted to Project Manager, and during 1½ years working there, I was promoted three times with three salary increases and each increase an average of 30%!

In 2005, I joined another company, and nine months later got promoted to a higher position plus a 30% increase in salary again.

In August 2006, I joined another company, starting in the position of Survey Manager. Eight months later, I got promoted, and have continued to be promoted with a salary increase every year with an average of a 28% increase each time.

Now, is that Lucky?

If it is one time, two times, we can say "Lucky." But I have always performed in different fields of business, in different companies and I keep being promoted every 8 – 10 months, and each time with a salary increase minimum of 20% and maximum of 40%! That is not "lucky."

After 13 years working, I've figured out the formula that keeps getting me promoted again and again and in any company (regardless that company may have a bad reputation about C&B system, process, etc…) Luckily, that method not only can apply to me; if you know and practice the same thing, I am sure you can do the same with your career.

THE FORMULA IS: TNT

Wow, it looks like a bomb, right? Yes! This is the bomb that blows away my poverty that blows all the barriers and blasted me from a dishwasher to a restaurant manager, and keeps me promoted fast in any company that I joined, and blasted me from employment at a small company to a big company. So, let's start with the first T:

1. THE FIRST WORD IS: TALK TO YOURSELF

Tell yourself, "this is the only choice you have – you have no better choice, therefore, you should do your best to retain *this* job and to grow within *this* company."

It means this: as soon as you join a company, please do not work for them and still be searching for another job. If you do that, you will lack focus and you will find a lot of negative reasons to not become an Excellent Performer.

Someone asked me, "If I have a better opportunity, why shouldn't I choose it?"

Yes you can, but remember where you will start. You are new in the industry, you can't find a better company to join, and you think that there is no fast way to become an expert plus you don't think you can get promoted after only eight months – it's the impossible mission.

So by talking to yourself, you will remind yourself that, "this is the best job that you can have with your current capabilities," and "you don't want to be jobless," or "you don't want to lose this job so that you have to take another job with a lower income."

So, my first motivating power was to not complain, not to feel the same as others. I talked to myself to say "I have no other choice. Therefore, I have to do my best, and I have to focus on what can I do? What can I contribute to *this* company?"

Then…

2. THE SECOND WORD IS: NEVER.

Never say: "I don't know", or "I cannot do it" when you get a task assigned from your boss.

Remember, you don't want to lose the job and you don't want to stay at the same position where you started. So, keep those two sentences away from any assigned task:

1. "I don't know" and
2. "I cannot do it"

What if I don't know? I have to say I don't know! I don't want to tell a lie!

Look, we all know that human beings use less than 5% of their real capabilities. If a person can do more than that, he or she will become outstanding compared with others. I don't ask you to tell a lie or to do something like a rock star. All I ask is, only say "I don't know" after you really do all your research, ask for support within your company or look for the answer on the internet etc…

To make it clear, before you say so:

- Get a clear understanding about your boss' concerns. Know clearly what your boss wants you to do and what results he wants?
- Then, spend time to figure out the gap between where you are now and where the target is that you need to achieve.
- List out all the obstacles and barriers and ask yourself, "How can I do it?"

Hey, I am new in this business, how can I know how to do it?

Sure, your experience is not enough; therefore, you must list out your obstacles and your solutions. Then, you come back to your boss and ask him, "Boss, based on my experience, this is my plan. Please guide me if you think that even if I do all those things, I still will not achieve what you want."

From that, you will get the chance for your boss to guide or teach you.

Let's look at it this way:

Imagine that you are the boss, you gave an instruction or your expectation or assigned tasks for your staff to do and your staff immediately replied, "Sorry boss, I don't know" or "I can't" or even worse your staff said, "Someone did it before and failed already." How do you feel? Do you want to promote staff like that?"

So, if you want to get promoted fast like me – in different companies, with different bosses and continue to get promoted after every eight or nine months – don't forget to stop yourself from saying the words "I don't know" or "I can't do it." For the person who works in a service industry, using this second word is also good for your reputation as well as for customer appreciation.

Small note, after I left the company, most of my customers would stop their contract three months after that. Reason? The new project manager would say "No" or "It is not possible to execute with that short a period of time."

And I do agree that "customers usually have a short period of time and always want something as fast as possible." However, imagine that you want to have a holiday trip from Europe to Vietnam. Of course you want to fly first class, stay in a 5-Star hotel, etc. …, but why do only a few people actually do that? Because the price they need to pay is more than they are willing to spend.

It is the same with customers. Customers describe their needs; they give a description of what they want, "first class, 5 stars." Instead of saying, "it's impossible with that short a time period," just go back to the office, calculate, and offer the "first class or 5 star" option. Also, have another "3-star hotel, coach flight seat" option and let the customer choose.

In real life, there are only a few things that are truly "impossible." Most are only "impossible" with the amount that the customer is willing to pay." Therefore, first, just calculate, make the plan then … let them choose.

What if they choose the "first class & 5 Star" option?

Then, you must be more than happy right? You must be happy because you have a chance to serve a premium service. If not, you also gain the knowledge, experience, and much more important you have a chance to learn from real life.

3. LASTLY, THE THIRD WORD IS: TAKE ACTION:

An idea is just an idea. Setting a goal or plan is just a preparation stage. Therefore, the only way to achieve what you want, such as: Promotion, Respect, etc… **You have to create your value by Taking Action.**

You don't know about your company's business: so spend your time to learn more.

You don't want to lose your job: so work harder.

You don't want to work long hours: so figure out a better way to do your job that much more efficiently! (This could be an entire course.)

You want to get promoted fast: so take on more tasks and achieve them, create more value for yourself.

You don't know what to do? Then do simple things such as: find your coach, your mentor and seek their advice. Do not just sit at one place and think: "If they care for me, they should come and tell me what to do." No, that's not correct. If you don't care for yourself, no one will.

How to ask for advice and approach is another subject entirely. However, I do get some questions like this:

"The owner is a jerk; he always wants me to work more but won't increase my salary. Why should I work more for a company like that?"

Let's look at my case. I worked in a company where everyone complained that the owner is stingy, that he wanted people to work harder, but he didn't want to pay more for anyone at all. But I had no other choice, so I had to accept it and work at that place.

The difference between my colleagues and me was this: I always do more than his expectation and agree to take on more tasks. After 6 months, the owner realizes that if he doesn't pay me more, he has to hire two more guys just to do my current job. So by increasing my salary 30% or 40% more, this is still better than hiring two persons to replace me – which means an increase of100%. And then there is nothing sure about the commitment or performance level of the new person.

That's the situation with the owner who's not good. How about a good company? Sure, they don't want to lose their good performers, and that's how I would just get promotion after promotion. And that is where I can easily jump from an unpopular company to a reputable company.

So, **TNT** is the first thing that has to happen with yourself to improve your situation. After that are attitude, then behavior, then any other soft skills courses. These will help you to achieve your career path faster than others.

Lastly, please understand that knowing it is only one part, the harder part is how to apply it in a real life situation, and how to make it become your habit. So, if you find it difficult to execute or practice, please visit my web page / Facebook regularly, where you will find more details on how to practice daily, or courses that will clear all the clouds away that stop you from achieving your goal.

The secret to luck isn't really luck at all. **It is TNT!**

ABOUT PHAP

Here's what they say about him:

"Phap is an extremely intelligent person, highly motivated and energetic while at work. His adaptability skill & process alignment is outstanding and he drives this with passion and commitment. Phap is clear with every step of audit process and leading the function very effectively. He is even better as a Trainer, since his communication is very clear and he has the energy to train a team continuously for more than 8-9 hours tirelessly.

Phap translates both in a meeting situation and also during public speaking immaculately. He does not only translate the matter, he can communicate the feeling & energy of the speaker also to the team."

Sangram Sinha, *Customer Development Director, THP Group*

Phap always show his strong commitment in bringing the success to company. Not stopping at the assigned duty: Managing Quality Center, Demonstration and Marketing, he was also willing to take challenging responsibility in setting up a new team for new division: Sales – technical Team and gained back Major Distributors in Ho Chi Minh City from our main competitors.

Dien Thi Lan Phuong, *General Manager, Puratos Vietnam Co, Ltd.*

I have always know Xuan Phap to be enthusiastic in his work, diligent and conscientious. He has a good sense of responsibility and for these reasons, demonstrates the ability to manage and provide consistency in our Brand that is famous around the world.

Kitson Choong, *Director General, KFC Vietnam*

Last position: **2006 – 2011: National Sales Audit cum Sales Training Manager – THP Group**

Monthly Audit more than 200 distributors nationwide (sales team: > 1,200 Sales Representatives)

In charge of Sales Training & regular training / evaluation for Distributors, Sales Supervisors, Area Sales Managers & Regional Sales Managers

A Super Team member that contributes to the successful of THP Group (grown from a small company to the Number One Beverage Company in Vietnam).

For more information about Phap Trinh, please visit:
http:// PhapTrinh.com
http://YogaCuoi.com
http://ClbSales.com

CHAPTER 33

THE LEADERSHIP MATRIX

9 HABITS OF BUSINESSES THAT EXECUTE

BY RICK WALLACE

THE LEADERSHIP MATRIX

After spending 15 years with 2 Fortune 1000 corporations and another 15 as a member of the Executive Management team of a midsized company I left to pursue my true passion – coaching small business owners. Interacting with small business owners across the country has brought me to some simple but significant conclusions. I have learned that the strategies for success are not unique to one industry, company, or business owner. Success is determined by the use of predictable, repeatable, simple actions and habits that ensure you follow through and execute the Right Actions.

That is a fact. The Bane of All Business, large and small is lack of *Follow-through* and *Execution*.

Whether your "big problem" is marketing, sales, too busy, etc., etc., the solution is the same. In its simplest form, the secret to a successful, smooth running, growth company comes from **Jim Collins** in his book, ***Good to Great*** – **"Get the Right People, Doing the Right Things, Right."**

So how do we do that? That is what this chapter is all about. The habits, process and tools you need to build a company in which you can proudly say YES, when asked if you have **the right people, doing the right things, right!**

I call it – *The Leadership Matrix*

Here is an outtake from a conversation I recently had with one of my best clients, see if it sounds familiar:

We have been working together for a year now and he finished with record sales and profits for 2010, a 28.8% growth over 2009. The first thing he told me when he answered the phone was, "Well, we blew away the 1st quarter numbers and we are up over 26% from first quarter in 2010."

So, of course, I asked him what he is doing differently, knowing full well we were still in the process of building his marketing plan.

That's right, we have not even implemented any new marketing ideas or plans.

I knew the answers but I wanted to hear from him. He said:

"Rick, I have been facing the same problems for 10 years. For years I set my goals and would wish and hope we'd get there. At the end of the year, we would have to pull the old goals out and see how we did against those goals. The difference is that we aligned the team, focused, and then followed through and executed. In the past, if you would have asked five of my guys what the goals were for the company, you would have gotten five different answers.

My people were running around working hard, very busy, but not on the right things and not doing most of them right. They didn't know where I was going much less where the company was going. Of course, I didn't either so it wasn't their fault. What changed? – ***you got me focused and refocused, you helped me document where we are going, our Goals, and the Actions to get us there.*** *Then you kept me focused on 3 to 5 Key Actions each quarter.*

I used the goals we set, communicated them to everyone and we got the whole company aligned. They get excited about the goals, they look forward to seeing how we are doing each week, we use dashboards and weekly huddles and we all are working together. We, as a team, are having fun again. We have celebrations each quarter when we meet certain goals. I had my best salesperson tell me the other day that "everyone is working like a real team, in the past some people were jealous when I got a big order, now they are excited and helpful."

So now you keep me ***focused*** *on the goals and the 3 to 5 Actions that we are going to* ***focus*** *on executing this quarter. We make one person accountable for each Action, we have meetings each week, use the dashboards for reporting, we update the progress against our goals and we get the Right Things done! We block our calendars each week and spend an hour here or there during the week and* ***focus*** *on our working on the Actions.*

We used to get distracted, try to do too much and never followed through. We stopped! Now we stopped stopping! *<u>We are Executing</u>."*

So, I have to ask, what would you say is your biggest problem, marketing, sales, the right people, etc. That is what we usually think. But skip that problem, peel the onion back and the real basic problem is Lack of Clarity, Focus and Execution. There is some level of Chaos that is holding everyone back. We have good intentions, but we get distracted, lose focus and STOP. Business owners know what they need to do to build a better business and make any part of the business better. The problem is that they just don't seem to be able to **focus, follow through** and **get it done**.

They stop!

<u>Anything you focus on GROWS!</u> Thus his revenues grew this last year. So let's go and find out the steps we take to make your business one that executes and brings some fun back.

THE LEADERSHIP MATRIX

I spent over 30 years in various leadership and management positions in corporations and mid-sized companies and have had the pleasure over the last few years to work with, study and conduct workshops for hundreds of small business owners. It is due to these experiences that I can, with credibility, say that the biggest issues we all deal with is not the ideas, strategies and "how to's". It is the follow through or execution of those Strategies, Tactics or Actions throughout the organization.

We all have documented processes for our employees so that we get certain functional things done properly, but how many companies have **Process** to manage the whole business?

Remember what Collins said – you really have to answer yes to just three simple questions about your organization to make it great.

1. Do you have the Right People?
2. Do they know what the Right Things are to be doing?
3. Do they do those Things Right?

That is all well and good, but what if the answer to any of these questions is no? How do you put in place a process to change for the better and get "yeses" across the board?

I believe there are three keys to making this happen.

1. Clarity
2. Focus
3. Execution

So I began to focus on these 6 points and eventually developed a matrix and then populated the matrix with the key points from the Strategic Planning Process Document I implement with my clients. This is not an event like traditional Strategic Plans with which we are so familiar. You know, you go offsite and come up with binder full of Strategies and Tactics and "#'s", and then return to work the next week and the dust builds up, as it sits on your desk waiting for someone to implement some of it.

As Eisenhower said, "The planning is priceless, the plan is worthless."

No, this is a real process that becomes ingrained into the business. So I married the six points above to the Strategic Planning Process and came up with a roadmap to implementing and actually executing those great ideas we have to make our business better.

So let's break down the matrix below:

	Right People	Right Things	Done Right
Clarity	Vision/Goals	Actions	Core Culture
Focus	Alignment	Accountability	Process
Execution	Rhythm/Huddles	Dashboards	Training

Let's take this one row at a time.

#1 – CLARITY

	Right People	Right Things	Done Right
Clarity	Vision/Goals	Actions	Core Culture

1. CLARITY – this is the first and most vital step in changing a company for the better. The leader must have a **Vision** and **Goals** that are **documented, tracked, measured and communicated to the People in the company.** Every company must have something to rally around and measure itself against – to achieve a high level of success.

"Vision without action is a dream, Action without Vision is Chaos"

~ Japanese Proverb

I never set any goals for myself when I worked for corporations. I told myself I did okay without them, why bother? When I left that world and started working with business owners, I had to ask myself if setting goals was so important for them, then why did I succeed without goals. After a lot of contemplation it occurred to me. The CEO set my goals. It came down the ladder and if I met and exceeded their goals I was rewarded with more responsibility, more money, etc.

Guess what? No one is coming to set the goals for you, the business owner. You must do it yourself. Your employees don't know where you want to go, or what they are supposed to do, so they need those goals set for them. So if goals are so important, how do I convince my clients to embrace the practice and commit to setting them?

Here is how I present my case:

Without a Vision and Goals, the employees of the company have no idea what they are supposed to be doing and how they can align and help the company succeed.

Over 23,000 employees were surveyed by Steven Covey and the results of the survey concluded:

- Only 17% said they have a clear understanding of what their organization is trying to achieve and why
- Only 20% were enthusiastic about their team's and their organization's goals
- Only 20% said they had a "clear line of sight" between their jobs and their team's and organization's goals
- Only 15% felt that their organization fully enables them to execute key goal's
- Only 20% fully trusted the organization they work for

Imagine a soccer team with those same stats:

- Only 2 of the 11 players on the field would know which goal is theirs and how to score
- Only 2 of 11 would care
- Only 2 of 11 would know what position they play and what they were supposed to do
- Only 2 would feel they had the coach's ok to pass the ball or kick it in the goal
- 9 players would be keeping the ball away from their own team members

How could a company or team really succeed with that lack of alignment?

So, goals established and communicated consistently to your team will make your business more successful simply by the fact that everyone knows the road to follow, where they are going, what they can do to get us there and that they are empowered to do it.

Actions tend to immediately flow from Goal setting. I've seen this time after time in client meetings. The owner sets the goals and the team immediately begins to talk about "what we have to do to make those goals".

The **Actions** are the Right Things that our People should be working on to achieve our goals. Not too many – just a few, 3 to 5 each quarter.

"If you have a house full of cats and you try to catch them all at once you will catch nary a one. But if you focus on one at a time you will eventually catch them all."

~ Jim Groh

The **Core Culture** of the company provides the answers to the "Should we or Shouldn't we" questions that arise within the company on a day-to-day basis. You know, the soul of the company, the "sayings" the owner is known for when something happens or a question arises and there is no one there to provide direction.

Clarity of this **Core Culture** provides the People guidance to make sure the **Right Things are Done Right.**

It is also important in recruiting and hiring to make sure you have the Right People.

#2 – FOCUS

	Right People	Right Things	Done Right
Focus	Alignment	Accountability	Process

2. FOCUS – When we talk about Focus and People we talk about **Alignment**. We need to get everyone on the same page and aligned with our Vision, Goals, Actions and Core Culture. Remember the soccer team from the discussion above.

We then need to Focus People on the doing the Right Things through making individuals **Accountable** for each key Action we have identified. That's right, only one individual is Accountable. That individual might need to get others to be responsible for and help accomplish the various tasks to complete the Action but the buck stops here. I have seen too many companies, including ones that I worked for where Actions or projects were assigned to a team or to two people to share. It does not work. Actions must be assigned to one person who is Accountable for its completion.

Lastly, we need to Focus on documenting **Processes** to provide guidance in how to Do Things Right. To ensure that the team becomes self sufficient we need processes that are documented.

#3 – EXECUTION

	Right People	Right Things	Done Right
Execution	Rhythm/Huddles	Dashboards	Training

3. EXECUTION – the bane of most companies. To Execute we need to communicate with our People. We need to build a Rhythm that ingrains processes, makes them consistent, provides consistent communications and tracking against goals and measurements. Thus the **Huddle** or meeting. A 5 minute meeting everyday and a 30 minute meeting per week.

Quarterly, we need a 2-hour meeting to update the Strategic Planning Process for the next quarter. This produces new Goals and new Actions we can now *Focus* upon for the next quarter. Too many meetings – forget it – they will reduce meetings in the long run.

To ensure we are Executing the Right Things we use **Dashboards** – simple, easy-to- update snapshots as to how the work on the Actions is progressing. These are used in our Weekly Huddles to show progress by those accountable for key Actions. Watch this 6 minute video on dashboards: http://www.youtube.com/watch?v=yADwLfROvYY.

The Weekly Meeting and the **Dashboard** reviews are the keystone to ensuring this whole process comes together and that the team is aligned and those Accountable for the Key Actions for the quarter report on their progress. There are no surprises at the end of the quarter.

Finally, to be sure we are doing the documented **Processes** Right, we need **Training**.

Looking down the columns, you have:

Right People – Vision/Goals – Alignment – Huddles/Rhythm

Right Things – Actions – Accountability – Dashboards
Done Right – Core Culture – Process – Training

Sounds like a lot? You may say "You're crazy, I don't have time for all of this!!! My people would never do it!!!"

"One can choose to go back toward safety or forward toward growth. Growth must be chosen again and again; fear must be overcome again and again."

~ Abraham Maslow, Psychologist

It is not easy, but then again, it is not hard if done over a period of time. Remember:

"Success – Doing the right things in small amounts over a long period of time"

This does not take as much time as it does commitment to doing it. I have been implementing this process with businesses of all types and sizes. It is the first time, in my long career, where I have seen actual change take place in a company, and actual follow-through on ideas and concepts until they are implemented and executed upon.

Now we understand the Matrix and the Habits we must instill in our business. You might ask, where does one start? First, whenever you are faced with an overwhelming task: Eat the elephant one bite at a time. Take that first step, take Action, any action toward your goal will give you tremendous energy. Then develop these habits and don't STOP!

"Knowing is not enough; we must apply. Wishing is not enough; we must do."

~ Johann Wolfgang Von Goethe, Author

(For more information and tools please find a recorded webinar on this process "The Leadership Matrix" at www.next-level-coaching.com)

NEXT LEVEL COACHING LLC

ABOUT RICK

Rick Wallace is a successful businessman with over 30 years of experience. He has held leadership and executive positions in sales, sales management, corporate training, product management and marketing at two Fortune 1000 companies..

Rick was a member of the Executive Management Team that built a $40 million domestic manufacturer into a global company whose **revenues almost tripled**. This team, **managed** as a private company, sold it to a public corporation and then completed their own management buyout in 2000.

In his former career, he has spoken all over the US, Europe and even Japan. Since 2008, he has presented to over 800 small business owners across the country and has worked directly with over 40 business owners and their teams in six states and Canada – to implement the programs and plans and build businesses that worked for them vs. relying on them to work. Businesses that execute.

He was awarded the Amherst Chamber of Commerce's Small Business Advocate Award for 2008. He is on the coaching steering committees at both the University of Buffalo's Center for Entrepreneurial Leadership and Canisius College's Women's Business Center.

Rick is available to provide one-on-one coaching, speaking and workshops for small business owners and organizations.

Use your smart phone QR app and see his short video:

Or go to his website for a wealth of complimentary educational tools from recorded webinars to blog posts and eBooks.

For more information and to sign up for his newsletter and blog visit:

www.next-level-coaching.com

Or, contact him at: rick@next-level-coaching.com or 716-479-7719